ALSO BY ROY MORRIS, JR.

*The Long Pursuit: Abraham Lincoln's Thirty-Year Struggle with
Stephen Douglas for the Heart and Soul of America*

*Fraud of the Century: Rutherford B. Hayes, Samuel Tilden,
and the Stolen Election of 1876*

The Better Angel: Walt Whitman in the Civil War

Ambrose Bierce: Alone in Bad Company

Sheridan: The Life and Wars of General Phil Sheridan

LIGHTING OUT FOR

Simon & Schuster

New York   London   Toronto   Sydney

THE TERRITORY

How SAMUEL CLEMENS Headed West
and Became MARK TWAIN

ROY MORRIS, JR.

Simon & Schuster
1230 Avenue of the Americas
New York, NY 10020

First Simon & Schuster hardcover edition March 2010

SIMON & SCHUSTER and colophon are registered trademarks
of Simon & Schuster, Inc.

For information about special discounts for bulk purchases,
please contact Simon & Schuster Special Sales at
1-866-506-1949 or business@simonandschuster.com.

The Simon & Schuster Speakers Bureau can bring authors
to your live event. For more information or to book an event,
contact the Simon & Schuster Speakers Bureau at
1-866-248-3049 or visit our website at www.simonspeakers.com.

Designed by Kyoko Watanabe
Map by Paul J. Pugliese

Manufactured in the United States of America

1 3 5 7 9 10 8 6 4 2

Library of Congress Cataloging-in-Publication Data

Morris, Roy.
Lighting out for the territory : how Samuel Clemens headed west and
became Mark Twain / Roy Morris, Jr.
p. cm.
Includes bibliographical references.
1. Twain, Mark, 1835–1910—Travel—West (U.S.) 2. Authors, American—Homes and
haunts—West (U.S.) 3. West (U.S.)—Intellectual life—19th century. 4. West (U.S.)—
Description and travel. 5. West (U.S.)—In literature. I. Title.
PS1342.W48M67 2010
818'.403—dc22
[B]
2009049221

ISBN 978-1-4165-9866-4
ISBN 978-1-4391-0137-7 (ebook)

ILLUSTRATION CREDITS: Mark Twain Project, The Bancroft Library, University of
California Berkeley: 1, 2, 10, 11, 17; National Archives: 3; Library of Congress: 4, 6,
7, 8, 14, 15, 18; The Bancroft Library, University of California, Berkeley: 5, 9, 12, 13;
The Mariners' Museum, Newport News, Virginia: 16

In memory of Susan Woodall Pierce,

1954–2008.

Nothing so liberalizes a man and expands the kindly instincts that nature put in him as travel and contact with many kinds of people.

—MARK TWAIN, 1867

CONTENTS

AUTHOR'S NOTE

ANYONE VENTURING TO WRITE ABOUT THE SIN-
gularly gifted and protean individual who began life on November 30, 1835, in northeastern Missouri as Samuel Langhorne
Clemens and became famous the world over as Mark Twain faces an
immediate and unavoidable problem: what to call him. His family and
his oldest friends called him Sam, or sometimes Sammy; newer friends
called him Mark; business associates called him Clemens; his daughters called him Papa; his wife called him Youth. Early in his writing
career he tried out various noms de plume, ranging from short and
pithy—Rambler, Grumbler, Josh, Sergeant Fathom—to long and
clumsy—W. Epaminondas Adrastus Perkins, W. Epaminondas Adrastus Blab, Thomas Jefferson Snodgrass, Peter Pencilcase's Son, even A
Dog-Be-Deviled Citizen. In February 1863, commencing his professional writing career on the Virginia City *Territorial Enterprise*, he
began signing himself "Mark Twain." That's how most people think
of him today. The name Mark Twain is as much a trademark, in its
way, as Coke or McDonald's or Mickey Mouse. He's that big.

The generally accepted way to identify Clemens/Twain is chronologically, calling him by whatever name he was using at the time. It makes for occasionally awkward reading, particularly when Mark Twain the writer is describing something he experienced years earlier as Sam Clemens the person, but there is no easier way to do it. Like most previous biographers, I will employ the admittedly arbitrary but convenient method of referring to the subject as "Sam" or "Clemens" during his youth and "Twain" or "Mark Twain" after he unveiled his famous pen name. As with everything else in this book, it's Mr. Mark Twain's fault, not mine, and all the blame attaches to him. Credit, where due, is optional.

LIGHTING
OUT FOR THE
TERRITORY

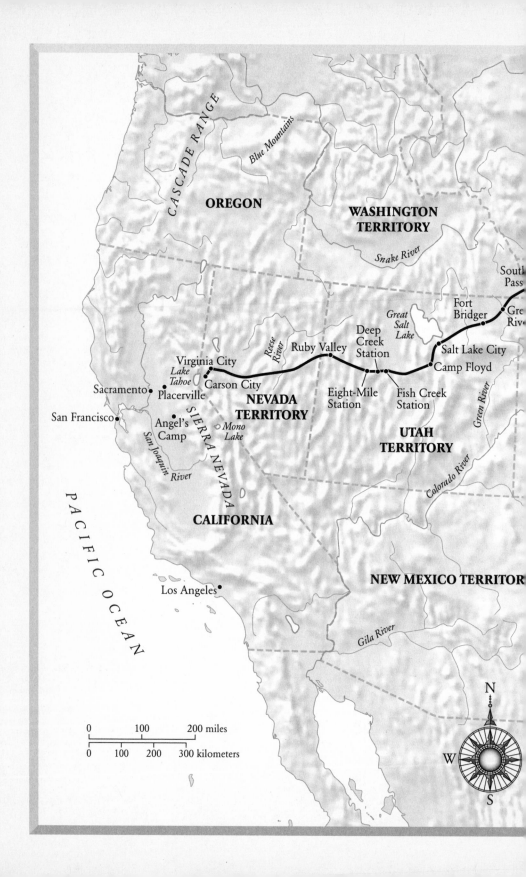

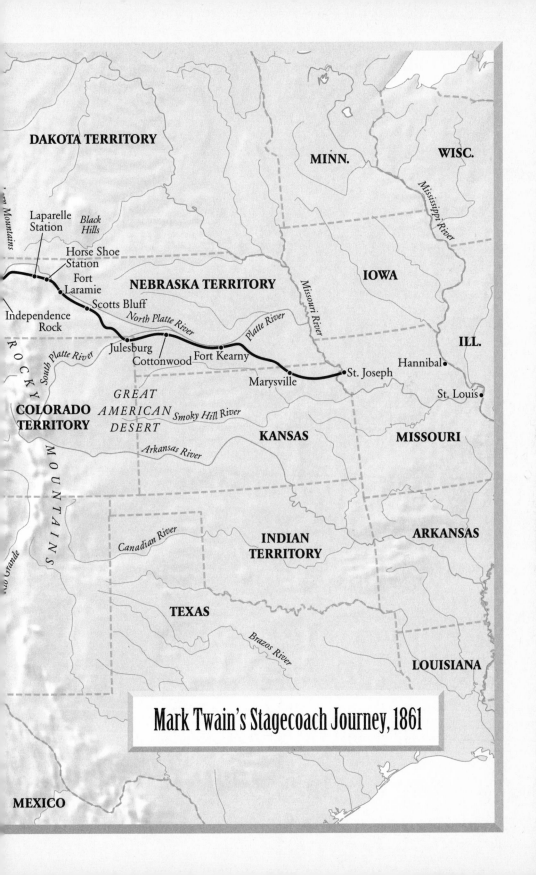

Mark Twain's Stagecoach Journey, 1861

INTRODUCTION

AT THE END OF HIS GREAT ADVENTURE DOWN THE Mississippi River and the joyless labor of trying to make a book out of it, a rather glum Huckleberry Finn pauses to take stock of the situation. Jim is free (and forty dollars richer, compliments of Tom Sawyer), Tom is recovering nicely from his recent gunshot wound, and the odious Pap is long since dead, last seen floating downriver in a ruined house. Everyone, it seems, is happy except Huck. He has his reasons. Tom's formidable Aunt Sally, on whose south Arkansas farm Jim finally found his long-delayed deliverance, is threatening to turn her stifling if well-meaning hand toward Huck; she aims, he says, to "sivilize" him. It is more than a boy can bear—this boy, anyway. He reckons it is time "to light out for the Territory ahead of the rest." Huck's creator had made a similar decision two decades earlier. He wasn't even Mark Twain then, but as Huck might have said, "That ain't no matter." In the ramshackle mining camps and raucous boom-towns of the West, free from feminine constraints and civilized soci-ety, Samuel Clemens would finally conclude his extended adolescence and assume the mantle—and burden—of "Mr. Mark Twain." Neither he nor American literature would ever be the same.

Lighting Out for the Territory: How Samuel Clemens Became Mark Twain is the story of how Samuel Clemens, itinerant printer, Mississippi riverboat pilot, and Confederate guerrilla, became Mark Twain, celebrated journalist, author, and stage performer. As with most of the events in his long and varied life, Twain told it best, recounting his western adventures in one of his most popular books, *Roughing It*, published in February 1872, a full decade after his trip out west. Like *Huckleberry Finn*, which appeared in 1885, *Roughing It* is "mostly a true book . . . with some stretchers" thrown in. It is an appropriately rambling and episodic account of the five and a half years the author spent traveling to and from Nevada, California, and Hawaii between July 1861 and December 1866—not coincidentally the same years that bracketed the American Civil War. There is virtually nothing about the war in the book—again not a coincidence, since leaving the war behind was Twain's primary motive for going west in the first place. Except for a brief paragraph about a Fourth of July celebration in Virginia City, Nevada, in 1863 and a slightly longer account of local fund-raising activities on behalf of the United States Sanitary Commission, Twain omits any reference to the greatest and most tragic event of his lifetime. Indeed, *Roughing It* could have taken place at any time after 1849, when the first gold rushers headed for California along pretty much the same route that Sam Clemens and his brother Orion (pronounced OR-ee-un) followed a dozen years later. It is a timeless book in more ways than one.

History aside, *Roughing It* is great fun, as Twain clearly intended it to be, but it is also carefully sanitized. The book was written not long after his marriage to an exceedingly proper young eastern lady, Olivia Langdon, who would not have wanted to know the full story of what went on in the mining camps, saloons, and brothels out west. With that in mind—she was always his first, most scrupulous reader—Twain produced a sort of modified *Adventures of Tom Sawyer*, with himself cast in the lead role of a slightly older but still wholesome and high-spirited Tom. It is a boy's book, written by and about an over-grown boy. There is just enough truth in it to spice up the story, but not enough to kill the flavor. Stretchers abound. And while no one in his right mind would ever try to outdo Mark Twain on the subject of Mark Twain, it is sometimes necessary, for the sake of the record, to correct, emend, or otherwise expand Twain's often contradictory accounts of his life. He was, after all, a novelist, and he rarely let the facts get in the way of the story. One of the central aims of this book, with the help of contemporaneous letters, diaries, and reminiscences, is to separate the fact from the fiction—to "de-stretcher" it, if you will—a noble ambition but one that in Mark Twain's case is more or less a full-time occupation.

Growing up in Hannibal, Missouri, on the western bank of the Mississippi River, Samuel Clemens knew all about the concept of lighting out for the Territory. As a boy, he regularly watched the steamboats threshing into view, offloading knots of travel-worn passengers whose dreams were bundled, along with their belong-ings, into a few threadbare carpetbags. Often these dreams involved making a new start of things in the West, that already legendary region beyond the next hill or bend in the river where a man with a past could successfully reinvent himself. In the spring of 1849, the thirteen-year-old Clemens witnessed the first wave of eastern gold rushers pouring through Hannibal en route to California. One of the transients fatally stabbed another in full view of the horrified youth, a murder that Mark Twain would chillingly re-create in the graveyard killing of Doctor Robinson by Injun Joe in *Tom Sawyer.* Eighty of his fellow townsmen subsequently joined the pack that frantic spring; six were dead, of Indians or illness, before summer came. In all, more than two hundred Hannibal natives became gold rushers themselves, including the town doctor, Hugh Meredith, and his son, John. Years later, Twain was still running into his old Hannibal neighbors out west.

His own route to the West was considerably less direct—in fact, it was in exactly the opposite direction. Before turning his sights westward, the inveterately restless Clemens spent the better part of a decade wandering the great cities of the East and Midwest, from St. Louis to New York to Philadelphia to Washington, then back to New York, to Cincinnati and New Orleans. He worked when he could as a journeyman printer, before becoming a pilot on the Mississippi River. Like Huckleberry Finn, he learned early on to light out at the first sign of trouble, and when the Civil War erupted he already had one foot out the door, so to speak. And while it is not entirely accurate to describe his subsequent journey west as a headlong flight, it was at the very least a headlong amble. By then he had proven to everyone's satisfaction, including his own, that he was manifestly unsuited to soldiering. It was good to know. Had he stayed on, Clemens might well have gotten himself killed—the guerrilla war in Missouri was particularly nasty—but his death would not have lengthened the life of the Confederacy (or the Union, either) by a single day. It would, however, have reduced the literary inheritance of the United States by an incalculable amount. By lighting out for the Territory when he did, Samuel Clemens lived to write another day, and American literature is infinitely richer and a good deal funnier because of it.

Lighting Out for the Territory traces the course of that comparatively narrow escape and the remarkable transformation—personal, professional, and artistic—that followed. Samuel Clemens went west in 1861; Mark Twain returned east six years later. This is the story of what happened in between.

CHAPTER 1

A CAMPAIGN THAT FAILED

I N THE CHAOTIC OPENING DAYS OF THE CIVIL WAR, a red-haired, gray-eyed, twenty-five-year-old Mississippi River pilot arrived in St. Louis after a harrowing four-day trip upriver from New Orleans. Already the war had rendered the pilot's profession too confused and dangerous for someone of his high-strung, rather morbid disposition. Boats were taking fire from troops on both sides of the water, their crews being impressed into military service at half the going rate. Samuel L. Clemens, late of Hannibal, Missouri, could not foresee what new course his life would take, but he could grasp all too clearly that his halcyon days as a riverboat pilot, "the only unfettered and entirely independent human being that lived on the earth," were over. The mighty river, with its triple-decker steamboats, moon-shadowed sandbars, and ink-black eddies, was closing down for the duration. Sam Clemens, for all intents and purposes, had been shipwrecked.

Unlike the majority of his fellow Americans, he never saw it coming. He tended toward dreaminess anyway, a lifelong inclination that long, languid hours on the river tacitly encouraged. Nor was he, at this stage of his life, particularly political. His hometown was a crossroads river port in a divided border state, its citizens a mixture (as was his own family) of proslavery and abolitionist elements. And while his piloting work on the Mississippi had exposed him to slavery in all its harshest forms, from Sisyphean dockworkers staggering under mounds of passengers' luggage to ragged field hands stoop-picking cotton on the great plantations along the river, the young pilot paid them little mind. He simply steamed past, his eyes fixed on the breaks and bends ahead. They had their work, he had his, and he fully expected "to follow the river the rest of my days, and die at the wheel when my mission was ended." And then, as Abraham Lincoln would say with eloquent simplicity a few years later, the war came.

Clemens, who had voted for compromise candidate John Bell in the recent presidential election, was in New Orleans in late January 1861 when word arrived of Louisiana's secession. "Great rejoicing. Flags, Dixie, Soldiers," he noted in his journal. Contrary to his later assertion, he did not leave the city for the North as soon as he heard the news. Although Louisiana was one of the first states to secede—a rash thing to do, given the vast amount of commerce New Orleans enjoyed with northern states—there were no immediate consequences, either commercial or military, to secession. No one knew what might happen; for the time being, people on both sides took a wait-and-see attitude. Clemens continued his piloting work aboard the side-wheeler *Alonzo Child*, where he and his closest childhood friend, Will Bowen, got into a fistfight one day, reportedly over an unpaid three-hundred-dollar loan and Will's overt "secesh" talk. Given Clemens's always complicated handling of finances and his comparatively fluid political sentiments, it was more likely the former than the latter.

As the shadows of war spread across every corner of the nation,

Clemens kept determinedly to the middle of the river. He speculated in the egg market, losing several hundred dollars when the bottom fell out—"So much for eggs," he shrugged—ran the *Alonzo Child* aground while recklessly racing another boat in the fog, and took his mother on a holiday cruise from Boonville, Missouri, to New Orleans. It proved to be a valedictory trip. *Alonzo Child*'s captain, David DeHaven, described by Clemens as "flamboyantly secessionist," had volunteered his boat for the southern cause, an act of impulsive patriotism that severely unnerved his less committed pilot. Clemens had no intention of steering Rebel supplies from New Orleans to Memphis between blasts from Union cannonballs, "perched all solitary and alone on high in a pilothouse, a target for Tom, Dick, and Harry."

After Confederate forces fired on Fort Sumter in mid-April, making such target practice inevitable, Clemens abandoned his post on the *Alonzo Child* and hitched a ride north on the *Nebraska*, which was heading upriver to St. Louis. It was the beginning of a nearly six-year-long odyssey of wandering, flight, and dislocation that would leave him as changed personally as the nation would be changed politically. For Clemens, as for all Americans of the era, the Civil War was the watershed moment of his life, even if he managed to avoid—as so many did not—being fatally swept away in the flood.

Heading northward with his friend Zeb Leavenworth at *Nebraska*'s wheel, the two young men were conversing idly in the pilothouse when the boat approached Jefferson Barracks, a military installation just south of St. Louis. The day before, their boat had passed safely through a Union blockade at Memphis—one of the last civilian vessels to do so—but the soldiers manning the defenses at Jefferson Barracks were not so open-minded. They fired a warning shot across the bow, and when *Nebraska* did not immediately stop, they sent another shot crashing into her pilothouse, splintering wood and breaking glass. Leavenworth threw himself into a corner, shouting, "Good Lord Almighty! Sam, what do they mean by that?" Clemens grabbed the lurching wheel, responding calmly (or so he claimed), "I guess they want us to wait a minute, Zeb."

Clemens's unlikely calm in the face of hostile cannon fire did not last long. As soon as the boat docked, he hastened to the home of his married sister, Pamela (pronounced Pa-MEE-la) Clemens Moffett, at 1312 Chestnut Street, where he sought refuge from what he imagined to be roving press-gangs of Union and Confederate toughs. His eight-year-old niece Annie watched in fascination as her distraught uncle paced the floor, obsessed, she said, "with the fear that he might be arrested by government agents and forced to act as pilot on a government gunboat while a man stood by with a pistol ready to shoot him if he showed the least sign of a false move."

Either side would have been happy to utilize Clemens's valuable piloting experience, but no one even knew he was in the city. Determined to keep it that way, Clemens lurked indoors, avoiding open windows like a wraith. His storekeeping brother-in-law, William Moffett, a dyed-in-the-wool southerner, jangled Sam's nerves one night by announcing with drawing-room bravado that he would rather go to jail than be drafted into the Union Army to fight his friends. Clemens was similarly torn. One night he and his niece were standing in the doorway when a group of boys paraded past, shouting, "Hurrah for Jeff Davis!" Caught up in the spirit of the moment, Sam sent Annie upstairs to find some red and white ribbons for the marchers. A few minutes later, another youth came down the street waving an American flag and was immediately set upon by the others. Clemens angrily chased away the attackers, but fumed afterward that the outnumbered patriot "should have guarded that flag with his life." The boy was eight.

Clemens's own internal struggle came to a head one afternoon when a mysterious stranger named Smith turned up on the doorstep seeking Confederate recruits to take back the state capital in Jefferson City. Clemens politely resisted the call, at least at first, focusing instead on winning his Masonic badge. He solemnly swore to "the Worshipful Master, Wardens, and Brethren of Polar Star Lodge No. 79 of the Ancient, Free, and Accepted Orders of Masons" that he was offering himself as "a candidate for the mysteries of Masonry" due to "a sincere wish of being serviceable to his fellow creatures," and he was duly enrolled as a third-degree Mason on July 10, 1861. Then he went back to Hannibal to collect the still-outstanding debt owed to him by Bowen, who had returned home to help his mother run the family boardinghouse. This time, at least, there were no fisticuffs. The two old friends resumed their carefree habits—as carefree as they could be in a town controlled by Union-leaning Home Guards who elbowed citizens off the sidewalk and filled the air with raucous patriotic songs. With the rest of his family long since gone from the small frame house at 206 Hill Street, where he had grown up, Samuel Clemens felt increasingly like a stranger in his own hometown.

In its fictional guise of St. Petersburg, Hannibal glows in perpetual sunlight, the idyllic home of Tom Sawyer, Huck Finn, Aunt Polly, Mary and Sid, Becky Thatcher, Joe Harper, Ben Rogers, the Widow Douglas, Miss Watson, and the villainous (but ultimately vanquished) Injun Joe. It is the realm of joyous boyhood, of pranks and adventures, camping and fishing, of Jackson's Island, Holliday's Hill, Lover's Leap, and McDougal's Cave. The twilight is lit by a spangle of fireflies; Halley's Comet is always winking out in the distance. The real Hannibal was larger and more complex. To begin with, unlike St. Petersburg, it actually had black people living in it besides Miss Watson's long-suffering man servant Jim. Approximately a quarter of the town's three thousand residents were slaves, including a handful of human chattel alternately owned, rented, or sold off by Clemens's

Virginia-born father, John Marshall Clemens. To the townsfolk, the peculiar institution was neither good nor evil—it simply was. "There was nothing about the slavery of the Hannibal region to rouse one's dozing humane instincts to activity," Mark Twain recalled years later in his autobiography. "It was a mild domestic slavery, not the brutal plantation article. Cruelties were very rare and exceedingly and wholesomely unpopular."

Yet cruelties there were. Marshall Clemens, not a particularly violent or demonstrative man, occasionally whipped or cuffed his slaves for various infractions. Constantly needing money, he eventually sold off the family's longtime household servant, Jennie, to an infamous slave trader when Sam was eight, even though Jennie had loyally nursed the boy through his sickly infancy and saved him from drowning in a nearby creek. Sam personally witnessed a neighbor fatally strike down his slave with a piece of iron ore, and when he was eleven he and some friends found the floating body of an escaped slave who had been murdered and mutilated by bounty hunters. Nor were the horrors all one-sided. The county's first legal execution was of a local slave with the Faulknerian name of Glascock's Ben, who had raped and murdered a twelve-year-old girl in a rock quarry. During his trial, Ben had boasted that he would never be hanged because he was worth too much to his master alive. He was wrong. Life on the fringe of the American frontier was hard, even in sunlight.

Nor was Sam Clemens's home life always as sunny as he remembered. His father was a distant, disappointed man who spent much of his time brooding over his numerous debts and the elusive fortune he expected to realize any day from the sale of seventy thousand acres of unimproved wilderness in north-central Tennessee. The "Tennessee land," as the property was invariably known within the family, had come into Marshall's hands in the late 1820s and early 1830s, when he bought up several parcels of acreage in Fentress County. He spent a total of four hundred dollars for the land, a not inconsiderable sum in Jacksonian-era America, and when he moved to Missouri in 1835 he held on to the land as a potential moneymaker. As was the case with most Clemens financial dealings, then and later, the Tennessee land would prove to be a stinging disappointment, serving mainly as a catch-all symbol of improvident hopes and cruelly dashed dreams.

Clemens's father, "a silent, austere man" who died in 1847 when Sam was eleven, would recur throughout his son's fiction, always as a chilly personage. "My own knowledge of him amounted to little more than an introduction," Twain lamented to a friend late in life. True to his namesake, John Marshall Clemens was also a judge, albeit of a rather less exalted variety than the first chief justice of the United States Supreme Court. As a circuit court judge in Monroe County, Missouri, the elder Clemens functioned mainly as a glorified justice of the peace, issuing subpoenas, taking depositions, and performing marriages. Judge Clemens appears in his son's writings as Judge Thatcher in *The Adventures of Tom Sawyer*, Judge Hawkins in *The Gilded Age*, and Judge Driscoll in *The Tragedy of Pudd'nhead Wilson*. Traces of him can also be found in the death-decreeing figures of Sir Kay the Seneschal in *A Connecticut Yankee in King Arthur's Court* and Bishop Cauchon, St. Joan's persecutor, in *Personal Recollections of Joan of Arc*. Some scholars even see his shadow lurking behind the menacing, mercurial figure of Pap Finn. All in all, Marshall Clemens is not a particularly likable ghost.

Fortunately for everyone, in looks, intellect, and basic temperament Sam took after his loquacious, fun-loving mother, Jane Lampton Clemens. Like her famous son, Jane was high-strung, emotional, quick-witted, and affectionate—everything her gloomy husband was not. She had married him on the rebound, after a tragic misunderstanding with a shy suitor who wrongly thought she had rejected him, when in fact she was merely playing hard to get. Marshall Clemens, a law clerk for Jane's uncle in her hometown of Columbia, Kentucky, happened to be available. She married him without loving him in the least, bore him seven children (three of whom lived past childhood), and followed him loyally if not enthusiastically from Kentucky to Tennessee and, ultimately, to Missouri. Samuel Langhorne Clemens, their sixth child, was born two months prematurely, on November 30, 1835. Twain's famous boast that he had arrived on the scene with Halley's Comet must, like many of his most memorable remarks, be taken with a grain of salt. The comet, in fact, arrived six weeks before him, peaking in visibility in mid-October and making an altogether more impressive entrance than the red-haired, underweight newborn mewling softly in its wake. "You don't expect to raise that babe, do you?" one of her neighbors asked the new mother after peering skeptically under Sam's blanket. Jane allowed that she would try.

Jane Clemens appears mostly winningly as Aunt Polly in *The Adventures of Tom Sawyer*, Twain's most personal and in some ways best book. Aunt Polly's patient, kind, and unfailingly shrewd insight into a boy's heart reflected her real-life model's generous approach to life. "She had a slender, small body but a large heart," her son remembered, "a heart so large that everybody's grief and everybody's joys found welcome in it. . . . Her interest in people and other animals was warm, personal, friendly. She always found something to excuse, and as a rule to love, in the toughest of them—even if she had to put it there herself." Twain would have a considerably harder time loving the human race, generally and particularly, than his mother, but he shared her interest in the world at large. He also shared—along with her red hair, gray eyes, and wide ironic mouth—Jane Clemens's fascination with language, music, and impersonations. "She was the most eloquent person I have heard speak," Twain recalled. "It was seldom eloquence of a fiery or violent sort, but gentle, pitying, persuasive, appealing; and so genuine and so nobly and simply worded and so touchingly uttered, that many times I have seen it win the reluctant and splendid applause of tears." He played it more for laughs himself, but he could appreciate his mother's kinder, gentler approach to an audience.

All traces of family—maternal, paternal, or otherwise—had long since vanished by the time Sam Clemens returned to Hannibal in the summer of 1861. It was his first trip home in exactly eight years, and it would prove to be a short visit. There was not much to hold him there—too much time and distance lay between.

The size and shape of his wanderings was a familiar coming-of-age story in antebellum America. It began in June 1853, when Clemens left home for the first time at the age of seventeen and went to St. Louis to try his luck as a printer's apprentice on the St. Louis *Evening News*. He had learned the rudiments of the trade at various local newspapers, including the Hannibal *Journal* and the Hannibal *Western Union*, then owned by his brother Orion, whose irritating habit of paying his workers in "uncashable promises" eventually induced Sam to seek employment elsewhere. He soon grew bored with his new job as well—all his life he would have trouble reining in his quicksilver enthusiasms and equally fungible disenchantments. That August he abruptly abandoned St. Louis for New York City, where the World's Fair was taking place inside the specially constructed Crystal Palace. Along the way, he passed by stagecoach through Springfield, Illinois, the adopted home of an obscure one-term congressman named Abraham Lincoln. The two future giants of the age did not meet, but Lincoln in time would play an important, if indirect, role in Clemens's slow-developing destiny.

Somehow, the unconnected teenager found work quickly in New York, signing on as a compositor in the printing shop of John A. Gray, whose two-hundred-man staff set type for a wide assortment of books and magazines, including the *Choral Advocate, Jewish Chronicles, Littell's Living Age*, and *Knickerbocker*. The first inkling his long-suffering mother had of her son's arrival in the big city was a letter postmarked New York (not St. Louis, where she thought he still was). "You will doubtless be a little surprised, and somewhat angry when you receive this, and find me so far from home," Sam began with guarded understatement. Professing himself still to be her "best boy," he proceeded to recount the exotic sights he had seen, beginning with showman P. T. Barnum's "Wild Men of Borneo," a set of unfortunate, probably retarded twins he had encountered in a cage on the city sidewalk and judged to be, a little uncharitably, somewhat less than human. "Their faces and eyes are those of the beast," he wrote, "and when they fix their glittering orbs on you with a steady, unflinching gaze, you instinctively draw back a step, and a very unpleasant sensation steals through your veins." What his eternally worrying mother made of her son's exposure to such extraordinary sights is anyone's guess.

Clemens went to some pains to reassure her that he was living right, recounting long days of honest typesetting followed by wholesome visits to the fruit market and cloistered, scholarly evenings in the free reading library a few blocks from his boardinghouse on Duane Street. "If books are not good company, where will I find it?" he asked piously. Sam visited the World's Fair (he found it something of a disappointment), saw the famous actor Edwin Forrest interpret *The Gladiator* on Broadway, and toured the recently constructed Croton Aqueduct, which he pronounced "the greatest wonder yet." Sharing the sidewalk with an undifferentiated throng of pushy New Yorkers, the newcomer found himself continually "borne, and rubbed, and crowded along" by a vexatious swarm of "trundle-bed trash. To wade through this mass of human vermin," he groused, "would raise the ire of the most patient person that ever lived." Even at seventeen, Sam Clemens was most definitely not that sort of person.

Two months later he went to Philadelphia—for some reason, he seemed to think it would be a warmer place to spend the winter. There he toured the usual historical sites, including Independence Hall, fellow printer Benjamin Franklin's gravesite, and the Liberty Bell. With his unquenchable taste for the grotesque, he also took the time to ogle the self-described "Largest Lady in the World," a sideshow attraction who admitted to a decidedly unladylike weight of 764 pounds. Sam, for his part, was unimpressed. "She is a pretty extensive piece of meat," he said, "but not much to brag about; however, I suppose she would bring a fair price in the Cannibal Islands." He complained to the broadminded but abstemious Orion about the "abominable foreigners" and "whisky-swilling, God-despising heathens" who infested the city, but undercut the temperance lecture by confessing his attendance at "free-and-easy" amusements—a sort of precursor to open-mic night at a modern comedy club—in the local saloons. If Orion caught the contradiction, he let it stand, running the letter unedited in the Hannibal *Journal.*

Orion was used to his brother's japes. Sam's first known foray into professional writing was a paragraph in the January 16, 1851, issue of the Hannibal *Western Union.* Titled "A Gallant Fireman," the item mercilessly mocked Sam's coworker, Jim Wolf, who had run off in panic the previous week after a fire broke out in the grocery store next to the newspaper. "Being of a *snaillish* disposition, even in his quickest moments, the fire had been extinguished during his absence," Sam wrote. "He returned in the course of an hour, nearly out of breath, and thinking he had immortalized himself, threw his giant frame in a tragic attitude, and exclaimed, with an eloquent expression: 'If that thar fire hadn't bin put out, thar'd a' bin the greatest *combination* of the age!'" Although hardly an immortal work of prose, the piece contained many aspects of Mark Twain's basic style: frontier setting, use of the vernacular, love of the ridiculous, play on words *(combination* for *conflagration),* true-life situation, and mean, or at least stinging, wit. In its humble way, "A Gallant Fireman" is a virtual checklist of Twainian literary effects.

Clemens's next journalistic venture, after disposing of Jim Wolf, was even more brutal—a brief but bitter feud with rival editor Josiah T. Hinton of the Hannibal *Tri-Weekly Messenger.* Hinton had raised Sam's hackles by daring to attack Orion in print for complaining, in Orion's mild and gentlemanly way, about stray dogs barking at night. From this, Hinton deduced "a fierce hater of the canine race pour[ing] out his vials of wrath." Hinton stood foursquare behind man's best friends. When Orion went to St. Louis on business for a few days in September 1852, leaving Sam temporarily in charge of the *Journal,* his brother saw an opening. Hinton had already become something of a laughingstock in Hannibal with his failed attempt to drown himself in Bear Creek—the same body of water from which Sam had been plucked by his alert nursemaid a few years earlier. Hinton's mistake was to leave behind a brokenhearted suicide note, then wade out chest-deep into the creek before thinking better of it and wading back to shore, a sadder but perhaps a wiser man.

With Orion gone, Sam sprang to the attack. Alongside a woodcut showing Hinton with the head of a dog, advancing stalwartly toward Bear Creek, liquor bottle in hand, the *Journal*'s acting editor printed a breaking news item, "Local Resolves to Commit Suicide." It was a "real *dog*-gerytype," Sam joked, wishing peace to Hinton's *"re*-manes" and signing the item, "A Dog-Be-Deviled Citizen." A follow-up editorial chided Hinton for "failing in the patriotic work of ridding the country of a nuisance . . . by feeding his carcass to the fishes of Bear Creek." Hinton attempted to fire back, complaining of his "obscene and despicable" treatment in the *Journal,* but by then the damage had been done. When Orion returned home and saw the smoldering remains of his rival, he immediately apologized in print for his brother's "rather rough" jokes at a fellow journalist's expense. There the matter died. But Sam, who never forgot either a slight or a joke, stored the event in his memory. For someone with at least the normal antipathy to physical violence, pencils at ten paces was a much more satisfying way to fight.

Sam took advantage of another Orion absence in May 1853 to typeset the first of what would become a lifelong series of hoaxes. "TERRIBLE ACCIDENT! 500 MEN KILLED AND MISSING!!!" the *Journal* headline screamed. Such mishaps were all too common along the river, and Hannibal residents were used to such waterborne calamities. With a mixture of relief, irritation, and grudging amusement—a typical reaction, one would assume, to Sam Clemens's relentless larks—they scanned the lead paragraph: "We had set the above head up, expecting . . . to use it, but as the accident hasn't yet happened, we'll say (To be Continued)." Journalism would never be a sacred calling for Mark Twain.

In the winter of 1854, midway through his eastern travels, Clemens paid a four-day visit to the nation's capital. He judged the famous Washington landmarks to be fine specimens of architecture, but "sadly out of place" among the muddy roads and ramshackle hovels that made up much of the city. The Capitol itself was fine enough, but the political discourse taking place inside the Senate chamber failed to impress the callow young visitor. Michigan senator Lewis Cass, he thought, was "a fine looking old man," but Illinois senator Stephen Douglas resembled a lawyer's clerk, and New York senator William Seward was "a slim, dark, bony individual, and looks like a respectable wind would blow him out of the country." Former Missouri senator Thomas Hart Benton, now sadly reduced to the House of the Representatives, was "a lion imprisoned in a cage of monkeys."

Had he been more politically aware, Clemens might have realized that the day's debate was far from commonplace. In fact, it was nothing less than epoch-making, the closing round of deliberations over the Kansas-Nebraska bill put forward by Douglas as a way around the ever-vexatious issue of slavery in the territories. By the time the full effects of the bill became apparent, the nation would find itself a long way down the slippery slope of civil war, with no clear way back to the top. Douglas, who was jockeying for the Democratic Party's 1856 presidential nomination, had somehow convinced himself that the best way to accomplish that ambition was by abrogating the Missouri Compromise, which for the past thirty-four years had tenuously held the slave and free states at arm's length, if not always at peace. The new act intended to put the slavery question directly into the hands of the people by means of what Douglas called "popular sovereignty," or majority rule. Within weeks of its passage, the bill would bring angry swarms of proslavery zealots pouring out of Clemens's home state into the adjacent Kansas Territory, where they would attempt to influence, at the point of a gun, their fellow citizens' imperfect understanding of Douglas-style democracy.

After his flying visit to Washington, Clemens returned to New York and continued to eke out a precarious living at the printers' table, earning a penurious twenty-three cents per "em" of type. A sudden downturn in the employment prospects of unconnected young printers, occasioned in part by a pair of ruinous fires at New York publishing houses, put him out of work that spring. Clemens returned reluctantly to the Midwest, rejoining his family in the riverfront village of Muscatine, Iowa, 220 miles north of Hannibal, where the always impecunious Orion had moved in search of another newspaper to run into the ground.

Sam made a dramatic entrance, wildly waving a secondhand pistol and threatening to use it "in self-defense." The family watched carefully. It was only a joke, referencing Orion's earlier refusal to loan him money to buy a gun, but it symbolized neatly the brothers' always uneasy relationship. Sam stuck around Muscatine for a few months, reading and loafing, but the unfamiliar village was not his home. His undeveloped fondness for his new surroundings was further impeded by a knife-wielding lunatic who cornered him in a field one day and "threatened to carve me up . . . unless I acknowledged him to be the only son of the Devil." Sam readily conceded the point.

Two months later he moved back to St. Louis and reclaimed his old job at the *Evening News*. Like much of the nation, St. Louis was enflamed just then by the specter of foreign immigrants clambering ashore in irresistible waves. The nativist Know-Nothing movement was in full swing, and Clemens arrived in the midst of a full-blown riot. Going with a friend to an armory near his boardinghouse, the would-be volunteer militiaman was issued a musket and sent out with the rest of his untrained company to put down a howling mob of local patriots. The riot lasted two days, but Clemens's service was somewhat briefer. Marching toward the scene of the fighting, he asked his friend to hold his musket for him while he went in search of something to drink, "then I branched off and went home." It was a pattern of behavior he would repeat often during his life.

While his brother was off fighting Know-Nothings on the streets of St. Louis, Orion married a nineteen-year-old Keokuk, Iowa, girl named Mary Eleanor "Mollie" Stotts and moved eighty miles downriver to her hometown, a tidy, brick-walled village atop a bluff overlooking the Des Moines and Mississippi rivers. There Orion took possession of a failed printing company, the Ben Franklin Book and Job Office, which was located on the third floor of a building on Keokuk's Main Street. With a contract in hand to print the city's first formal directory, Orion put his youngest brother, Henry, to work on the press and implored Sam to join them in the growing family concern.

Partly to escape the civic strife in St. Louis, Sam accepted Orion's offer, and for the next thirteen months he labored more or less diligently at the printing press, sharing a room with Henry on the premises and smoking an enormous Oriental-style water pipe in bed at night like a prairie-grown pasha. From time to time, the brothers annoyed the sharp-eared tenant below them, music teacher Oliver Isbell, by clomping about the premises in their boots. When Isbell complained one night about the noise, Sam immediately organized an impromptu militia unit and marched it back and forth for hours above Isbell's studio. The teacher surrendered good-naturedly and promised Clemens free piano and banjo lessons in return for a little peace and quiet.

Keokuk, "a hotbed of rest," in biographer Ron Powers's happy phrase, provided Clemens with few other opportunities for mischief. He did what he could, simultaneously courting two girls named Ella and even escorting one of them to church. "I believe it was the first time I ever went to church; it was either the first time or the last time, I don't know which," he recalled a little vaguely. (It was neither.) He developed a serious crush on a bookish young student at nearby Iowa Wesleyan College, Ann Elizabeth Taylor, the daughter of a local alderman. The mostly theoretical affair eventually petered out, a casualty of time and distance, much to her father's undoubted relief. The frustrated suitor, between dashing off bits of romantic doggerel, helped his brothers fill desultory job orders for cards, circulars, bills, posters, wedding invitations, and something rather vaguely described as "colored work."

With a newfound interest in the life of the mind, Sam purchased a book on phrenology by St. Louis minister George Summer Weaver and carefully copied out the reverend's description of the "sanguine temperament." Phrenology, the divining of supposed character traits by feeling the lumps on one's head, was something of a national craze. The poet Walt Whitman was an early convert, cataloguing his traits in "Song of the Broad-Axe" as "voluptuous, inhabitive, combative, conscientious, alimentive, intuitive, of copious friendship, sublimity, firmness, self-esteem, comparison, individuality, form, locality, eventuality." Clemens's own phrenological characteristics, Sam noted proudly, indicated "activity, quickness, suppleness to all the motions of the body and mind; great elasticity and buoyancy of spirit; readiness, and even fondness for change; suddenness and intensity of feelings; impulsiveness, and hastiness in character, great warmth of both anger and love. . . . It loves excitement, noise, bluster, fun, frolic, high times, great days, mass meetings, camp meetings, big crowds." Orion, by contrast, was a classic case of the "nervous temperament," which, in contradiction of its somewhat negative name, supposedly produced "geniuses, precocious children, and people of purely intellectual habits and tastes." Orion, it must be said, was none of these.

Epitomizing perhaps his sanguine temperament, Sam considered going to South America and opening up "a trade in coca," a wondrous and still little known plant whose energy-enhancing qualities he had read about in a government pamphlet. With the help of a fifty-dollar bill he miraculously found plastered against the wall of a Keokuk house (so he claimed, at any rate), Clemens intended to work his way down the Mississippi River to New Orleans, where he would board a vessel bound for Brazil. He made it as far as Cincinnati. After a few unfulfilling months setting type in the Queen City for T. Wrightson & Company, the would-be cocaine baron boarded the steamboat *Paul Jones* and resumed his journey to South America. By the time the boat docked in New Orleans twelve days later, his career plans had changed dramatically.

A quarter of a century later, writing as Mark Twain, Clemens would describe that change in loving, evocative detail in his bestselling memoir, *Life on the Mississippi*. In that book, Twain recounted his transformation from itinerant typesetter to "good average St. Louis and New Orleans pilot," introducing the world to the agent of that miraculous change, Captain Horace Bixby, and dozens of other vivid characters, not least of whom was Twain himself. He would meet the first real love of his life, a little slip of a girl named Laura Wright, on the river, but it was the Mississippi itself that he fell most deeply in love with, and he would remember that attachment with undiluted, misty-eyed affection for the rest of his life.

Bixby was a good if idiosyncratic teacher, and Clemens quickly became his prize pupil. They got off to a stumbling start (Sam thought Bixby was just making conversation when he carefully pointed out various Mississippi River landmarks and danger spots), causing the captain to explode: "Taking you by and large, you do seem to be more different kinds of an ass than any creature I ever saw before."

The neophyte riverman soon learned his lesson, purchasing a small memorandum book and carefully jotting down Bixby's every offhand observation. There was a lot to learn. Bixby's empire stretched from New Orleans to St. Louis, twelve hundred miles on the lower Mississippi, each mile menaced by ever-shifting currents, riptides, shallows, sandbars, quicksand, floating islands, sunken rocks, sunken trees, sunken boats, loose debris, and the ever-present dangers of collisions with other boats, shipboard fires, and boiler explosions.

Still, with all its attendant dangers, the life of a steamboat pilot was grandly romantic, particularly for a young man who had grown up beside the river. Gradually, Sam learned how to be a pilot. "The face of the water, in time, became a wonderful book," he remembered fondly, "a book that was a dead language to the uneducated passenger, but which told its mind to me without reserve, delivering its most cherished secrets as clearly as if it uttered them with a voice." After two years of learning the river as an unpaid cub for Bixby and other experienced pilots, Clemens became fully licensed on April 9, 1859, an achievement that remained ever afterward the single proudest moment of his life. "Your true pilot cares nothing about anything on earth but the river, and his pride in his occupation surpasses the pride of kings," he observed

Moving regularly between a room at the Pilots' Association club in New Orleans and his sister's house in St. Louis, Clemens over the next two years made no fewer than 120 trips up and down the river. An average trip took about twenty-five days, not counting time spent in port. Some nine hundred steamboats plied the Mississippi below St. Louis, carrying loads of cotton, tobacco, sugar, livestock, farming equipment, even the U.S. mail. A boat could accommodate some two hundred passengers, many of them professional gamblers or prostitutes. Loaded to the gunnels, the flat-bottomed boats barely cleared the surface of the river. They needed twelve feet of water to float freely, hence the steersman's welcome cry of "Mark twain!" or two fathoms, signifying at least temporary safety. Even the most careful of pilots could run into trouble, natural or man-made, on a typical trip. Clemens was at the wheel for three such mishaps: crashing the *City of Memphis* into another steamboat in New Orleans harbor, running the *A. B. Chambers* onto a sandbar in the fog, and grounding the *Alonzo Child* during a race with another boat. Despite his somewhat mixed record, Clemens retained the confidence of his fellow professionals, although in retrospect his assessment of himself as a "good average" pilot seems, if anything, a trifle generous.

It was the golden age of steamboating, before railroads supplanted rivers as the nation's chief conduit of the goods, and Sam and his fellow pilots were lords of all they surveyed. At a princely salary of $250 a month, he could afford to live well, dining on oysters, shrimp, mushrooms, and brandy in fine New Orleans restaurants, and sending money home to his always impoverished mother. (He even sent Orion a pair of twelve-dollar alligator boots.) To his everlasting regret, Sam brought his eighteen-year-old brother Henry into the life, finding him an entry-level position as mud clerk, an unpaid job that mainly involved checking off inventory as it was loaded onto boats. In the summer of 1858, the two brothers were working together on the *Pennsylvania* when Sam got into an altercation with another pilot over Henry's alleged malfeasance of duty. Put off the boat by Captain John Klinefelter to avoid further fisticuffs, Sam was spared a gruesome fate. On June 13, seventy miles below Memphis, *Pennsylvania*'s steam boiler exploded, killing 120 passengers and crew, including Henry Clemens, who fatally inhaled white-hot steam while trying to rescue others. Sam, following two days behind his brother's boat, passed the bloated bodies of victims still bobbing unrecovered in the water. Henry, who had been taken to a hospital in Memphis, died eight days later without regaining consciousness.

Henry's death permanently haunted Sam, who blamed himself for his brother's fate. (The date of Henry's death, June 21, is the same date on which Hank Morgan, the antihero of *A Connecticut Yankee in King Arthur's Court*, is scheduled to die at the stake as a heretic.)

Even so, he could not stay away from the river for long. Over the course of the next three years, he served aboard eighteen different steamboats, beginning with the *Colonel Crossman* and ending with the *Alonzo Child*. His close brush with death won Clemens the unwanted nickname of "Lucky."

Sam briefly adopted another river-inspired sobriquet, "Sergeant Fathom," when he published a spoof in the New Orleans *Daily Crescent* in May 1859. Titled "River Intelligence," the piece lampooned fellow pilot Isaiah Sellers, a self-important old windbag who frequently unburdened himself of unsought advice and interminable reminiscence in the pages of the New Orleans *Picayune*. Clemens had sailed with Sellers aboard the *William M. Morrison*, and the older man had struck him one night with a boot. Now came the payback. Writing in Sellers's familiar sententious voice, Clemens recounted a ridiculous trip upriver in 1763 with a Chinese captain and a howling crew of Choctaw Indians, one of the sergeant's 1,450 trips upriver since "me and De Soto discovered the Mississippi." The broadly written burlesque drew blood as well as laughs, and the humiliated Sellers never published another column. As he had discovered with his written attack on Josiah T. Hinton in Hannibal a few years earlier, Clemens with a few well-chosen words could blast an unsuspecting target into oblivion. It was an experience that would never grow old.

However satisfying, "River Intelligence" would be Clemens's last piece of writing for several years. He was too busy piloting steamboats to poke fun at other pilots, most of whom he liked well enough, anyway. He rejected, as usual, Orion's advice, this time to write travel letters for newspapers, noting that "I cannot correspond with a newspaper, because when one is learning the river, he is not allowed to do or think of anything else." He did take the time to attend Mardi Gras in New Orleans, where he observed hundreds of men, women, and children "in fine, fancy, splendid, ugly, coarse, ridiculous, grotesque laughable costumes. . . . [A]n American has not seen the United States until he has seen the Mardi-Gras in New Orleans."

He further delved into the flamboyant underside of New Orleans life in February 1861 when he visited a fortune-teller, Madame Caprell, who for the bargain price of two dollars foretold with some accuracy both his immediate and long-term future. Her subject, she said, had been thrown into a wandering life by the sudden death of his father. (Not strictly true, but close enough.) He had written a great deal—"You write well," she said, in what constitutes the first known literary criticism of Mark Twain—and he would write even more in the future. He was in love with a young girl (Laura Wright, presumably) who was "not remarkably pretty, but very intelligent, educated, and accomplished." That girl would always be his first love, the mystic foresaw, but the lovers would "never break through the ice" between them since "you are both entirely too proud." Madame Caprell also had some advice for Orion, which Clemens happily passed along. Orion, she said, was "too visionary—always flying off on a new hobby." If only he would devote himself fully to politics, he might hold government office one day, even run for Congress. The image of hangdog, perpetually underachieving Orion bestriding the halls of the nation's capital was too rich to be believed. Sam, for his part, found it hilarious.

Four months after his visit to Madame Caprell's salon, Clemens was back in Hannibal, idling about the docks with his boyhood friends. The erstwhile riverboat pilot understood that, for the foreseeable future at least, the most glorious part of his life was over. Irresistibly drawn back to the river, Sam was slouching about the levee one afternoon with Sam Bowen, Will's younger brother, and another out-of-work pilot, Absalom Grimes, when an arriving steamboat slid into place, unloading a troop of blue-clad soldiers. Their commanding officer, a spruce young lieutenant, approached the three able-bodied Missourians, demanded to know their identities, and brusquely informed them that they were to be drafted into the Union Army. He had orders to see to it himself, taking them to St. Louis to be sworn into service. It was Clemens's worst nightmare sprung suddenly to life.

After a quick trip downriver aboard the *Harry Johnson*, the dispirited trio was escorted into the headquarters of Brigadier General John B. Grey, commander of the District of St. Louis. Appealing to their patriotism, Grey told the three friends they were needed to pilot Union troopships up the Missouri River to Boonville. They protested that they only knew the Mississippi, but the general was unmoved. "You could follow another boat up the Missouri River if she had a Missouri pilot on her, could you not?" he asked. They admitted as much. "That is all that is necessary," Grey said. Just then a pair of stylishly dressed ladies appeared at the general's door and asked for a word in private. When he stepped across the hall to see what they wanted, Clemens, Bowen, and Grimes took the heaven-sent opportunity to hightail it out the side door and escape to Hannibal. Their unexpected brush with Union service had the immediate effect of driving the young men into the waiting arms of the Confederate Army, or what passed for the Confederate Army at the time, the newly formed Marion Rangers.

Named for the county of its nativity, the Marion Rangers was the brainchild of Hannibal attorney John Robards, or RoBards, as he grandly styled himself *pour la guerre*. At its height, the company numbered a mere fifteen members, including Robards, Clemens, Grimes, Sam Bowen, and assorted other friends. In late June, the Rangers assembled on the farm of Mexican War veteran John Ralls, a former colonel who swore them into service in the name of Missouri governor Claiborne Jackson. (Jackson was busy, just then, retreating from the Union forces that had defeated him at Boonville on June 17.) The

Rangers, a very democratic group of guerrillas, immediately held an election for officers. William Ely was elected captain, Asa Glascock first lieutenant, and Sam Clemens second lieutenant. Sam Bowen, who had nominated Clemens, was selected first sergeant. By the time all the officers and noncommissioned officers had been chosen, there were only three or four men left over to serve as privates—which was probably just as well, since no one deigned to take orders from anyone else. Clemens, mounted precariously atop a fractious yellow mule named "Paint Brush," rode to war equipped with a valise, a carpetbag, a pair of blankets, a quilt, a frying pan, an old-fashioned Kentucky squirrel rifle, twenty yards of rope, and an umbrella. (The would-be Mars was prone to sunburn.)

As with the rest of the country, the military situation in Missouri at the beginning of the war was in a confused state of flux. Thanks to the quick actions of an alert young Army captain named Nathaniel Lyon, who had seized the federal armory in St. Louis and kept sixty thousand rifles, pistols, bayonets, and cannons out of the hands of homegrown Rebels, Union forces still held St. Louis and the upper Mississippi above Cairo, Illinois. But the southern part of the state belonged, however tenuously, to the Confederacy. Governor Jackson—Old Claib to admirers—installed a pro-southern legislature at Neosho, near the Arkansas border, and passed an ordinance of secession, which the Confederate Congress in Richmond, Virginia, readily accepted. Meanwhile, a rump legislature in Jefferson City deposed Jackson and replaced him with a pro-Union governor, setting the stage for some of the most brutal combat of the entire war.

In time, Missouri would witness more than eleven hundred battles and skirmishes, the third most of any state behind Virginia and Tennessee. Murderous guerrilla fighting of a very different sort than the gallant Napoleonic-era minuet the Rangers thought they were volunteering for would spawn reprisals and counterreprisals across Missouri that lasted long after the war was over, giving rise to the train-robbing deviltry of Jesse James and his henchmen, who had learned their dark skills in the Civil War. At this point, however, most of the fighting in Missouri was still being done with words—weapons that Sam Clemens and the other Marion Rangers were altogether better equipped to handle.

A quarter of a century later, Mark Twain recounted his military adventures in *Century Magazine*'s ongoing series, "Battles and Leaders of the Civil War." The series, one of the most successful ventures in publishing history, featured firsthand accounts by veterans of the war, both Union and Confederate, from General Ulysses S. Grant down to the most humble and unexceptional volunteer. Among the latter was Samuel Clemens, whose personal war story, part fact and part fiction, appeared in the magazine's December 1885 issue under the title "The Private History of a Campaign That Failed." When cross-referenced with Absalom Grimes's equally spurious account, "Campaigning with Mark Twain," published posthumously by Yale University Press in 1926, what emerges most clearly is a vision of the war's early days as a skylarking misadventure. The Rangers resemble nothing so much as Tom Sawyer's capering band of pirates.

Poorly led—Captain Glascock never even reported for duty—and insufficiently motivated, the Rangers thrashed about in the rain-drenched Missouri underbrush, arguing over strategy and literally picking names out of a hat to stand watch at night. Unlike their fellow guerrilla unit, the ferociously named Salt River Tigers, the Rangers had no long-handled sabers to carry with them and no three-piece company band to inspire them on the march. They did what they could, chopping off each other's hair with a pair of rusty sheep shears in anticipation of close-quarter, eye-gouging combat with the enemy, who seemed to be lurking devilishly behind every rock or tree. Like Stephen Crane's young private, Henry Fleming, in *The Red Badge of Courage*, the men were gripped by an obsessive fear of their unseen foes. One night on picket duty, Grimes cut down a clump of dangerous snapdragons with a blast from his double-barrel shotgun. Another night, a well-lubricated Ranger named Dave Young shot and killed his own horse, which had failed to give the proper password.

Their waxing and waning thirst for blood expressed itself mainly in a constant search for food, usually at the expense of long-suffering farmers. Clemens, impressively belted and sheathed by Colonel Ralls with a sword worn by his late neighbor, Colonel Brown, in the Mexican War, led the company "to a shady and pleasant piece of woods on the border of the far-reaching expanses of a flowery prairie. It was an enchanting region for war—our kind of war." Half the troop immediately jumped into the creek to go swimming; the other half began fishing. The Frenchified RoBards, called d'Unlap in the story, wanted to give the location a fittingly romantic name, but the other Rangers simply called it Camp Ralls.

Once safely installed amid the ruins of an abandoned maple sugar camp, the Rangers set about learning to ride the horses and mules brought to them by patriotic farmers in the neighborhood. "We did learn to ride, after some days' practice," Mark Twain recalled, "but never well. We could not learn to like our animals." It was no wonder: Clemens's mule threw him at every opportunity, while Bowen's horse was given to biting him in the leg whenever it sensed him falling asleep, as he did frequently, in the saddle. When Sam ordered Bowen (called Bowers in the story) to feed his mule for him, Bowen retorted "that if I [Sam] reckoned he went to war to be a dry-nurse to a mule, it wouldn't take me very long to find out my mistake."

The idyllic camp life, so reminiscent of Tom Sawyer's adventures with Huck Finn and Joe Harper on Jackson's Island, was regularly interrupted by fresh alarums of enemy activity in the area. Much panicky marching and countermarching ensued—so much, in fact, that a skeptical farmer observed drolly that the Rangers would undoubtedly win the war all by themselves "because no government could stand the expense of the shoe-leather we should cost it trying to follow

[them] around." On one occasion, the entire company managed to tumble down a rain-slick hill into a creek. Another night, lost again in the darkness, the men were set upon by a pack of farm dogs, each of which "took a soldier by the slack of the trousers and began to back away with him." The Rangers were unable to shoot the dogs for fear of hitting each other. At length, the dogs' owner woke up and managed to free the victims from their grip, all except Bowers. "They couldn't undo his dog," Twain recalled; "they didn't know the combination; he was of the bull kind, and seemed to be set with a Yale time-lock; but they got him loose at last with some scalding water, of which Bowers got his share and returned thanks."

During the course of his campaigning, Sam developed a painful saddle sore—he was never a very good rider—and sprained his ankle jumping out of a burning hayloft. The Rangers moved to another camp, which they dubbed Camp Devastation in honor of their ever-worsening prospects. Once again Sam attempted to pull rank, ordering Bowen to stand watch; he only agreed to do so after Clemens promised to switch places with him for the night. In due time, the newly appointed commander of their part of Missouri, Colonel Thomas A. Harris, arrived for an inspection. Harris, a fellow Hannibal resident, was "a first-rate fellow, and well liked," observed Twain, "but we had all familiarly known him as the sole and modest-salaried operator in our telegraph office, where he had to send about one dispatch a week in ordinary times, and two when there was a rush of business." He had no more luck issuing orders than anyone else.

Harris's Union counterpart was a freshly minted colonel from Illinois, Ulysses S. Grant, commanding the equally green 21st Illinois Infantry. Grant, like Harris, was a Mexican War veteran. In Mexico, the hitherto unprepossessing Grant had won several promotions for bravery, but he had ruined his postwar career and wasted his expensive West Point education by indulging in bouts of homesick binge drinking. He resigned impulsively from the army for a woefully misconceived career in business, a decision that would eventually reduce him to selling firewood on a St. Louis street corner. His penultimate position, before going to work for his brothers in a Galena, Illinois, hardware store, was that of a bill collector. To avoid calling on clients, Grant hung around the next-door office of William Moffett, Sam Clemens's brother-in-law. If the two future giants of the age ever laid eyes on each other then, neither remembered it later. Now, riding at the head of a veritable enemy juggernaut, Grant was said to be drawing ever closer to Camp Devastation. Once again, the Rangers moved.

What happened next, in Mark Twain's retelling, was nothing less than a tragedy. It was also untrue. "Presently," Twain wrote in his private history, "a muffled sound caught our ears, and we recognized it as the hoof-beats of a horse or horses. And right away a figure appeared in the forest path. . . . It was a man on horseback, and it seemed to me that there were others behind him. I got hold a gun in the dark, and pushed it through a crack between the logs, hardly knowing what I was doing, I was so dazed with fright. Somebody said, 'Fire!' I pulled the trigger." Half a dozen gunshots rang out and the man tumbled from his saddle. Sam and the others warily approached their victim, who was gasping for breath, his white shirt splashed with blood. The man soon expired, muttering pitifully about his wife and child. It gave them all pause. "The thought shot through me that I was a murderer; that I had killed a man—a man who had never done me any harm," Twain wrote. "It seemed an epitome of war; that all war must be just that—the killing of strangers against whom you feel no personal animosity; strangers whom, in other circumstances, you would help if you found them in trouble, and who would help you if you needed it. My campaign was spoiled. It seemed to me that I was not rightly equipped for this awful business."

The killing of the unarmed civilian was supposedly the last straw for Clemens and his fellow Rangers. When Colonel Harris arrived on the scene again and urged them to advance, they refused. "We told him there was a Union colonel coming with a whole regiment in his wake," Twain recalled, "and it looked as if there was going to be a disturbance; so we had concluded to go home. . . . We had done our share; had killed one man, exterminated one army, such as it was; let him go and kill the rest, and that would end the war." A few days later they disbanded. Half the Rangers would stay on and serve out the war, including Absalom Grimes, who subsequently put his guerrilla skills to work smuggling mail past Union checkpoints, and Sam Bowen, who became a Confederate gunboat pilot. As for Clemens, "I could have become a soldier myself, if I had waited. I had got part of it learned; I knew more about retreating than the man that invented retreating." He put that knowledge to immediate use, dodging enemy forces, real or imagined, all the way from northern Missouri back to St. Louis, where he again went into hiding at his sister's house.

"The Private History of a Campaign That Failed," though eventually read by *Century Magazine*'s 225,000 readers, was written, in fact, for an audience of one: Ulysses S. Grant. While Twain was finishing the rough draft of the article in May 1885, the former president was dying of throat cancer at a borrowed cottage in upstate New York. Twain showed the manuscript to the general, who was writing his own, much longer remembrance of the war for Charles L. Webster & Company, a publishing company owned, not coincidentally, by Twain and his nephew-in-law. A few months earlier, the author had induced Grant to back out of his contract with *Century Magazine* and sign an agreement with Webster & Company to publish his memoirs. Grant, in a valiant race against the clock, completed his two-volume book mere days before dying on July 23, 1885. It was a private joke between the two that they had just missed running into each other in Missouri in the summer of 1861; Twain even considered calling his story "My Campaign Against Grant." In fact, the Marion Rangers had already broken up and dispersed several weeks before Grant advanced southward into Missouri, and by that time Harris had retreated even farther south. Clemens was long gone when Grant won his first military victory, a glorified skirmish at Belmont, Missouri, on November 7, 1861.

But if Sam Clemens the reluctant Confederate had missed crossing swords with the greatest general in the Civil War, he had also avoided becoming part of an even more brutal war inside his home state. Despite all his after-the-fact joking about his innate military potential, there is simply no way that fun-loving Sam Clemens could have shared a campfire with the pitiless likes of William Clarke Quantrill, "Bloody Bill" Anderson, Frank and Jesse James, Cole Younger, "Little Arch" Clements, and dozens of other hardened bushwhackers who came together in the shadowy woods and rocky ravines of western Missouri in late 1861 and early 1862 to rob, pillage, and murder in the name of the Confederacy. (Union-leaning guerrillas such as Charles R. Jennison's Jayhawkers were just as bad.) Except for the fictitious killing of the civilian in "The Private History of a Campaign That Failed," Clemens was no killer—not with bullets, anyway. His weapon of choice was words, and he was about to relocate to a more congenial environment, one in which his natural abilities would be free to develop without the inconvenient intrusion of civil war.

For the time being, however, professing himself to be "incapacitated by fatigue from persistent retreating," the shaken Clemens stayed close to home. Once again, eight-year-old Annie Moffett was his daily companion. He called her "Old Horse" when he was pleased with her and "Trundle-bed Trash" when he wasn't. Her uncle's brief brush with "death-on-the-pale-horse-with-hell-following-after" did not have the immediate effect of increasing his attendance at the local Methodist church. Annie, a good Christian girl, encouraged Clemens to go to services with her and her parents. "I thought he needed a little religious instruction and started to tell him the story of Moses," she remembered. "Uncle Sam . . . said he knew Moses very well, that he kept a secondhand store on Market Street. I tried very hard to explain that it wasn't the Moses I meant, but he just couldn't understand." It would take more than the Civil War to get her uncle back to church.

Deliverance of a more worldly kind came from the unlikeliest of sources: Orion Clemens. In mid-July, Orion turned up at the Moffett house proudly flourishing a piece of paper that he considered his long-deferred ticket to the big time, a patronage appointment as secretary to the governor of the newly created Nevada Territory. As a longtime Whig turned Republican, Orion had kept in touch with St. Louis lawyer Edward Bates, an early mentor, and had campaigned hard for Abraham Lincoln in northern Missouri. True to form, Orion had failed to help Lincoln carry Missouri, which was the only state to give its electoral votes to Democratic nominee Stephen Douglas in the 1860 election. Nevertheless, as a sop to the southern border states with large Unionist populations, Lincoln selected Bates as his attorney general. (He could not resist joking, however, that Bates's dark head of hair and snow-white beard suggested that he "used his chin more than his head.") Bates, in turn, rewarded Orion for his long years of service to the abolitionist cause. In a letter of recommendation to Secretary of State William Seward that was remarkable chiefly for its lack of enthusiasm, Bates described Orion as "an honest man of fair mediocrity of talents & learning—more indeed of both, than I have seen in several Territorial secretaries. Without being very urgent with you, I commend Mr. Clemens to you, as a worthy & competent man, who will be grateful for a favor."

Whatever Bates's level of enthusiasm, Orion was immensely grateful for the favor, and so was his unemployed brother. At a family meeting at Pamela's home, where their mother Jane now was living, Orion detailed the grand particulars of his appointment. He was to receive a salary of $1,800 a year while serving as the second-highest government official in Nevada. (New York machine politician James W. Nye, Seward's erstwhile campaign manager during his failed presidential campaign, had been named territorial governor, possibly to get him as far away from New York City as Lincoln could manage for the duration of the war.) Mark Twain joked that his brother's appointment was one of "such majesty that it concentrated in itself the duties and dignities of Treasurer, Comptroller, Secretary of State, and Acting Governor in the governor's absence. . . . [T]he title of 'Mr. Secretary' gave to the great position an air of wild and imposing grandeur."

There was just one problem: Orion didn't have enough money to pay his way across country to Carson City, Nevada, where his lofty secretariat awaited him. Sam offered to help. He had saved $1,200 from his piloting days, money he had intended to live on for the next six months. But St. Louis was too dangerous for a militarily unaffiliated young man like Clemens; whoever controlled the city—Federals or Confederates—would soon put him back to work on a gunboat on the river. Expecting the trouble to blow over in a few months, anyway, Sam offered to pay for both their riverboat and stagecoach tickets if Orion would take him along to Nevada. Orion was agreeable, and Jane Clemens, although still a southerner at heart, was glad to have her two surviving sons out of harm's way. It was settled.

On July 11, 1861, Orion, proudly bearing his certificate with Abraham Lincoln's signature at the bottom, appeared before a Missouri Supreme Court justice in St. Louis and officially took his oath of office. Then he and his brother began preparing for their trip out west. Since they would be traveling mainly by stagecoach, they packed light—twenty-five pounds each, including one heavy suit, a few dress shirts, one wool "army shirt," boots, tobacco, pipes, and underwear. "It was a sad parting," remarked Twain, "for now we had no swallow-tail coats and white kid gloves to wear at Pawnee receptions in the Rocky Mountains, and no stove-pipe hats nor patent-leather boots nor anything else necessary to make life calm and peaceful. We were reduced to a war-footing." For future sustenance, they took along a bag full of coins to pay for their meals along the way, as well as two canteens for water and several boxes of "Acetous Extract of Lemons," contributed by their practical-minded mother to help ward off scurvy.

Orion also carried with him ten pounds' worth of federal statutes and an unabridged dictionary, unaware that such things could be purchased in San Francisco and shipped overnight to Carson City. (In his autobiography, Twain estimated that the dictionary "weighed about a thousand pounds and . . . it wasn't a good dictionary, anyway—didn't have any modern words in it—only had obsolete ones that they used to use when Noah Webster was a child.") Orion brought along fourteen pages of handwritten instructions from U.S. Treasury comptroller Elisha Whittlesey detailing his duties as territorial secretary. Sam, for his part, "was armed to the teeth with a pitiful little Smith & Wesson's seven-shooter, which carried a ball like a homeopathic pill, and took the whole seven shots to make a dose for an adult." The pistol, a .22-caliber 1857 model breechloader, had a four-inch barrel and was not accurate beyond a range of fifteen yards. Not to be outgunned, Orion strapped a small Colt revolver to his hip, western-style, but left it unloaded "to guard against accidents." Thus suitably armed and accoutered, the Clemens brothers set out for the wild and woolly West. Henceforth, the Confederacy would have to make do without Samuel Clemens. He was lighting out for the Territory.

A FINE PLEASURE TRIP

BEFORE SAM AND ORION COULD GET TO NEVADA, they first had to reach St. Joseph, Missouri, the jumping-off point for the western frontier. On July 18, they went down to the St. Louis levee and boarded the *Sioux City*, a ramshackle packet boat, for a six-day trip up the Missouri River, the same river Sam Clemens had nearly been drafted to navigate for the Union Navy. Orion had left his wife, Mollie, and their five-year-old daughter, Jennie, with Mollie's parents in Keokuk; they would rejoin him in Carson City once he got properly situated.

The Missouri, the longest river on the North American continent, is a notoriously winding and treacherous waterway. Its three-thousand-mile course traces an elliptical loop from just above St. Louis to Fort Benton, Montana, a bluff-lined, ever-changing river that makes the Mississippi look tame in comparison. "The Big Muddy," as it was—and still is—called by travelers with no particular fondness for its turbid, dingy-brown appearance, was "unpoetic and repulsive—a stream of flowing mud studded with dead tree trunks and broken by bars," in the words of New York *Tribune* reporter Albert Richardson. It rose twice yearly, in April and June, when the snowmelt from the Nebraska prairies and the Rocky Mountains uprooted trees and sent them flying like javelins through the silt-thick water. "I have seen nothing more frightful," French explorer Jacques Marquette observed in 1673, and in his travels he had seen a lot of frightening things.

In many ways, the Missouri was more dangerous than the Mississippi. Except for its annual flood time, the Missouri baked down during the summer to a trickle of quicksand-studded shallows beneath glowering treeless bluffs. Many pilots relied too readily on "a wad of steam" to get them through the occasional rapids or over sandbars. The consequences could be deadly; dozens of Missouri River steamers blew up each year from boiler explosions. On Good Friday, April 9, 1852, the paddle wheeler *Saluda* exploded near Lexington, Missouri. Ill-fated Captain Francis Belt, leaning against the ship's bell when the mishap occurred, found himself tumbling head over heels down a bluff several hundred yards inland, the bell clanging madly as it rolled downhill alongside him. The ship's safe, with a watchdog still chained to it, and an unlucky clerk who happened to be passing by, were flung two hundred yards ashore, and a local butcher had the abject misfortune to be dismembered by a flying boiler flue. In all, the bodies of more than one hundred *Saluda* crewmen and passengers were eventually recovered up and down the Lexington wharf, making it the worst single disaster in the river's disaster-strewn history.

The current trip was somewhat less perilous. Indeed, it was "so dull and sleepy," recalled Twain, "that it has left no more impression on my memory than if its duration had been six minutes instead of that many days." Perhaps not, but he remembered enough about the trip to jab his professional judgment a decade later. The river, he said, presented "a confused jumble of savage-looking snags, which we deliberately walked over with one wheel or the other; and of reefs which we butted and butted, and then retired from and climbed over in some softer place; and of sand-bars which we roosted on occasionally, and rested, and then got out our crutches and sparred over." The boat might as well have traveled to St. Joseph by land, said Twain, since "she was walking most of the time, anyhow." The boat's captain bragged that she was "a bully boat," needing only more shear and a bigger wheel to make her perfect. Twain, with his jaundiced pilot's eye, thought the boat actually needed a pair of stilts, but he "had the deep sagacity not to say so." Richardson, who had made a similar voyage upriver four years earlier, had no such compunction. "Navigating the Missouri, at low water," he wrote, "is like putting a steamer upon dry land, and sending a boy ahead with a sprinkling pot."

The brothers arrived safely in St. Joseph on July 24 and went immediately to the business office of the Central Overland California & Pike's Peak Express stagecoach line, where Sam purchased tickets for the pair of them, at $150 apiece. Counting boat fare, he was now four hundred dollars out of pocket, with only a vague promise from his brother—he knew all about those—to put him on the government payroll once they reached Nevada. In choosing as their carrier the COC&PP, as it was known, the brothers had opted for the northernmost of the five established routes to the West Coast. (The Oregon Trail, which their route followed, diverged at Fort Bridger, Wyoming, and continued through the upper Northwest, but did not go through all the way to the coast.) Their itinerary followed the Little Blue River from Kansas into Nebraska, passing through Fort Kearny, then shadowed the Platte River to Cottonwood before cutting across the edge of Colorado and back into Nebraska to Fort Laramie, Wyoming, down to Fort Bridger, then to Salt Lake City, Utah, across the Great Salt Lake, and finally a straight shot across Nevada to Carson City. The trip was scheduled to take seventeen days and average a hundred miles per day. Passengers were expected to sleep sitting up inside the coach. It was a wearying prospect, but there was no other option;

the first transcontinental railroad line would not be completed for another decade.

The fact that the stage line pulled into so many different forts along the way reflected the smoldering unrest, not yet a full-blown prairie fire, that was kindling within the various Plains Indian tribes whose ancestral homelands were being trampled daily by numberless thousands of white travelers. (On one day alone in August 1850, soldiers at Fort Laramie counted some 39,506 travelers rumbling westward aboard 9,927 wagons.) Among the tribes claiming territory abutting the COC&PP route were the Cheyennes, Pawnees, Poncas, Arapahos, Utes, Paiutes, and Gosiutes. Most had attended the great 1851 peace parley at Fort Laramie, where representatives of the American government, in return for the right to build roads and army posts on their land, had promised to pay the tribes annuities of fifty thousand dollars each for the next fifty years. The parsimonious U.S. Senate soon cut the number down to ten years.

It took less than three years for trouble to flare. In August 1854, a young Miniconjou Sioux warrior named High Forehead, summering with his tribesmen outside Fort Laramie, shot a stray cow that had wandered into their camp and (according to the Indians) run amok. The cow belonged to a passing party of Danish immigrants, who complained to the fort's overworked commander, Lieutenant Hugh Fleming. Against his better judgment, Fleming sent Second Lieutenant John L. Grattan to investigate. Grattan, fresh out of West Point, was given to bragging that with ten good men he could defeat the entire Cheyenne nation. As it developed, he never got the chance (these were Sioux, anyway). On the morning of August 19, he rode out to arrest High Forehead. The warrior demurred. By the time negotiations had concluded, Grattan and his entire thirty-man force lay dead, Grattan's body by grim coincidence bristling with twenty-four arrows—one for each year of his abruptly terminated life.

Sam Clemens may have heard about the Grattan massacre—he was in St. Louis at the time—and he certainly knew a garbled version of a second Indian massacre that had taken place two years later near Fort Kearny and involved a particularly luckless territorial secretary named Almon Whiting Babbitt. It was Babbitt's remarkable misfortune to be attacked twice by Cheyennes within the space of thirteen days. He survived the first attack by managing to be absent when a war party set upon his supply train and killed various of his companions. Forewarned but not forearmed, the secretary was attacked again two weeks later, apparently by a different group of Cheyennes. This time he was killed. In his subsequent account of the episode in *Roughing It*, Mark Twain mislocated Babbitt's attack by a good hundred miles and added: "I was personally acquainted with a hundred and thirty-three or four people who were wounded during that massacre, and barely escaped with their lives. . . . One of these parties told me that he kept coming across arrow-heads in his system for nearly seven years after the massacre." According to Twain, Babbitt survived the massacre by crawling away on his hands and knees for forty hours, a singular feat since Babbitt was dead at the time.

With images of Indians dancing in his head (a drawing on page three of *Roughing It* shows the sleeping author innocently dreaming of Indians, wagon trains, buffalo hunts, steamboats, and gold mining, all lit by the rising sun), Sam climbed aboard a Concord stagecoach with Orion for the first leg of their journey. The Concord, named for the New Hampshire city where it was produced by the Abbot-Downing Company, was "a great swinging and swaying . . . cradle on wheels." It weighed more than a ton, stood eight feet high, and could accommodate as many as twenty-one passengers—nine seated inside and a dozen more hanging precariously from the roof. Drawn by six horses, the Concord's chief innovation was its flexible leather thoroughbraces, a pair of stiff, three-inch-thick leather strips that acted as primitive shock absorbers and produced the coach's characteristic rocking motion. A conductor rode beside the driver, functioning more or less as his counterpart did on a railroad train, overseeing the driver, passengers, and bags of mail entrusted to his care. The body of the stagecoach was painted English vermilion, with scenic pictures decorating the outside door panels and the likenesses of well-known actresses painted on the footboards or driver's seat much as pinup art would grace the nose cones of air force bombers in World War II.

Trading, no doubt, on Sam's noticeable jumpiness, the "facetious" driver of their stage immediately brought up the subject of Indians. The interior of the coach was loaded down with twenty-seven hundred pounds of mail, "a perpendicular wall" of mailbags that jostled the brothers' knees inside the passenger compartment; the rest was stowed in the front and rear boots. Some of the mail, said the driver, was intended for Salt Lake City, some for Carson City, and some for San Francisco, but most of it was set aside "for the Injuns, which is powerful troublesome 'thout they get plenty of truck to read." Earlier that same month, the stage line had undertaken a contract with the federal government to make daily mail deliveries between St. Joseph and Salt Lake City, a task that was greatly complicated by Confederate depredations in southern Missouri, which caused some twelve tons of undelivered mail to pile up at the company's St. Joseph office. To lighten their loads, many of the drivers had taken to abandoning mailbags on the side of the road, particularly those containing non-personal mail such as *Harper's Weekly, Atlantic Monthly*, and *Godey's* magazines, thus depriving culture-starved frontier matrons of the latest fashion news from the East. Sometimes the drivers disguised themselves as Indians and set fire to the bags to give their stories the plausible appearance of truth.

At this point in his life, the only authentic Native American that Sam Clemens had met personally was his old Hannibal neighbor "Injun Joe" Douglas, an Osage Indian who had survived a scalping from some less than fraternal Pawnees as a teenager and had been brought to Hannibal for his own safety by some sympathetic drovers.

The real Injun Joe was a pleasant enough person (he even bought ice cream for the local children), but that did not stop Mark Twain from making him the memorably murderous villain of *The Adventures of Tom Sawyer*, the slayer of grave-robbing Doctor Robinson and the perjured accuser of town drunk Muff Potter. For all his various misdeeds, subsequently punished by the author when "I starved him entirely to death in the cave," Injun Joe was a mere piker compared to the literally hair-raising Indians in Twain's unfinished 1884 novel, *Huck Finn and Tom Sawyer Among the Indians*, which takes place in the same Platte River valley that their stagecoach was just now in the act of crossing.

Intended as a direct sequel to *Huckleberry Finn*, the eighteen-thousand-word manuscript picks up with Huck and Tom, accompanied by Jim, "lighting out for the Territory"—in this case, Nebraska—where they join a Missouri family named Mills that is bound for Oregon. Along the Platte River, they camp with a small group of Oglala Sioux warriors. Initially friendly, the Indians suddenly attack and kill all the men in the party except Huck and Tom, who escape, and Jim, who is taken prisoner along with the two Mills girls. The book meanders on, with Huck and Tom searching for their friends with late-arriving frontiersman Brace Johnson, the older girl's fiancé. The specter of miscegenational rape is hinted at throughout the story, which may be why Twain was unable to finish it. By then he was the father of three young girls himself, and he could not bring himself to carry the book through to its logical and tragic conclusion: the rape and murder of the Mills girls by their captors.

Given his famous disdain for statistics, it probably would not have mattered to Clemens that fewer than four hundred of the nearly thirty thousand deaths suffered by western emigrants between 1842 and 1859 came at the hands of hostile Indians. Cholera alone killed ten times that many—to say nothing of dysentery, tuberculosis, small-pox, measles, mumps, Rocky Mountain spotted fever, and scurvy, the latter caused by insufficient fruits and vegetables in the travelers' diet.

Accidental shootings, drownings (one historian has estimated that nearly as many travelers drowned in the various rivers as were killed by Indians), wagon mishaps, falls, lightning strikes, tornadoes, whirlwinds, blizzards, quicksand, wild animal attacks, snakebites, starvation, exhaustion, exposure, and sometimes sheer "melancholy" were steady—if less colorful—killers on the trail. Four hapless immigrants were killed by a falling oak tree in 1849; another was scalded to death in the hot springs at Truckee, Nevada. "To enjoy such a trip," said one anonymous overlander a few years earlier, "a man must be able to endure heat like a salamander, mud and water like a muskrat, dust like a toad, and labor like a jackass. . . . It is a hardship without glory, to be sick without a home, to die and be buried like a dog." Luckily, perhaps, as another traveler noted: "The air of the plains is glorious, pure and dry. There is no odor to a dead body here, as it does not decay but simply dries up."

The brothers saw their first live Indians on July 29, four days into the trip and 370 miles out of St. Joseph, near Fort Kearny. Twain, oddly, does not mention the sighting in *Roughing It*, but Orion took note of the event at the time, reporting to his wife that they had visited the camp, priced some "beautifully dressed" buffalo robes—the Indians wanted between three and six dollars—and seen the burial scaffold, eight feet high, of an Indian child. At this point of their journey, the Indians were almost certainly Pawnees, which was good luck for Sam and Orion since the Pawnees were unwavering allies of the white man and sworn enemies of the Sioux and Cheyenne, with whom they were contesting ownership of the rapidly dwindling Plains. (Not for nothing was one of the principal Sioux chiefs named Pawnee Killer.) The Pawnee men wore their hair in a distinctive high, bristling scalp lock, not unlike a mid-seventies punk rocker, and other Indians called them the Horn People. With typical Indian humility, they called themselves the Men of Men. They were particularly avid astronomers, worshipping the morning and evening stars and annually sacrificing a captured virgin to the morning star, until a reform-minded chief named Petalesharo put an end to the practice, presumably because it was upsetting the white men.

Sam and Orion were also lucky in the timing of their trip. The trail passed just south of the area claimed by the fierce Santee Sioux, who were within a few months of going on the warpath in Minnesota and massacring upwards of 250 white men, women, and children in the worst such incident in western history. The brothers also passed within one hundred miles of the future site of an even more infamous massacre, the rubbing out in June 1876 of Lieutenant Colonel George Armstrong Custer and 263 of his men in the 7th Cavalry at the Little Bighorn. Santee were there that day, too.

Indians aside, the first leg of the stagecoach trip brought the brothers "an exhilarating sense of emancipation from all sorts of cares and responsibilities, that almost made us feel that the years we had spent in the close, hot city, toiling and slaving, had been wasted and thrown away." Forgetting the fact that he had spent most of the last four years on the wide-open Mississippi River, as the captain of all he surveyed from the three-story-high pilothouse of a steamboat, Sam acted as though he had been delivered from one of Charles Dickens's poorhouses or William Blake's dark satanic mills. It was a bit of a stretch, but no matter. The brothers, for the time being at least, were free. "Our perfect enjoyment took the form of a tranquil and contented ecstasy," noted Twain. "The cradle swayed and swung luxuriously. . . . As we lay and smoked the pipe of peace and compared all this luxury with the years of tiresome city life that had gone before it, we felt that there was only one complete and satisfying happiness in the world, and we had found it."

In many ways, Sam and Orion were mismatched traveling partners. Ten years apart in age, they had never played together as children; Sam and the lost Henry were much closer playmates. After their father's death, Orion had become the family breadwinner, a role he was congenitally unsuited to fill. The three brothers had worked together on Orion's newspapers and at his printing company, but never as equals—Orion was always the boss. When Sam became a riverboat pilot the interpersonal balance of power tipped, but thanks to the outbreak of the war, Sam had a short reign on top. Now, once again, the older brother was dominant, and Sam could only look on with the usual mixture of affection, exasperation, and wonder at Orion's frangible nature. "He was the only person I have ever known in whom pessimism and optimism were lodged in exactly equal proportions," Twain would write. "Except in the matter of grounded principle, he was as unstable as water. You could dash his spirits with a single word; you could raise them into the sky again with another one. . . . He was always truthful; he was always sincere; he was always honest and honorable. But in light matters—matters of small consequence, like religion and politics and such things—he never acquired a conviction that could survive a disapproving remark from a cat." Given the obvious differences in their natures and the contrasting similarities they bore to their parents, it was almost as if their mother and father were traveling with them on opposite sides of the stage.

For reasons of filial mercy and artistic necessity—he couldn't very well make Orion the butt of his jokes—Mark Twain invented a third passenger on their stagecoach, a Falstaffian character named George Bemis. Like them, Bemis came armed, in his case with a comically impractical Allen pistol, known as a "pepper-box" for its unique appearance. With six revolving barrels, the unwieldy Allen did resemble a pepper shaker, more or less, and it was about as effective as a hand-gun. "To aim along the turning barrel and hit the thing aimed at," said Twain, "was a feat which was probably never done with an 'Allen' in the world. . . . It was a cheerful weapon—the 'Allen.' Sometimes all its six barrels would go off at once, and then there was no safe place in all the region round about, but behind it." Demonstrating the weapon for his fellow travelers, Bemis nails a deuce of spades to a tree and accidentally shoots a mule standing thirty yards to the left. "Bemis did not want the mule," remembered Twain, "but the owner came out with a double-barreled shotgun and persuaded him to buy it, anyhow."

In *Roughing It*, Bemis provides comedy relief, or at any rate comedic companionship, during the first part of the brothers' journey west. At one point he is conked on the head by Orion's half-ton unabridged dictionary, which "tilted Bemis's nose up till he could look down his nostrils." On another occasion, he joins an impromptu buffalo hunt, only to be chased for two miles by an enraged bull, which follows him up the only tree still standing within sight of nine counties. Bemis, in his recounting, says he lassoed the bull when it drew too near to his tree limb, and fired off his Allen, which missed the bull but scared it enough to send it into convulsions and allowed him to escape. When Twain expresses doubt about the story, Bemis forces him to admit that the story must be true, since he (Bemis) is missing his lariat, his horse, and the bull buffalo—thus proving his point.

At South Pass City, Utah, astride the Continental Divide, the travelers meet the resident postmaster, who combines within his person the offices of hotel keeper, blacksmith, mayor, constable, city marshal, and principal citizen. "Bemis said he was 'a perfect Allen's revolver of dignities,'" Twain recalled. When last seen, a drunken Bemis has taken to his bed in Salt Lake City, still wearing his boots and "talking loosely, disjointedly and indiscriminately, and every now and then tugging out a ragged word by the roots that had more hiccups than syllables in it." A victim of "valley tan," a local whiskey made from wheat and considered by one authority to be "the vilest whisky I remember tasting," Bemis is heard no more. Like the fool in *King Lear*, he simply disappears from the play.

When not communing with the imaginary Bemis, the brothers kept a close eye on the real-life flora and fauna outside the stagecoach windows. For comfort's sake, they stripped down to their cotton underwear—it was truly a man's world inside the coach—and reclined on the mailbags, smoking their pipes and dodging periodically "the uneasy Dictionary" when it "made an assault" upon them. Side by side, wrote Twain, they "leveled an outlook over the world-wide carpet about us for things new and strange to gaze at. Even at this day it thrills me through and through to think of the life, the gladness and the wild sense of freedom that used to make the blood dance in my being on those fine overland mornings!" The countryside went from gently rolling plains to flat, horizonless prairie broken only by the hardy sagebrush, or "greasewood," which made for a smokeless campfire "and consequently no swearing." As a comestible, however, Twain found the sagebrush "a distinguished failure. Nothing can abide the taste of it but the jackass and his illegitimate child the mule. But their testimony to its nutritiousness is worth nothing, for they will eat pine knots, or anthracite coal, or brass filings, or lead pipe, or old bottles, or anything that comes handy, and then go off looking as grateful as if they had had oysters for dinner."

Orion's maddening habit of whistling drove the fidgeting Sam to frequent transports of imagined murder. "His diabolical notions of time and tune [are] worse than the itch," Sam wrote to their mother. "Providence has ordained that he shall whistle when he feels pleasant—notwithstanding the fact that the barbarous sounds he produces are bound to drive comfort away from everyone else within hear-shot of them. I have to sit still and be tortured with his infernal discords, and fag-ends of tunes which were worn out and discarded before 'Roll on—Sil-ver Moo-oon' became popular, strung together without regard to taste, time, melody, or the eternal fitness of things."

Orion's whistling aside, it was "a fine pleasure trip," and the brothers "supped daily on wonders." Near Big Sandy Creek in Nebraska, they saw their first jackrabbit, or "jackass rabbit," as Twain called it.

The stage driver encouraged them to make the unoffending animal "hump himself," or take off running, and the brothers opened fire with their pistols. "It is not putting it too strong to stay that the rabbit was frantic," wrote Twain. "He dropped his ears, set up his tail, and left for San Francisco at a speed which can only be described as a flash and a vanish! Long after he was out of sight we could hear him whiz."

Besides jackrabbits, they also saw wolves, antelopes, prairie dogs, and coyotes. The coyote—he continually misspelled it "cayote"—afforded Twain an opportunity for a fine set piece of descriptive writing. The coyote, he said, "is a long, slim, sick and sorry-looking skeleton, with a gray wolf-skin stretched over it, a tolerably bushy tail that forever sags down with a despairing expression of forsakenness and misery, a furtive and evil eye, and a long, sharp face, with a slightly lifted lip and exposed teeth. He has a general slinking expression all over. The cayote is a living, breathing allegory of Want. He is *always* hungry. He is always, poor, out of luck and friendless. The meanest creatures despise him, and even the fleas would desert him for a velocipede. He is so spiritless and cowardly that even while his exposed teeth are pretending a threat, the rest of his face is apologizing for it." The coyote's only companions are lizards, jackrabbits, ravens, and "his first cousins, the desert-frequenting . . . Indians." Like them, "he will eat anything [he] can bite. . . . He does not mind going a hundred miles to breakfast, and a hundred and fifty to dinner, because he is sure to have three or four days between meals, and he can just as well be traveling and looking at the scenery as lying around doing nothing and adding to the burdens of his parents."

The brothers were often hungry themselves, owing to the gruesome fare provided to passengers at COC&PP way stations. Stagecoaches would stop every ten or twelve miles to change horses, but passengers could alight only every forty or fifty miles to relieve and refresh themselves at a station. The stations, so familiar to future generations of motion picture and television shows, were a jumble of long, low adobe huts connected to wooden barns and stables.

Watering troughs and hitching posts stood in front of the main building, which doubled as a dining room and bunkhouse for the station keeper and assorted hostlers, blacksmiths, and hangers-on. To Twain, the station men were "unspeakably picturesque" in their invariable outfits of buckskin leggings, blue-and-yellow pants, high-heeled boots, and Spanish spurs. Long navy revolvers were worn on leather belts, the handles reversed for easy drawing; horn-handled bowie knives projected from their boots. The station men scarcely noticed the interchangeable travelers, reserving their attention for the stage-coach driver—"a great and shining dignitary, the world's favorite son, the envy of the people, the observed of the nations."

The driver, for his part, considered the station men "a sort of good enough low creatures, useful in their place, and helping to make up a world, but not the kind of beings which a person of distinction could afford to concern himself with." When he did deign to speak to them, uttering a joke "old as the hills, coarse, profane, witless, and inflicted on the same audience, in the same language, every time his coach drove up there—the varlets roared, and slapped their thighs, and swore it was the best thing they'd ever heard in all their lives." The meals at the stations were no better than the jokes. Served at a communal table where the conversation typically boiled down to a muttered "Pass the bread, you son of a bitch," the fare consisted of "a disk of last week's bread, of the size and shape of an old-time cheese," a slice of rancid bacon bought cheap from the army after it had been condemned as unfit to serve to enlisted men, a cruet of fly-specked vinegar, and a uniquely western beverage called "slumgullion," which "pretended to be tea, but there was too much dish-rag, and sand, and old bacon-rind in it to deceive the intelligent traveler." Once, Twain asked for coffee instead, rendering the station keeper momentarily speechless. "At last, when he came to, he turned away and said, as one who communes with himself upon a matter too vast to grasp: '*Coffee*! Well, if that don't go clean ahead of me, I'm damned.'"

British explorer Sir Richard Burton, co-discover of the source of the Nile, infiltrator of Mecca, and translator of *The Arabian Nights*, made a similar stagecoach trip west eleven months before Sam and Orion, and he too found the station food virtually inedible, the coffee simmered "till every noxious principle was duly extracted from it," the bacon "rusty," the antelope steak "cut off a corpse suspended for the benefit of flies outside," and the bread prepared with sour milk, carbonate of soda, or alkali, "which communicates to the food the green-yellow tinge, and suggests many of the properties of poison."

Burton's itinerary mirrored the brothers' route. Like them, he had boarded a Central Overland stage in St. Joseph, bound initially for Salt Lake City. And, like Sam, Burton was leaving behind a conflict, in his case a nasty row with his erstwhile exploring partner John Hanning Speke over which man had actually discovered the headwaters of the Nile at Lake Victoria. (Opinions still vary.) Speke beat Burton back to London and took the lion's share of the credit for himself, and a depressed, demoralized Burton abandoned England for a cross-country tour of America. "It'll be a most interesting experiment," Burton noted in his journal. "I want to see whether after a life of 3 or 4 months, I can drink and eat myself to the level of the aborigines." To guard against such aborigines, Burton wore a brace of Colt revolvers on his hips, with extra bullets stuffed into the oversized pockets of an English tweed shooting jacket and a bowie knife jammed into his boot.

Armed, too, with letters of introduction from Secretary of War John B. Floyd to the commanders of the various forts along the way, Burton hoped to join the army in hostile encounters with the Indians. To his disappointment, the main tribes in the area—the Comanches, Kiowas, and Cheyennes—had lapsed into a temporary period of quiet, and Burton had to settle for turning his sharp brown eyes to an anthropological study of the Indians, whom he found quite similar to the desert Bedouins of North Africa. "Both have the same wild chivalry, the same fiery sense of honor, and the same boundless hospitality," he wrote. "The blood feud and the vendetta are common to the two. Both are grave and cautious in demeanor and formal in manner—princes in rags or paint. The Arabs plunder pilgrims; the Indians, bands of trappers. And both rob according to certain rules." At one point Burton tried unsuccessfully to get a Sioux warrior to show him how to scalp someone, but the Indian "refused indignantly." A glass of whiskey would have changed his mind, thought Burton, "but I was unwilling to break through the wholesome law that prohibits it."

Another prominent mid-century figure who traversed the Plains at about the same time did not share Burton's admiration, however tempered, of the Indians. New York *Tribune* editor Horace Greeley, who a few years earlier had famously urged his fellow Americans, "Go West, young man, and grow up with the country," took his own advice in 1859 and crossed the country in a stagecoach. En route from Quincy, Illinois, to the jumping-off point at St. Joseph, Greeley passed through Hannibal, which he found "a bustling, growing village," although he advised the residents to get a better wharf before he returned. Much of what Greeley saw disappointed him, particularly the Native Americans he passed along the way. "The Indians are children," Greeley wrote. "Their arts, wars, treaties, alliances, habitations, crafts, properties, commerce, comforts, all belong to the very lowest and rudest ages of human existence." Indian men, he said, were "squalid and conceited, proud and worthless, lazy and lousy," while their women were "degraded and filthy" and treated no better than a beast of burden by their husbands. Summing up, Greeley wrote: "I could not help saying, 'These people must die out—there is no help for them.' . . . [T]hey will strut out or drink out their miserable existence, and at length afford the world a sensible relief by dying out of it."

The Indians were not alone in disappointing Greeley. "There are too many idle, shiftless people in Kansas," he informed his readers. "They live a little and lie a little." The Mormons, although hardworking and abstemious, "assumed that [they] were God's peculiar, chosen, beloved people, and that all the rest of mankind are out of the ark of safety and floundering in heathen darkness. I am not edified by this sort of preaching." As for California, Greeley found the Indians living there "generally idle and depraved, while the white men who come in contact with them are often rascals and ruffians." The state was sorely lacking in "virtuous, educated, energetic women" and the chances of young men "making their pile . . . have nearly ceased to exist."

Even the majestic countryside failed to impress the sophisticated New Yorker. The Great Plains were "nearly destitute of human inhabitants," Greeley wrote, and the wind blew incessantly for fifty miles in either direction, threatening to literally blow the wheels off wagons. "The broad landscape remains treeless, cheerless, forbidding," he shuddered. Farther west, the Humboldt River in northern Nevada was "the meanest river of its length on earth. . . . Its water, for at least the lower half of its course, is about the most detestable I ever tasted. I mainly chose to suffer thirst rather than drink it." On the first point, at least, Mark Twain would agree: in *Roughing It*, he would describe the Humboldt as "a sickly rivulet," only one-fourth as deep as the Erie Canal. It was not completely useless, however, since "one of the pleasantest and most invigorating exercises one can contrive is to run and jump across the Humboldt River till he is overheated, and then drink it dry."

Like Greeley and Burton before them, Sam and Orion spent the vast majority of their time inside the stagecoach. On the open road, the coach changed drivers once a day, or every seventy-five miles, and conductors every 250 miles, which was the limit of their fiefdom in a "division," or area of responsibility. The Clemens brothers rarely got to know their drivers, but they did on occasion become friendly with the conductors, who were as regal in bearing and absolute in power as a mogul, sultan, or king, and "in whose presence common men were modest of speech and manner, and in the glare of whose greatness even the dazzling stage-driver dwindled to a penny dip." There were, Twain estimated, sixteen to eighteen conductors on the overland route, one coming and one going at all times.

Overseeing the entire 1,900-mile operation was another larger-than-life character, Ben Holladay. Known without exaggeration as "the Stagecoach King," the Kentucky-born Holladay had immigrated to Missouri as a teenager and variously operated a tavern, a drugstore, and a dirt-floor hotel before entering the transportation business. Mortgaging his property, he bought a handful of wagons and mules and began running goods to and from the Mississippi River to Santa Fe, New Mexico. Eventually taking control of the Central Overland stage line, Holladay cornered the market on passenger traffic between the Mississippi and Salt Lake City, bullion deliveries from California and Nevada, and U.S. mail delivery everywhere in between. After the outbreak of the Civil War closed the more southerly Oxbow Route, operated by his chief competitor, John Butterfield, between St. Louis and San Francisco, Holladay enjoyed a virtual monopoly for the next five years. During that time, his stage line raked in an estimated $200,000 per month in cargo and passenger fees, along with an additional two million dollars in total payments from the federal government for mail deliveries.

One brief but romantic part of Holladay's empire was the hell-for-leather mail delivery system that came to be known as the Pony Express. Although it operated for only eighteen months before being rendered obsolete by the transcontinental telegraph, the Pony Express captured—and still captures—the American imagination as a vivid and breathless chapter of the western experience. Begun in April 1860 by Holladay's predecessor, William H. Russell, head of Russell, Majors & Waddell freight company, the Pony Express was intended to answer the national demand for swifter, more dependable coast-to-coast mail service. Prior to 1860, there were only two ways for mail to reach the West Coast: the southwesterly Oxbow Route, which took three weeks, and a land-sea route from New York City to San Francisco, via the Isthmus of Panama, which took twice that long. Russell proposed to cut the time to thirteen days by means of an interlocking relay system of horseback riders dashing cross-country at breakneck speed over the central route between Sacramento and St. Joseph. Each rider would cover between seventy-five and a hundred miles on his run, with quicksilver stops to change horses every dozen or so miles. The fee per letter was five dollars per half ounce, not including the ten-cent postage stamp required by the U.S. Treasury Department. The mail was carried in a specially designed four-pouch container called a *mochila* (Spanish for "rucksack"), which fit over the saddle horn and could be transferred from one horse to another in a matter of seconds. A small bugle, soon discarded, was carried by the riders to announce their impending approach.

Russell placed an ad for potential riders in leading newspapers throughout the West. The ad itself became legendary: "Wanted: Young, skinny, wiry fellows not over eighteen. Must be expert riders, willing to risk death daily. Orphans preferred." Hundreds of adventure-seeking young men who met all or part of the qualifications quickly responded, including a teenager named William F. Cody, still a few years' shy of acquiring his indelible nickname, Buffalo Bill. Deliveries commenced on April 3, 1860, starting out of St. Joseph. From the beginning, the riders' heroic feats of bravery, stoicism, and devotion to duty spread across the country more quickly than the mail they delivered. One such feat involved the aptly named "Pony Bob" Haslam, an express rider making the Nevada run between Friday's Station and Fort Churchill. On May 11, 1860, Haslam set out on his route, only to discover that all the stations had been abandoned by their panicky keepers or destroyed by marauding Paiute Indians, who had killed and scalped several unlucky station employees. By the time he reached Smith's Creek Station on early May 12, Haslam had ridden 190 miles in eighteen hours. After grabbing a few hours' sleep, he was back in the saddle for the return trip; in thirty-six hours, he covered an astonishing 380 miles. It was all in a day's work for Haslam, who once rode 120 miles in Utah Territory with his jaw broken by an Indian arrow and one arm shattered by a bullet.

Despite such superhuman accomplishments, the Pony Express was already on its last legs, so to speak, when Sam and Orion set out for Nevada. The overland telegraph was leapfrogging them along the way; telegraph stations already had been established as far west as fifty miles beyond Fort Kearny. Another crew was busily stringing wire eastward from Carson City, the brothers' ultimate destination. On the sixth day of their trip, 580 miles out of St. Joseph outside Scott's Bluff Pass, Nebraska, they got their first and only look at a Pony Express rider. Before then, Twain wrote, "We had had a consuming desire, from the beginning, to see a pony-rider, but somehow or other all that passed us and all that met us managed to streak by in the night, and so we heard only a whiz and a hail, and the swift phantom of the desert was gone before we could stick our heads out of the window." Now, in full daylight, they heard their driver cry, "Here he comes!" and they saw, in the distance, a black speck rising and falling as it approached them from the opposite direction. It was a brief encounter: "A whoop and a hurrah from our upper deck, a wave of the rider's hand, but no reply, and man and horse burst past our excited faces, and go winging away like a belated fragment of a storm! So sudden is it all, and so like a flash of unreal fancy . . . we might have doubted whether we had seen an actual horse and man at all."

Other adventures real or imagined broke up the monotony of their trip. One rainy, ink-black night, the brothers jolted awake from a restless sleep to hear their stage driver cry out: "Help! Help! Help! I'm being murdered! Will no man lend me a pistol?" Seconds later they heard two pistol shots, followed by confused voices, trampling feet, heavy, dull thumps, and the driver groaning, "Don't, gentlemen, please don't—I'm a dead man!" The next morning, when they asked the conductor about the disturbance, he shrugged it off, hinting darkly that some of the many outlaws who infested the area had been "laying for" the now-missing driver. The hair-raising experience was likely a hoax, one of the "play killings" that drivers and conductors performed on occasion to frighten tenderfeet such as the Clemenses. On one occasion, however, Orion reported an actual violent altercation between their conductor and four drunken stagecoach drivers at a station in the Black Hills near La Prele, Nebraska Territory. The conductor had come up to Orion and asked to borrow his pistol, "but before I could hand it to him, one of the men got up and commenced cursing him. Another then came up and knocked the conductor down, cutting a bad gash in his upper lip, and telling him he would have killed him if he had had his boots on." Neither Orion nor Sam, probably wisely, tried to intervene.

A very real outlaw whom they did encounter on their journey was Joseph A. Slade, trail master for the stage line between Julesburg, Colorado, and Rocky Ridge Station, Nebraska. Jack Slade, perfectly named for a gunfighter, was already a legend around those parts. Originally from Carlyle, Illinois, the wastrel son of a former congressman, Slade had run off to the West at the age of thirteen after killing a man with a rock during an argument. He subsequently served in the Mexican War and drove freight wagons for several years before becoming a division superintendent for the COC&PP in 1859. By all accounts, Slade was an efficient and fearless superintendent, contending with both outlaws and Indians along his route. One of the former, his predecessor at Julesburg, was a bearish French-Canadian fur trader named Jules Beni, who had given (oddly) his first name to the settlement on the South Platte River where the overland road branched off to Denver. Beni, feeling perhaps underappreciated as a city father, shot the unarmed Slade several times with a double-barreled shotgun but made the fatal mistake of not finishing him off when he had the chance. After recovering from his wounds, Slade sought revenge, taking care not to repeat Beni's mistake. He shot and killed his rival, either dispatching him instantly with two rounds to the head or else tying him to a fence post and potshotting him at his leisure, depending on who was telling the story. Either way, he cut off one of his victim's ears afterward and wore it as a watch fob, to the horrified fascination of local children to whom he displayed it frequently as a curiosity, talisman, and object lesson.

By the time Sam sat down to share a cup of coffee with the famous badman at Rocky Ridge Station, he had comically inflated the real Slade into an outsized bogeyman for the purposes of underlining their argument over a last cup of coffee. "Slade was about to take it when he saw that my cup was empty," wrote Twain. "He politely offered to fill it, but . . . I politely declined. I was afraid he had not killed anybody that morning and might be needing diversion." Slade insisted that Sam take the coffee, "but it gave me no comfort, for I could not feel sure that he would not be sorry, presently, that he had given it away, and proceed to kill me to distract his thoughts from the loss."

Twain, of course, survived the confrontation, but Slade eventually met a bad end. Three years later, having moved to Montana, he was hanged by his fellow vigilantes for repeated but nonspecific disturbances of the peace, usually after he had been drinking. His sympathetic biographer, transplanted Englishman Thomas J. Dimsdale, noted that Slade was usually a courteous gentleman, but that "those who met him when maddened with liquor and surrounded by a gang of armed roughs, would pronounce him a fiend incarnate. From Fort Kearny west, he was feared a great deal more than the Almighty." Buffalo Bill Cody, not in attendance for the execution, testified later that he had worked for Slade for two years as a Pony Express rider and stage driver and knew him to be "kind, generous, and concerned for the welfare of his employees." By then, it was a little late for character references.

The peripatetic Richard Burton, who encountered the gunman about the same time that Clemens did, also found him to be gallant and solicitous. Burton could not say the same for Slade's common-law wife, Virginia, whom the Englishman considered "cold and disagreeable," perhaps because she, a former dance hall girl in frontier saloons, was more or less immune to his flashing Old World charm and required Burton and his fellow male travelers to sleep in a barn at the station. Orion Clemens remembered Slade more clearly than his brother, leaving behind a good physical description: "He had gray eyes, very light straight hair, no beard, and a hard-looking face seamed like a man of 60," wrote Orion. "His face was thin, his nose straight and ordinarily prominent—lips rather thinner than usual—otherwise nothing unusual."

On their way across Nebraska, the brothers just missed running into another soon to be notorious gunslinger, James Butler "Wild Bill" Hickok. Less than a week before Sam and Orion departed St. Joseph, the twenty-four-year-old Hickok, not yet dubbed "the Prince of the Pistoleers," had been involved in a deadly shootout at Rock Creek Station, near Beatrice, Nebraska, the circumstances of which remain murky to this day. As with many such incidents, then and later, it began with a woman, in this case the sometime girlfriend of a nearby rancher named Dave McCanles. Hickok, a humble stock tender at the time, was a romantic rival for the favors of the complaisant local girl, one Sarah Shull, notwithstanding the nickname McCanles had hung on Hickok—Duck Bill—an unflattering reference to Hickok's protruding upper lip.

When McCanles and two henchmen showed up at the station on the afternoon of July 12, 1861, threatening to "clean up on the people at the station," Hickok somewhat unvalorously hid behind a curtain in the bedroom and shot McCanles through the curtain and heart, respectively, when McCanles peeked into the station. Hickok then wounded McCanles's two companions, who were quickly dispatched with axes and hoes by other station workers before they could get away. Somehow, the sordid little frontier murders grew into a heroic account of derring-do in which the gallant Hickok single-handedly killed ten desperadoes, while himself suffering a fractured skull, thirteen knife wounds, and fourteen bullet wounds in the process. It was a reputation Hickok would spend the rest of his life—almost exactly fifteen years—attempting to live down, or live up to, before he was shot in the back of the head by a skulking assassin in a Deadwood, South Dakota, saloon while holding the poker hand ever afterward known as Dead Man's Hand—two aces, two eights, and the queen of hearts.

Passing unscathed around the Black Hills into Utah, the brothers entered Mormon country. They were beyond the reach of marauding Indians, at least the formidable Sioux and Cheyenne, but the Mormons were no walk in the park themselves. In the summer of 1857, disguised as Indians, members of the sect had waylaid a wagon train of 140 Missouri and Arkansas emigrants at Mountain Meadows in southern Utah, tricked them into surrendering their weapons, and killed everyone in the party except for seventeen infants deemed too young to identify their attackers. It was long-delayed revenge for the rough treatment the Mormons had endured at the hands of the Clemenses' fellow Missourians two decades earlier, which had occasioned their trek westward in the first place.

Resettled in Utah after an epic 1,400-mile odyssey from the Midwest, the Mormons and their indomitable leader, Brigham Young, had built a new Zion, initially called Deseret, on the alkali flats around the Great Salt Lake. Resisting the demands of the federal government that they stop practicing polygamy (Young alone had seventeen wives), the Mormons forced normally languid President James Buchanan to send in the army and remove Young from his official post as territorial governor, although Young retained his grip on power.

Fully half of the Mormons' territory was carved away and shaped into Nevada Territory, a vivisection that had only become official in March 1861. Tensions remained high on both sides, although the new president, Abraham Lincoln, promised to leave the Mormons alone if they would leave him alone while he turned his attention to his fellow Christians in the South.

Orion's only official duty before taking his seat in Nevada was to meet with Brigham Young in Salt Lake City and ascertain his willingness to be left alone. A meeting was arranged for August 5, and Sam tagged along to see firsthand the notorious defier of federal and biblical authority. The night before, the brothers had shared supper with one of the so-called Destroying Angels, or Sons of Dan, a Mormon paramilitary group "set apart by the church to conduct permanent disappearances of obnoxious citizens." Richard Burton had seen tangible evidence of the Danites' destructive ability when he was shown the remains of two suspected horse thieves who had been gunned down and left to hang as a warning to other potential miscreants. "This wild, unflinching, and unerring justice, secret and sudden, is the rod of iron which protects the good," Burton noted approvingly.

Twain, for his part, was not as impressed. Their host "was murderous enough, possibly to fill the bill of a Destroyer," he recalled, "but could you abide an Angel in an unclean shirt and no suspenders? Could you respect an Angel with a horse-laugh and a swagger like a buccaneer?" As for Young, whom Burton considered "no common man," Twain found him "quiet, kindly, easy-mannered, dignified, [and] self-possessed." When he tried to draw him out on questions of governmental authority, Young "merely looked around at me . . . as I have seen a benignant old cat look around to see which kitten was meddling with her tail." Young's second in command, Heber C. Kimball, was more forthcoming, telling the brothers bluntly that he would like to see the North and the South give each other "a grubbing. It's my opinion," he continued, "you won't see peace any more; the United States will go all to pieces, and the Mormons will take charge of and rule all the country." Kimball could not say precisely when that time would come, but he ended with a blunt personal warning to Orion: "You are going to have trouble in Nevada." He did not say from which direction such trouble would come. In private, Kimball relished the American war. "Now the yoke is off our neck and on theirs," he said.

The remainder of the brothers' two-day visit was spent taking in the sights around Salt Lake City. The cosmopolitan, well-traveled Burton, who had toured cities from London to Cairo, found the Mormon capital "a vast improvement upon its contemporaries in the valleys of the Mississippi and the Missouri." Two decades later, Burton's fellow Anglo-Irish writer, Oscar Wilde, would include Salt Lake City on his triumphal speaking tour of America. To Wilde, the Mormon Tabernacle "looked like a soup-kettle . . . an enormous affair about the size of Covent Gardens that holds with ease fourteen Mormon families." Twain was less interested in local architecture than in the controversial practice of polygamy, which he described in delighted detail in *Roughing It*: "Some portly old frog of an elder, or a bishop, marries a girl—likes her, marries her sister—likes her, marries another sister—likes her, takes another—likes her, marries her mother—likes her, marries her father, grandfather great grandfather, and then comes back hungry and asks for more."

Quoting a made-up source named "Johnson," Twain depicted a comically set-upon Brigham Young, whose squadron of wives had given him an uncountable number of children, so many that Young could not remember all their names or faces, and simply assumed that any child he passed on the street was one of his. To accommodate all seventy-two of his wives, said Twain, the Mormon leader had constructed a ninety-six-foot-wide bed for them to sleep in, but the sound of their combined snoring proved deafening. "Take my word for it," says Young, "ten or eleven wives is all you need—never go over it." Twain, for his part, endorsed polygamy, at least for the Mormons. Seeing the "poor, ungainly and pathetically homely" women thronging the streets of Salt Lake City, the author judged that "the man that marries one of them has done an act of Christian charity which entitles him to the kindly applause of mankind . . . and the man that marries sixty of them has done a deed of open-handed generosity so sublime that the nations should stand uncovered in his presence and worship in silence."

Twain was less impressed by the *Book of Mormon*, which he considered nothing less than "chloroform in print." If Mormon founder Joseph Smith had actually written the book, said Twain, "the act was a miracle—keeping awake while he did it." Having learned, however unwillingly, much of the Bible as a boy in his Methodist mother's lap, Twain found the Mormon version of Christianity "a prosy detail of imaginary history, with the Old Testament for a model; followed by a tedious plagiarism of the New Testament." The Mormon Bible, he concluded, "is rather stupid and tiresome to read, but there is nothing vicious in its teachings." Twain's somewhat mixed view of Mormons was more tolerant than that of U.S. Army Colonel Patrick Connor, an Irish Catholic immigrant who was charged with protecting overland mail routes during the Civil War. The Mormons, said Connor, were nothing less than "a community of traitors, murderers, fanatics, and whores." Connor's opinion, by no means a minority in the rest of the Union, did not prevent him from making common cause with the Saints to slaughter more than 250 Shoshone men, women, and children at Bear River, Utah, on January 29, 1863—one of the worst, if least remembered, massacres in western history.

Having completed their visit, the brothers left Salt Lake City and crossed the southern edge of the Great Salt Lake, sixty-eight miles of "concentrated hideousness" littered with animal bones and suffused with alkali dust that burned their eyes and made their noses bleed for the entire twenty-two hours it took them to make the journey. At the mouth of Rocky, or Egan, Canyon, 250 miles west of the Mormon capital, they encountered the forlorn Gosiute Indians, a literally dirt-poor tribe whose very name meant "parched earth." Owing perhaps to the miseries he and Orion had just encountered, Sam had little patience with the tribe, whose members he considered "the wretchedest type of mankind I have ever seen."

The Gosiutes, relatives of the Paiutes and Shoshones, were the epitome of what other Indians called "Sit-arounds," meaning they sat around reservations and begged for handouts of food and liquor. In the Gosiutes' case, such behavior was understandable—they inhabited some of the least salubrious real estate in North America, land they shared exclusively with insects and rodents. To Twain, they were "a silent, sneaking, treacherous looking race . . . having no higher ambition than to kill and eat jackass rabbits, crickets and grasshoppers, and embezzle carrion from the buzzards and cayotes . . . manifestly descended from the self-same gorilla, or kangaroo, or Norway rat . . . the Darwinians trace them to." Army Captain James H. Simpson, exploring a wagon route through the area, shared that sentiment, watching with disgusted fascination as one hospitable Gosiute woman gutted a rat, squeezed out its intestines, and "threw the animal, entrails and all, into the pot." Simpson quickly found that he had lost his appetite.

Contradicting Twain's initial impression that "one would as soon expect the rabbits to fight as the Goshoots [*sic*]," tribesmen did occasionally attack stray stagecoaches and way stations, and two years' after the Clemenses' visit they went on the warpath briefly against the U.S. Army before suing for peace. Their chief role in *Roughing It* is to disabuse the credulous Clemens of his romantic image of Indians, which he traces back to his boyhood reading of James Fenimore Cooper's novels. As a direct, if delayed, result of his encounter with the Gosiutes, Mark Twain in 1895 would publish one of his funniest and most devastating essays, "Fenimore Cooper's Literary Offenses," in which he indicted the author of *The Last of the Mohicans, The Deer-*

slayer, and the rest of the *Leatherstocking Tales* for breaking eighteen of the nineteen accepted rules for fiction writing. Some of these rules concerned the art of writing, particularly in a clear, vernacular style—an art that Twain majored in, so to speak, while Cooper took it as a Saturday morning elective. As for Cooper's celebrated depiction of Indians, "The difference between a Cooper Indian and the Indian that stands in front of the cigar-shop is not spacious." Horace Greeley concurred. "The poetic Indian—the Indian of Cooper and Longfellow—is only visible to the poet's eye," he wrote. "To the prosaic observer, the average Indian of the woods and prairies is a being who does little credit to human nature—a slave of appetite and sloth, never emancipated from the tyranny of one animal passion save by the more ravenous demands of another."

The brothers were nearing the end of their journey, but they still had one more desert to cross, the Great American Desert, also known as the Forty-Mile Desert. ("They are called deserts because there is no water in them," Orion helpfully explained to his prairie-born wife in a letter describing their cross-country trip.) Beginning at Dry Sandy Springs and concluding at the appropriately named Ragtown, where earlier pilgrims had left behind their ruined clothing, the desert was "one prodigious boneyard," noted Twain, its roadway littered with the sand-blasted bones of horses and oxen. The entire basin, wrote journalist Samuel Bowles, was "a region whose uses are unimaginable, unless to hold the rest of the globe together, or to teach patience to travelers, or to keep close-locked in its mountain ranges those mineral treasures that the world did not need or was not ready for until now."

The day before reaching Ragtown, Sam and Orion had passed telegraph builders working their way east and had sent a message to Governor Nye announcing their imminent arrival. They did not wait for a reply—just as well, since none was forthcoming. On the morning of August 14, twenty days after departing St. Joseph, they got their first look at their destination. It was not overly impressive. Carson City, said Twain, was an "assemblage of mere white spots in the shadow of a grim range of mountains overlooking it." Still, like the Israelites in Canaan and the Mormons in Utah, they too had reached the promised land—smack in the middle of a broiling desert. There was no milk and honey, and no harem of compliant wives, waiting for them at the end of their journey, but for the time being, at least, it would have to do.

CHAPTER 3

THE DAMNEDEST COUNTRY UNDER THE SUN

UPON THEIR ARRIVAL IN CARSON CITY, SAM AND Orion were met by a welcoming committee, a gunfight, and a windstorm. It was a normal day in the Nevada capital.

As their stage pulled up in front of the three-story Ormsby House, the brothers tumbled out, dusty, disheveled, and coated with a fine furze of alkali dust. The official greeters took one look at "His Majesty the Secretary," presumably fully dressed and not still wearing his traveling outfit of pipe and underwear, and instantly melted away. It was not easy to do, given the surroundings. The main drag, imaginatively named Carson Street, "consisted of four or five blocks of little white frame stores which were too high to sit down on, but not too high for various other purposes," recalled Twain. The plaza around which the stores huddled was "a large, unfenced, level vacancy with a liberty pole in it," used mainly for public auctions, horse trading, and mass meetings of the vigilante sort. The predominant color palette was brown.

Carson City, tucked into the crooked left elbow where Nevada abuts California, owed its name to the intrepid explorer and Indian fighter Christopher "Kit" Carson, who had single-handedly kept "Pathfinder" John C. Frémont and his men from starving to death during their various mapmaking expeditions a decade earlier. Carson had also located many of the paths later claimed by the sinuous and not overly straightforward Frémont en route to his 1856 presidential nomination by the newly formed Republican Party. The city was founded by Major William S. Ormsby, a transplanted Californian who had been one of the leaders in the movement by the newly arrived Gentiles to secede from Mormon-dominated Utah Territory in 1857. Ormsby and his business partner, Abraham S. V. Curry, laid out the nascent town around a four-acre plaza in the Eagle Valley, near an old Mormon trading post at the base of the Sierra Nevada mountains. In a burst of civic optimism, Ormsby constructed a hotel on the western edge of the plaza, at the corner of Carson and Second streets, while Curry built a two-story combination hotel and bathhouse of his own directly above warm springs a couple of miles away. He called it the Warm Springs Hotel.

Ormsby, as it turned out, did not have long to enjoy his newfound career as a hotelier. On May 9, 1860, he led an expedition to punish a rogue element of the Pyramid Lake Indians, Paiute tribesmen who had burned down a trading post at Williams Station and killed five white men in retaliation for the kidnapping and rape of two young Indian girls. One week later, his brother located the major's arrow-filled body on the banks of the Truckee River, alongside those of forty-five other posse members. In the somewhat ambiguous words of one Nevada historian, "His death was generally mourned."

Carson City in itself was lively enough, but it sat on the edge of a veritable volcano of activity. Twelve miles to the northeast, the richest silver strike in American history, the Comstock Lode, had been made in June 1859. Two scruffy prospectors, Peter O'Riley and Patrick McLaughlin, were placer mining for gold on the side of Mount Davidson, a 7,800-foot-high mountain above Gold Canyon, when they scraped out a pile of thick blue mud from a hole in the ground. Placer mining required only a pick, a pan, a stream of water, and a good pair of eyes. O'Riley and McLaughlin had all those things, if nothing else, and they quickly discerned a number of gold nuggets amid the muck. When they sent off the specimen to be assayed, it yielded $3,876 per ton—three-fourths of which was not gold, but silver.

They were rich—or should have been. But in the typical way of western finance, a Canadian-born fur trader turned prospector, Henry T. P. Comstock, somehow persuaded the duo that he owned title to the entire mountainside, including their claim. After a brief partnership in which he "did all the talking and none of the working," Comstock bought out O'Riley and McLaughlin with forty dollars cash, a bottle of whiskey, and a blind horse. Called "Old Pancake" because he was too lazy to bake his own bread, the supposedly wily Comstock did not fully realize what he had finagled. He sold his stock for $10,000, a comfortable profit in those days but somewhat short of the $400 million the fabulous Comstock Lode would earn in the next three decades. In the meantime, thousands of other would-be Comstocks began scrabbling up and down Mount Davidson, and a new town, Virginia City, sprang up at the base. A full-bore silver rush was taking place a stone's throw from the Clemenses' new home.

Sam and Orion claimed their baggage at the freight office and headed back across the plaza to Ormsby's hotel. They couldn't miss it—the name was painted in three-foot-high block letters on either side of the building. En route, they received their first friendly—if necessarily brief—greeting. A badman named Jack Harris, passing by on horseback, stopped to welcome them to the city. Harris had barely gotten past hello when he begged leave to interrupt himself. "I'll have to get you to excuse me for a minute," he said. "Yonder is the witness that swore I helped to rob the California coach—a piece of impertinent intermeddling, sir, for I am not even acquainted with the man."

Harris did not contradict the man's testimony, only his meddling. In all likelihood, he could not. Harris was Carson City's resident desperado, specializing in just the sort of stagecoach robbery his accuser had described. Despite his various depredations, the outlaw was held in "general esteem" by his neighbors, who considered the stage company an even bigger gang of robbers. Eventually, things got so bad after Harris moved to Pioche, in eastern Nevada, that Wells, Fargo & Company simply hired him to protect it from himself. Even that didn't work—Harris continued to rob stages with regularity, doubling back to the station under cover of darkness and meeting the new arrival, all injured sympathy, when it pulled up in front without its green-painted strongbox. In time, the company began putting live rattlesnakes in its strongboxes and molding silver coins into immovably heavy seven-hundred-pound cannonballs to deter Harris and such fellow highwaymen as Rattlesnake Dick and Black Bart from lifting them. It also formed its own private police force, which operated under the indelible motto, "Wells Fargo never forgets."

While the brothers looked on with disinterested curiosity, Harris rode over to the other man, whose name was Julien, "and began to rebuke the stranger with a six-shooter, and the stranger began to explain with another." The exchange of opposing views was brief. Julien resumed repairing a hitching post and Harris rode away, nodding politely to the Clemenses "with a bullet through one of his lungs, and several in his hips." Blood poured down the sides of the outlaw's horse—Twain found it "quite picturesque"—and the incident ended as swiftly as it had begun. The Virginia City *Territorial Enterprise* duly reported the gunfight in an article titled "Shooting Scrape," and it was picked up as far away as San Francisco. Harris continued his lively career until he died in 1875, worn out and shot to pieces by various business rivals, confessing on his deathbed that his real name was not Jack Harris but the rather more prosaic Amos Huxford, and that he had grown up about as far from the western frontier as it was possible to get and still remain on the North American continent—the state of Maine. Once again, San Francisco newspapers took note of his passing; the *Alta California* headlined it "Death of a Noted Character." He was that. "I never saw Harris shoot a man after that but it recalled to mind that first day in Carson," Twain remembered.

A natural disturbance quickly followed the man-made one. At about two o'clock, following local custom, the daily "Washoe Zephyr" blew through town. It was "a pretty regular wind," said Twain. "Its office hours are from two in the afternoon till two the next morning; and anybody venturing abroad during those twelve hours needs to allow for the wind or will bring up a mile or two to leeward of the point he was aiming at." Named after the Greek god of the wind, zephyrs are normally gentle breezes originating over the Pacific Ocean and puffing eastward. But the steep-sided mountains around Carson City deflected the wind currents straight up and straight down. The effect, recalled Twain, was "a soaring dust-drift about the size of the United States set up edgewise . . . and the capital of Nevada Territory disappeared from view." It was not wholly uninteresting, he added, since "the vast dust-cloud was thickly freckled with things strange to the upper air—things living and dead that flitted hither and thither, going and coming, appearing and disappearing among the rolling billows of dust." He could just pick out (or so he said) a variety of blown-by items: hats, chickens, parasols, blankets, tin signs, sagebrush, shingles, door mats, buffalo robes, shovels and coal scuttles, glass doors, lumber, buggies, wheelbarrows, and little children. "It was something to see."

Irish-born traveler John Ross Browne, a former government revenue agent from San Francisco who had joined the silver rush in 1860 and preceded the Clemens brothers to Carson City, left a similar account of the daily windstorm, which he said "came from the four quarters of the compass, tearing away signs, capsizing tents, scattering the grit from the gravel-banks . . . and sweeping furiously around every crook and corner in search of some sinner to smite. Never was there such a wind as this—so scathing, so searching, so given to penetrating the very core of suffering humanity." The zephyr seemed almost human—or inhuman—in its viciousness, Browne noted. "It actually seemed to double up, twist, pull, push, and screw the unfortunate biped till his muscles cracked and his bones rattled—following him wherever he sought refuge, pursuing him down the back of the neck up the coat-sleeves, through the legs of his pantaloons, into his boots—in short, it was the most villainous and persecuting wind that ever blew, and I boldly protest that it did nobody good."

It was called a Washoe Zephyr after the Washoe Indians, who actually called themselves Washiu, meaning people. The Washoe lived near Lake Tahoe, in the elbow of Nevada, and were part of the larger group of Great Basin Indians who, because they had to dig out whatever they could eat from the alkali flats and bone-dry water beds of the region, were known generically as Diggers. The Washoe did not manage to dig much—by the end of 1859 there were less than nine hundred of them still in existence. It is an interesting etymological speculation that the word *Washiu* bears a close resemblance to the word *wasichu*, which was the pejorative name the Plains Indians gave to white men. (The Wasco Indians, a tribe of Chinook Indians that roamed The Dalles region of Oregon, were unrelated to either group.) When Nevada successfully petitioned to become a state in 1864, the federal government overruled local residents who wanted to call the new state Washoe. The government felt that such a name was undignified, which may be the only time in American history that a state, city, county, river, lake, creek, or gambling casino was not given an Indian name. Nevadans, a stubborn race, later preserved the name as a county in the northwestern part of the state between Reno and the Oregon-California border.

Thrashing their way through the zephyr, Sam and Orion managed to locate the "state palace" of the newly installed territorial governor. The brothers were not initially impressed. The governor's residence, in reality, was merely "a white frame one-story house with two small rooms in it and a stanchion supported shed in front—for grandeur," Twain reported. "It compelled the respect of the citizen and inspired the Indians with awe." The chief justice of the territory and his judicial associates and other governmental officers "were domiciled with less splendor," he added, taking quarters in local boardinghouses and issuing formal decrees from offices in their bedrooms.

Nevada was a brand-new territory, having been absorbed by the Union on March 3, 1861. Abraham Lincoln, with an eye toward gathering some of the territory's ongoing landslide of gold and silver profits into the imperiled government's empty coffers, had welcomed the establishing bill. In Nye, he had chosen the right man for the job. As a brave in good standing in New York's Tammany Hall "wigwam," Nye understood fund raising, if nothing else about good governance. He had been president of the Metropolitan Board of Police before becoming New York senator William Seward's campaign manager during the recent Republican presidential race. Despite the fact that Seward had failed miserably in his attempt to capture the party's nomination, he had gotten Lincoln to reward Nye with a generous sliver of the patronage pie once the Republicans were in control of the White House. Nye also understood, if Orion Clemens did not, that Nevada was a mere stepping-stone to greater things—in Nye's case, the United States Senate—once Nevada became a state. Until then, Nye intended to spend as little time as possible in the benighted backwater. While he was off making regular state visits to California, he would leave Nevada to Orion to run—a prospect that must have been terrifying to both Orion and

Sam, who had seen firsthand Orion's managerial, organizational, and financial skills.

Nye had been in Nevada for a little over a month when the brothers arrived. During that time he had already named territorial officials, set up courts, provided for the first official census, and drawn up electoral districts for a territorial legislature. He described his progress to Orion in their first meeting; Sam took the opportunity to measure the governor with his quick gray eyes. "He was a fine physical specimen," Twain wrote. "He had a winningly friendly face and deep lustrous brown eyes that could talk as a native language the tongue of every feeling, every passion, every emotion. His eyes could outtalk his tongue and that is saying a good deal, for he was a very remarkable talker." Like most good politicians, Nye had developed the knack of remembering names and faces. "By the time he had been Governor a year," Twain continued, "he had shaken hands with every human being in the Territory of Nevada, and after that he always knew these people instantly at sight and could call them by name. The whole population, of 20,000 persons, were his personal friends."

Nye had brought along with him to Nevada a veritable tribe's worth of Irish-American followers from New York City, including a properly ethnic housekeeper named Marget Murphy to look after them. Mrs. Murphy opened a boardinghouse on the north side of the plaza in Carson City, and the New York Brigade, as Twain called it, moved into a shared dormitory on the second floor. "The Governor's official menagerie had been drawn from the humblest ranks of his constituents at home," he noted, "harmless good fellows who had helped in his campaigns, and now they had their reward in petty salaries payable in greenbacks that were worth next to nothing."

The original sketch of the fourteen brigade members in *Roughing It* by artist True W. Williams depicts them as variously bearded, bewhiskered, or clean-shaven, most smiling craftily, and at least four displaying traces of the telltale simian facial characteristics that Thomas

Nast made notorious in his anti-Irish illustrations for *Harper's Weekly* during and after the Civil War. Only three of the men's names have survived: Will H. Wagner, James Neary, and Clement T. Rice, the last of whom would reappear hilariously as a rival newspaper correspondent during the latter stages of Sam Clemens's western career. Two of Nye's nephews, Robert Howland and Thomas Nye, also turned up in Nevada, but were not founding members of the New York Brigade. There were whispered rumors that the brigade members, one and all, "were paid assassins . . . brought along to quietly reduce the Democratic vote."

Sam and Orion moved into Mrs. Murphy's as well, taking a room on the first floor facing the plaza. There was just enough space for a bed, a small table, two chairs, a fireproof safe for government dispersals, and the infamous unabridged dictionary from their stagecoach trip. The interior walls were made of "cotton domestic," stitched together from old flour sacks. "If you stood in a dark room and your neighbors in the next had lights, the shadows on your canvas told queer secrets sometimes," recalled Twain. The common folk in Carson City used unornamented sacks for their walls, while the local aristocrats sported rudimentary frescoes made from red-and-blue flour sacks.

To give his brother more room, Sam moved upstairs with the Irishmen, although he did not take part in their various make-work projects, one of which involved surveying eastward for a prospective railroad. The surveying job, said Governor Nye, was intended to provide the men "with recreation amid noble landscapes, and afford you never ceasing opportunities for enriching your minds by observation and study." Twain described it as "recreation with a vengeance." One result of the brigade's outdoor work was a formidable collection of desert tarantulas, which the men kept inside large glass specimen jars. One night a slightly worse for wear Bob Howland staggered into the dormitory and knocked over the jars, unloosing the captives in the dark. "Turn out, boys," he warned, "the tarantulas is loose!"

Every man, recalled Twain, jumped on top of a bed or trunk. "Then followed the strangest silence—a silence of grisly suspense," as the men peered into the darkness for signs of the spiders. "Presently you would hear a gasping voice say: 'Su-su-something's crawling up the back of my neck!' Every now and then you could hear a little subdued scramble and a sorrowful 'O Lord!'"

When Mrs. Murphy finally climbed the stairs with a lantern to survey the damage, she found the members of the brigade, along with Twain, clinging to their perches in their bed shirts. No sign of the tarantulas was ever found; they had taken the first opportunity to escape. As for Twain, "I know I am not capable of suffering more than I did during those few minutes of suspense in the dark, surrounded by those creeping, bloody-minded tarantulas. I had skipped from bed to bed and from box to box in a cold agony and every time I touched anything that was furzy I fancied I felt the fangs. I had rather go to war than live that episode over again." The men stayed awake the rest of the night, playing desultory hands of cribbage and keeping a nervous lookout for returning spiders.

Nye took advantage of Orion's arrival by immediately going off to Sacramento for a few weeks to confer with California officials about mining statutes and "a festering border dispute." Orion was left with the task of locating a building that was big enough to handle the new, twenty-five-man legislature when it met for the first time on October 1. Abraham Curry, owner of the Warm Springs Hotel, offered his spa free of charge, but the unfurnished second floor needed furniture and—ironically enough—heating stoves. Orion borrowed the stoves from government officials in Salt Lake City and had them shipped by overland freight to Carson City. He also ordered plain pine desks, wooden benches, writing paper, envelopes, pens, penknives, spittoons, sawdust (in lieu of rugs), and two large American flags, all of which he duly vouchered to Washington.

Anything that the government refused to pay would have to come out of Orion's own pocket. The next year, federal bookkeepers disallowed $1,330.08 in printing costs for territorial documents, beginning a decade-long process of hounding Orion for the money and threatening legal action if he did not pay up (he never did). Next he designed an official state seal, which he bragged to his wife was "the prettiest seal in the Union." It was certainly the busiest. The foreground showed a miner holding a pick in one hand and an American flag in the other, with a mining pan at his feet. The background featured a mountain stream turning the water wheel of a quartz mill, while a second miner pushed a car loaded with presumably precious ore. The motto beneath read *Volens et Potens*—willing and able. Sam, noting that there were more buzzards than quartz mills in Nevada at that time, suggested replacing the mine with the bird, but Orion termed the idea "disgusting."

While Orion drudged away on government work, Sam began to grow restless. He knew all about the Comstock strikes, and he wanted to get in on the second floor, so to speak, of the silver boom. First he needed to look the part. He outfitted himself in the loose-fitting blue shirt, denim dungarees, slouch hat, and high boots of the typical miner. He felt "rowdyish and bully." To complete the ensemble he needed a partner, or pard, in the lingua franca. He found one in the person of John D. Kinney—called "Johnny K"—the son of a Cincinnati banker, who, like Clemens, had left the Civil War behind (although, unlike Clemens, he would return to it later as a captain in the 7th Ohio Cavalry). Kinney was "a first-rate fellow," Sam told his mother in a letter, and the new sidekicks set off to seek their fortune, not in gold or silver, but in timber. Members of the Irish Brigade had told them of a rich forest on the shores of Lake Tahoe (then called Lake Bigler), a few miles west of Carson City. The partners reckoned that the building boom in Virginia City, where there were already some ten thousand people clamoring for rooms, would increase demand on the sort of virgin yellow pines that sprouted in profusion down to the very shores of the lake.

Clemens and Kinney made the trip on foot, climbing up and down mountains they estimated conservatively were "three or four thousand miles high," before coming upon Lake Tahoe, the largest freshwater lake in the western United States and perhaps the loveliest. The young men found a skiff belonging to the Irish Brigade, and Sam "superintended" Kinney as he rowed them across the lake. It was the sort of unspoiled scenery that "expand[ed] your soul like a bladder," Twain said, and ever afterward he judged all lakes in Tahoe's shadow, from Italy's Lake Como to the Sea of Galilee. "Three months of camp life on Lake Tahoe would restore an Egyptian mummy to his pristine vigor, and give him an appetite like an alligator," Twain wrote, claiming that he had heard of a consumptive bag of bones who went there to die, but "made a failure of it. . . . Three months later he was sleeping out of doors regularly, eating all he could hold, three times a day, and chasing game over mountains three thousand feet high for recreation." Twain recommended the experience to other skeletons.

The partners established a base camp, posted a few scattered claim notices, and chopped down half a dozen trees to "fence" their property. They fished for trout with little success (the water was so clear, said Twain, that the fish could see them coming), and slept out under the stars, smoking, reading, and playing cards before turning in. Their idyll ended abruptly after Sam left a campfire unattended one morning and set the entire mountainside ablaze with a frying pan: "Within half an hour all before us was a tossing, blinding tempest of flame! It went surging up adjacent ridges—surmounted them and disappeared in the cañons beyond . . . threw out skirmishing parties of fire here and there, and sent them trailing their crimson spirals away among remote ramparts and ribs and gorges, till as far as the eye could reach the lofty mountain-fronts were webbed as it were with a tangled network of red lava streams."

Somehow, the young men managed to make it down to their boat and row out of harm's way. They watched the fire rage for the next four hours, until "hunger asserted itself now, but there was nothing to eat. The provisions were all cooked, no doubt, but we did not go see." They returned to Carson City—no poorer, if no richer, for their efforts. The close call adversely affected Sam's enthusiasm for his new home. In a letter to his mother, he detailed Nevada's questionable charms. "This is the damnedest country under the sun," he wrote. "It never rains here, and the dew never falls. No flowers grow here, and no green thing gladdens the eye. The birds that fly over the land carry their provisions with them. Only the crow and the raven tarry with us. Our city lies in the midst of a desert of the purest—most unadulterated, and uncompromising *sand*—in which infernal soil nothing than that fag-end of vegetable creation, 'sage-brush,' ventures to grow." Nevertheless, he said, the country was fabulously rich in natural minerals and unnatural immigrants—"thieves, murderers, desperadoes, ladies, children, lawyers, Christians, Indians, Chinamen, Spaniards, gamblers, sharpers, cuyotes [*sic*], poets, preachers, and jackass rabbits."

Sam set aside his brief career as a lumber tycoon to work as an eight-dollar-a-day clerk for Orion during the two-month-long opening session of the Nevada Territorial Legislature, which got under way on October 1, 1861. Nye, as usual, was away from his post, leaving Orion to chair the proceedings. Predictably, Orion managed immediately to annoy the lawmakers, who did not appreciate the fact that they had to make a daily four-mile round-trip to Abraham Curry's Warm Springs Hotel to conduct their legislative deliberations. A few days into the session, the lawmakers felt the sudden need to confer with Orion, who was back at his office wrangling with the federal government over unvouchered expenditures. When the sergeant at arms went to fetch him, Orion told him to inform the legislature that he "would come tomorrow." The legislature sent a posse to encourage him to come today. Orion took the hint, apologizing in person to the solons for his absence and explaining, perhaps ill-advisedly, that he thought they "had other business to attend to." It was a weak apology, but better than none.

Another difference of opinion arose concerning Orion's unilateral editing of the legislative minutes to remove any mention of the body's elected president and secretary—Miles N. Mitchell and William M. Gillespie, respectively. This was a serious matter to the lawmakers, who passed almost unanimously (one legislator voting nay) a resolution condemning Orion for abuse of power: "The Secretary of the Territory, from the commencement of the present legislative session, has, by assumption of dictatorial power in various ways, continued to annoy and perplex the operations of the Legislature, in matters pertaining solely to their own business." Sam, who had been annoyed and perplexed often enough by his brother in the past to sympathize with the lawmakers, watched the proceedings with a characteristic mixture of amusement and disgust. "There is something solemnly funny about the struggles of a new-born territorial government to get a start in this world," he wrote. "Ours had a trying time of it." Taking it as a whole, he considered the legislature "a fine collection of sovereigns. . . . They levied taxes to the amount of thirty or forty thousand dollars and ordered expenditures to the extent of about a million."

To save money, one legislative member, Virginia City representative Jacob L. Van Bokkelen, moved to dispense with an official chaplain, a grand savings of three dollars a day. Van Bokkelen added that he had "sat under prayers costing ten thousand a year and did not know that they did him much good." As it turned out, he might have been well advised to pray. When a fellow legislator, John Winters of Carson City, took issue with him over a nonreligious matter, Van Bokkelen challenged him to a duel with pistols. Abjuring the formal choice of weapons, Winters grabbed a piece of firewood from a box beside the stove and proceeded to beat the distinguished member from Virginia City over the head with it, knocking Van Bokkelen to the floor and stomping on him with his boots. The assault was so severe that Van Bokkelen stopped breathing momentarily before doctors managed to revive him and was hors de combat for the next several days.

Firewood also figured prominently in a dispute between Orion and Treasury Department blue pencils in Washington. In yet another money-saving move, Orion had contracted with a local Indian, one Waw-ho-no-loah, to saw and stack wood for the legislature at the cost of $1.50 a day, about half the going rate for white men. Despite its thrift, the expenditure was disallowed for lack of a proper signature and because, as Twain said, "The United States was too much accustomed to employing dollar-and-a-half thieves in all manner of official capacities to regard his explanation of the voucher as having any foundation in fact." To rectify matters, Sam, in his quasi-official capacity as assistant secretary of state, made out another voucher and had the Indian mark it with a cross—"it looked like a cross that had been drunk a year"—and sent it back to Washington. "It went through all right," he said. "The United States never said a word. I was sorry I had not made the voucher for a thousand loads of wood instead of one. The government of my country snubs honest simplicity but fondles artistic villainy," Twain observed, "and I think I might have developed into a very capable pickpocket if I had remained in the public service a year or two."

Government bookkeepers even haggled with Orion over the cost of a piece of sewn canvas—$3.40—to divide the legislative meeting room into upper and lower houses, explaining with perfect bureaucratic logic that the government had allotted funds to rent an assembly hall, but not to divide it into rooms. The fact that Curry was not charging them a penny to rent the hall did not seem to matter to the government. "Nothing in this world is palled in such impenetrable obscurity as a U.S. Treasury Comptroller's understanding," Twain noted. That obscurity was underscored when Orion was billed for giving an extra penknife to the clerk of the legislature—another three dollars out of his own pocket. And when he sought to defend the high cost of printing by pointing out that everything cost more in the territory and enclosed a copy of the current market report showing hay going for $250 a ton, Orion was tartly informed that "nothing in his instructions required him to purchase hay." Sam sympathized with his brother but confided privately to their mother that Orion "hasn't business talent enough to carry on a peanut stand." As for the lawmakers themselves, from the governor down they considered the territorial secretary "a prissy chucklehead." It was the story of Orion's life.

As a break from his legislative duties, Sam decided to buy a horse, a glorious misadventure he detailed memorably in a stand-alone chapter of *Roughing It*. At an auction in the plaza, he purchased a "Genuine Mexican Plug" for twenty-seven dollars (the only bid) and attempted to mount and ride the black, mean-eyed animal, which "had as many humps and corners on him as a dromedary." After being shot straight up into the air three or four times—"Oh, *don't* he buck though!" said an onlooker admiringly—Sam loaned the horse to a California youth and sat down to take stock of the situation. "Imagination cannot conceive how disjoined I was," he noted, "how internally, externally and universally I was unsettled, mixed up and ruptured."

Abraham Curry informed Sam, no doubt unnecessarily, that he had been taken in: "Any child, any Injun, could have told you that he'd buck; he is the very worst devil to buck on the continent of America." Clemens tried unsuccessfully to sell the horse; the only taker was "a notoriously substanceless bummer" who had been put up to bid on the horse by the unscrupulous auctioneer. He subsequently loaned the animal to various members of the legislature, "my idea being to get him crippled, and throw him on the borrower's hands, or killed, and make the borrower pay for him." Nothing ever happened to the horse, although "everybody I loaned him to always walked back; they never could get enough exercise any other way." Eventually, Sam gave the horse to a passing Arkansas emigrant "whom fortune delivered into my hand." He paid off the livery stable—fifteen dollars for the horse's stall, $250 for the ton of hay he had consumed—and turned his attention to silver mining, a more productive occupation.

Inspired by a report in the Virginia City *Territorial Enterprise* touting the West Humboldt Mountains as "the richest mineral region upon God's footstool," Clemens rounded up three companions, including an old Keokuk neighbor named Billy Clagett, who had recently arrived in the territory, and set out by wagon in early December for the area's newest boomtown, Unionville, 175 miles northeast of Carson City. His companions were a variously accomplished group. Clagett, a newly wed lawyer whose wife, Mary, would accompany Orion's wife, Mollie, to Carson City a few months hence, had been appointed notary public for Unionville, a plum political post given a notary's importance in approving, recording, registering, and filing miners' claims. Another member of the party, Augustus W. "Gus" Oliver, was also a lawyer and political appointee; he had been named probate judge for Humboldt County by Governor Nye after attracting favorable attention while working as a Carson City journalist.

Completing the foursome was a sixty-year-old blacksmith and jack of all trades named Cornbury S. Tillou, who went along to drive the wagon and help the others build a cabin for the winter. The men packed their wagon full of eighteen hundred pounds of the bare essentials, including ten pounds of tobacco, two books of sacred hymns, fourteen decks of cards, a cribbage board, a small keg of lager beer, a copy of Charles Dickens's latest novel, *Dombey and Son*, and two dogs. The tobacco, in particular, was a necessity, if not perhaps a delicacy. It was, said Twain, "composed of equal parts of tobacco stems, chopped straw . . . fine shavings, oak leaves, dog-fennel, corn-shucks, sun-flower petals, outside leaves of the cabbage plant, and any refuse of any description whatever that costs nothing and will burn." Sprinkled with fragrant Scotch snuff, the noxious mixture was pack-aged as "Genuine Killickinick" and sold to consumers for a dollar a pound.

The wagon was pulled—generously speaking—by two horses, one of which was named Bunker after the territory's notoriously slow-thinking attorney general, Benjamin B. Bunker. The other horse in the team was none other than Sam's Genuine Mexican Plug, which he had in fact not given away to an unwary Arkansas traveler after all, but had sold to an equally unwary Clagett. The dogs were Tom, a seven-month-old puppy "much addicted to fleas," which they had liberated from Carson City's minuscule Chinatown and named after the absent governor, and Tillou's ill-tempered white terrier Colonel, or Curney, "a little mean, white, curly, grinning whelp, no bigger than a cat—with a wretched, envious, snappish, selfish disposition, and a tail like an all-wood Capital O, curled immodestly over his back."

It took the party fifteen days to reach Unionville, mainly because the lead horse, Bunker, tended to stop in his tracks whenever they reached a rough stretch of road, which was often. Other miners they met along the trail suggested drolly that they load the horses onto the wagon as well, but Tillou said they were too "bituminous from long deprivation" for that. Tillou, a transplanted Frenchman, was a character out of an old western movie. He was stereotypically lusty (Clagett wanted to find him a copy of *Fanny Hill*, and Clemens wor-ried that he might ravish a Paiute woman along the way and start another Indian war), and much given to using big words, even when he did not know what they meant. "If a word was long and grand and resonant," recalled Twain, "that was sufficient to win the old man's love, and he would drop that word into the most out-of-the-way place in a sentence or a subject, and be as pleased with it as if it were perfectly luminous with meaning." Tillou described one of the dogs, presumably Tom, as "meretricious in his movements and . . . organic in his emotions," and refused to drink coffee made with alkaline water because it was "too technical for him."

The party pulled into Unionville in a driving snowstorm in mid-December. The scraggly boomtown sprawled across the Buena Vista valley, with scraggly trails snaking up the mountainside to silver claims bearing such grand-sounding names as National, Alba Nueva, Peru, Delirio, Congress, and Independence. The town itself had been called Dixie before the fortunes of war turned against the Confederacy in late 1861 and residents voted to change the town's moniker to the more republican—and Republican—Unionville. When the party arrived, the settlement consisted of eleven huts and one enormous American flag. They pitched in and made it an even dozen, constructing a three-sided log and stone cabin and topping it with a canvas roof turned up in one corner for a primitive chimney. The area, wrote an alliteration-loving correspondent for the *Mining and Scientific Press*, was "well stocked in liquor, lice and loafers; and at the same time is greatly in want of water power, wood and women." Sam and his friends had brought some, if not all, of the same stock with them when they arrived.

Led by Tillou, who had actually done some prospecting before, the party scoured the hills for a promising claim of their own. Sam, a self-confessed tinhorn, "expected to find masses of silver lying all about the ground [and] glittering in the sun on the mountain summits." One day he picked up a shiny piece of stone and carried it back proudly to the campsite, presenting it with a flourish as the answer to their dreams. Tillou took one look at the rock and pronounced it "a lot of granite rubbish and nasty glittering mica that isn't worth ten cents an acre." Amending Shakespeare, he gave Sam and the others a crash course in mineralogy, pointing out that "nothing that glitters is gold . . . gold in its native state is dull, unornamental stuff, and that only low-born metals excite the admiration of the ignorant with an ostentatious glitter."

After several more days of fruitless searching through snow and wind, the party managed to locate a ledge outcropping of quartz, which Tillou said might contain silver. Sam was not enthused: "*Contained* it! I had thought at least it would be caked on the outside of it like a kind of veneering." Undeterred, the friends stuck up paper notices for three claims of three hundred feet each, along with an additional fifty feet of ground on either side. They dubbed their find "Monarch of the Mountains." Tillou explained that successful silver mining involved months of digging, drilling, boring, and blasting—the purest veins were usually the deepest. It was only a start.

After a week of gamely scratching away at the surface, the party finally managed to dig a tunnel "about deep enough to hide a hogshead in." Sam quit in disgust; Clagett and Oliver followed. "We wanted a ledge that was already 'developed,'" Twain observed. "There were none in the camp." As an alternative, they decided to trade in "feet," a highly speculative venture that consisted entirely of buying and selling shares, on paper, of largely nonexistent mines such as their own. The entire camp was engaged in the same practice, and the place swarmed with "bloated millionaires . . . who had not twenty-five dollars in the world." The trick, said Twain, was "not to mine the silver ourselves by the sweat of our brows and the labor of our hands, but to sell the ledges to the dull slaves of toil and let them do the mining."

Soon, they had amassed thirty thousand feet in such phantom holdings as the Gray Eagle, the Columbiana, the Branch Mint, the Maria Jane, the Universe, the Root-Hog-or-Die, the Samson and Delilah, the Treasure Trove, the Golconda, the Sultana, the Boomerang, the Great Republic, and the Grand Mogul. They were "drunk with happiness—smothered under mountains of prospective wealth." Before leaving Carson City, Sam had used some of his rapidly depleted savings to buy shares for himself and Orion in several mines in the Esmeralda mining district at Aurora, three hundred miles south of Unionville in the opposite direction. The mines were being worked by two acquaintances of the brothers, Bob Howland and Horatio

"Raish" Phillips, whom they had met at Mrs. Murphy's boarding-house while the miners were in town for the territorial convention. In early January 1862, Sam decided to leave Unionville and look in on his other fabulous holdings in the south.

In the company of two new associates, "Colonel" John B. Onstine and "Captain" Hugo Pfersdorff, he set off in yet another driving snowstorm. (In his description of the journey in *Roughing It*, Twain claimed that the unranked Cornbury Tillou also made the trip from Unionville, but that seems to have been a fictional device for comic effect.) The party subsequently spent eight days marooned with other vagabonds at the Honey Lake Smith stage line and trading post on the north bank of the snow-flooded Carson River. "By'm-by, heap water," the weather-savvy Paiutes told them before clearing out ahead of time. Sam and the others stayed, convinced that it was some sort of inscrutable Indian ruse, only to be awakened that night by "a great turmoil. . . . The crooked Carson was full to the brim, and its waters were raging and foaming in the wildest way—sweeping around the sharp bends at a furious speed, and bearing on their surface a chaos of logs, brush and all sorts of rubbish." They were marooned.

Cooped up inside the station, the travelers passed the time in the usual western way: swearing, drinking, and playing cards. In a tour de force passage in *Roughing It* that prefigured by more than two decades Stephen Crane's great short story "The Blue Hotel," Twain described a fight between a young Swedish immigrant and a pistol-sporting, bowie-knife-wielding ruffian calling himself "Arkansas." When the mild-mannered landlord attempted to intervene, Arkansas turned his guns on him, sending the landlord crashing through a glass door before the innkeeper's wife appeared, armed with a pair of scissors, and cowed the bully into embarrassed submission.

A short time later, Clemens and his friends escaped by canoe and resumed their journey to Esmeralda, only to get lost in the furious snowfall, following a steadily growing set of tracks. "Boys," said Til-lou, "these are our own tracks, and we've actually been circussing round and round in a circle for more than two hours, out here in this blind desert! By George this is perfectly hydraulic!" Down to their last match, which soon guttered out in the wind, the men resolved to die bravely together. Each poignantly renounced a particular vice—in Clemens's case, it was tobacco—and laid down in the snow to await oblivion. They awakened, still alive, to discover that they were within a few steps of another stagecoach station. "I have scarcely exaggerated a detail of this curious and absurd adventure," Twain swore. "It occurred almost exactly as I have stated it"—*almost* being the operative word.

However he actually made the journey back to Carson City, Clemens arrived in time to become embroiled in a nasty feud between Orion and Nye. The two were at loggerheads, predictably enough, over the governor's more elastic and creative interpretation of federal funding and dispensations. The more politically experienced Nye argued that the government, preoccupied just then with the Civil War, was unlikely to quibble over how every nickel of its money was being spent out west. It wanted, he said, the appearance of economy more than actual economy. Orion, who had endured several long months of just such nickel-and-diming while Nye was away, begged to differ. When Nye suggested that Orion juggle the books a little to account for "necessary adjustments," the secretary refused, complaining afterward to his mother that "a man can't hold public office and be honest."

Sam, freshly returned to town, stomped off to see the governor and favored him with a proper Mississippi riverboat dressing-down in Orion's behalf, but privately he was inclined to agree with Nye. For months he had been urging Orion to rent an office commensurate with his status as territorial secretary and de facto lieutenant governor. His threadbare rooms at Mrs. Murphy's boardinghouse were hurting him with the public, Sam argued. At length Orion gave in, renting a corner office and furnishing it with silk damask curtains and a fine Brussels carpet. Once again government bookkeepers questioned his expenses, and Orion was forced to repay the $339.25 he had spent on the curtains.

Sam spent the rest of the winter lounging and loafing around Carson City, growing a beard, smoking a pipe, and propping up a corner of the Ormsby House. He looked and acted the part of a seasoned prospector, clomping into saloons in high-top Spanish boots, linen shirt, and blue jeans and sporting a revolver on his hip "in deference to popular sentiment, and in order that I might not, by its absence be offensively conspicuous." While his actual money, a few hundred dollars in savings, steadily dribbled away, Sam counted and spent his paper millions, bragging to his mother, sister, and sister-in-law that he would soon be rich and hitting up his brother-in-law, William Moffett, for a thousand-dollar loan to buy yet more feet. To whet his appetite, Sam sent Moffett a lump of gold from his National holdings in Unionville and a silver-bearing piece of quartz from the Ophir mine, which he had visited briefly in Virginia City. "The Ophir," he confided, "has $2,000,000 worth of ore lying on the ground at the mouth of their incline." He did not own an interest in the mine, but that was beside the point. He managed to wheedle a tour by telling the mine foreman that he was the secretary of the territory, that is, Orion. In such hopeful diversions he passed the time.

In mid-April, while the Union and Confederate armies back east were still reeling from the cataclysmic Battle of Shiloh, a determinedly unmilitary Clemens set out by horseback for Aurora with Governor Nye's brother, Captain John Nye, and others to examine his holdings in the Esmeralda mining district. Although they had been discovered at roughly the same time, Aurora was a bigger boomtown than Unionville. It boasted a population of two thousand people, twenty-two saloons, sixteen ore mills, ten restaurants, two churches, one newspaper, a Masonic hall, an Odd Fellows hall, and an unspecified number of whorehouses. Everything, secular and religious, was buried under several feet of snow—"It always snows here," Clemens complained—and the first matter of business was finding a warm place to live. With his on-site business partners, Bob Howland and Horatio Phillips, Sam appropriated a ten-by-twelve-foot cabin in Chinatown and decided to move it to a better location uptown. The partners enlisted fifteen or twenty friends to help with the relocation, and the movers dragged the cabin down Main Street until they reached the Exchange Saloon, where they immediately put it down and went inside to refresh themselves. By the time Clemens and his associates had finished buying a round of drinks, Howland estimated that some 250 "helpers" had bellied up to the bar. It would have been cheaper, he said, to have simply bought a new cabin with a mansard roof and attached observatory.

Sam and Orion owned shares in several Aurora mines, including the Horatio and Derby, the Black Warrior, the Dashaway, the Flyaway, the Monitor, and the Annipolitan. It did not take Clemens long to realize that most, if not all, were utterly worthless. Over the winter, Howland and Phillips had dug a fifty-two-foot tunnel for the Horatio and Derby. They had not yet struck silver, but they had tapped into several underground springs. If all else failed, they assured Clemens, they could always sell the water.

In the meantime, Clemens acclimated himself to his new surroundings. Besides being larger than Unionville, Aurora was also more dangerous. Ranchers in the Owens River valley south of town had engaged all winter in a running battle with Digger Indians, who were attempting in their usual desultory way to defend their homeland against white incursions. That March, Aurora sheriff N. F. Scott had led a force of eighteen men to reinforce the ranchers, who were barricaded in a stone fort at Owens Lake. Fifty troopers from the 2nd Cavalry, California Volunteers, came up from Fort Churchill to lend a hand, and another forty troopers from as far away as Los Angeles arrived as well. The whites attacked in three columns, but the badly coordinated assault failed, and Scott and several others were killed. The standoff with the Indians remained unresolved until a treaty was signed with the Diggers in October 1862.

Closer to home, a gunfight between rival mine owners the same week that Clemens arrived resulted in the fatal wounding of a man named Gebhart on the all too aptly named Last Chance Hill. Gebhart died a few days later. The next month, claim jumpers literally jumped into Clemens's Monitor mine—a shallow hole in the ground—while he was scraping for gold and pulled guns on him, saying they were willing to die if necessary to assert their rights. Clemens was not. The matter was referred to Circuit Court, which eventually ruled in favor of Clemens and his partners, awarding them seven-eighths of the eight-hundred-foot holding, which in the end proved to be worth about what they paid for it—mere paper.

Undeterred by his close call, Clemens took up a pick and shovel and worked himself to a bloody pulp (to hear him tell it) on his various holdings in and around Aurora. No one was really sure who owned what—Aurora itself was variously claimed by the states of California and Nevada, before coming down finally in the Nevada column in 1864. Sam and Phillips, two-thirds of the grandly named Clemens Gold and Silver Mining Company, chipped away at the two hundred feet of outcroppings they owned in the Annipolitan mine, whose ledge adjoined two other more promising mines, the Wide West and the Pride of Utah. The Annipolitan was "a dead sure thing," Clemens told his brother, although he cautioned the easily impressed Orion that "it's the damnedest country for disappointments the world ever saw." Meanwhile, his mother and sister, who were armed with the full Clemens family complement of common sense, which is to say none, had become so enthralled by Sam's optimistic descriptions of mining life in southwestern Nevada that they decided they wanted to see it for themselves. It took all of Sam's persuasive powers to rid them of that misguided notion. People of his "uncongealable sanguine personality," Sam explained, falling back on his old phrenological diagnosis, were "very apt to go to extremes, and exaggerate." There was nothing, really, for them to see.

Like much American enterprise at the midway point of the nineteenth century, silver mining was in the process of transforming itself from individual effort to mass production. Sixteen ore-grinding mills had begun operating in Aurora, the most efficient of which was Joshua E. Clayton's twelve-stamp mill on Martinez Hill, which operated around the clock, seven days a week. Early millers used the "arrastre," or Mexican, method of ore extraction, hitching horses or mules to the wooden spokes of a large wheel and walking them in a continuous, infernal circle to grind down the ore into extractable nuggets. Clayton's mill used the stamping method, dropping ore through a chute into a large box, or battery, and crushing it with six-ton steel stamps. The crushed ore was then mixed in vats of water, mercury, and other chemicals, and the gold and silver were amalgamated with the mercury and separated. Clayton offered to teach the method to Clemens and Phillips, in return for them puffing the process to other miners.

Clayton estimated it would take them five or six weeks to learn the method; Clemens lasted one. "It is a pity that Adam could not have gone straight out of Eden into a quartz mill," he wrote, "in order to understand the full force of his doom to 'earn his bread by the sweat of his brow.'" At the end of the week, having caught a bad cold, he asked Clayton for a raise. Sam was making ten dollars a week; he asked for four hundred thousand. "I was ordered off the premises," he remembered. "And yet, when I look back to those days and call to mind the exceeding hardness of the labor . . . I only regret that I did not ask him for seven hundred thousand."

Actually, Clayton did not fire Clemens; he quit. As Sam explained to Orion, "I came near getting salivated, working the quicksilver and chemicals. I hardly think I shall try the experiment again. It is a confining business, and I will not be confined, for love nor money."

He was finding his partnership with Phillips confining as well, and by late July he had dissolved their connection like so much mercury or phosphate of copper. "He is a damned rascal," Sam told Orion, "and I can get the signatures of 25 men in this sentiment whenever I want them." He advised his brother not to pay Phillips for any more of their claims. "He can have his ground back," Clemens fumed. "It isn't worth a damn, except that the work on it will hold it until the next great convulsion of nature injects gold and silver into it."

Clemens located a new partner, an experienced and indefatigable civil engineer named Calvin Higbie, "a large, strong man [who] has the perseverance of the devil." In August 1862, the two went down to Mono Lake, twenty-five miles southwest of Aurora, where they embarked on a fruitless search for the fabled "Lost Cement Gold Mine," a regional chimera since its supposed discovery several years earlier by three lost survivors from a doomed Death Valley wagon train. The cement in question was not the modern paving compound, but a conglomerate rock comprised mostly of lava and containing "lumps of virgin gold thick as raisins in a slice of fruit cake," as Clemens put it. Supposedly, the wanderers had chanced on a vein of dull-yellow cement in a lost mountain gorge. "The vein was about as wide as a curbstone, and fully two-thirds of it was pure gold," Twain wrote. "Every pound of the wonderful cement was worth well-nigh two hundred dollars." Two of the men died, but a third reportedly gave a map of the fabulous find to a desert rat named Whiteman, who became a sort of one-man Lost Dutchman Mine, wandering the region for years in search of the site.

After Whiteman was allegedly spotted in Aurora earlier that month, wearing a disguise and pretending for some reason to be intoxicated, the entire community went into a frenzy. The local correspondent for the Sacramento *Bee* reported that miners by the dozen were sneaking out of Aurora "during the still hours of the night" and heading for Mono Lake, where "the news was whispered round in a few private circles that mines of gold had been discovered." Soon, Aurora was a virtual ghost town, the population having resettled around the shores of Mono Lake, the so-called Dead Sea of California. The name came from the resident Monache Indians, an offshoot of the Shoshone tribe who were known to their neighbors as "the fly people" for their reliance on the pupae of brine flies that darkened the lakeshore by the tens of thousand. Dried and crushed into a sort of flour, the flies were mixed with nuts and berries and baked into a bread called *cuchaba*. It was "not unpleasant to the taste," said a California geologist of the period who was brave enough to try it.

Perhaps because he almost drowned in it during the course of his visit, Clemens did not find Mono Lake transportingly beautiful. The lake, he said later, "lies in a lifeless, treeless, hideous desert, eight thousand feet above the level of the sea, and is guarded by mountains two thousand feet higher, whose summits are always clothed in clouds. This solemn, silent, sailless sea—this lonely tenant of the loneliest spot on earth—is little graced with the picturesque." The water in the lake was so strongly alkaline in content that it was undrinkable; indeed, it was almost bleach. Clemens had a dog with him (it is unclear whether this was the same dog Tom that had accompanied him to Unionville). One day the dog, which was covered with sores, jumped into the lake to get away from the flies. "It was bad judgment," said his master. "In his condition, it would have been just as comfortable to jump into the fire. The alkali water nipped him in all the raw places simultaneously, and he struck out for the shore with considerable interest. . . . He was not a demonstrative dog, as a general thing, but rather of a grave and serious turn of mind, and I never saw him take so much interest in anything before. He finally struck out over the mountains, at a gait which we estimated at about two hundred and fifty miles an hour, and he is going yet."

The lake was notorious for the changeability of its weather, dropping from ninety degrees during the day to forty degrees at night and turning in seconds from a calm glassy surface into a foaming maelstrom of whitecaps. Clemens and Higbie were out sailing one afternoon when they ran into trouble. A storm kicked up and they struck for shore, panicking all the while that they would be capsized. "Once capsized," Sam recalled, "death would ensue in spite of the bravest swimming, for that venomous water would eat a man's eyes out like fire, and burn him out inside, too. . . . [I]n less than five minutes we would have a hundred gallons of soap-suds in us and be eaten up so quickly that we could not even be present at our own inquest." Thanks to Higbie's superhuman strength, they managed to get close enough to shore to thrash landward, yelping every step of the way, before the boat capsized. Clemens also narrowly avoided being killed when a cooking stove exploded—someone had hidden six cans of gunpowder inside it—and the lid went whizzing past his head. "Dam stove heap gone!" their Indian helper observed unhelpfully.

In *Roughing It*, which he dedicated to Higbie, Mark Twain conflated the search for the lost cement mine with the equally unsuccessful denouement of the Annipolitan mining venture. The author's flavorful but not particularly accurate account begins with Higbie discovering a "blind lead" inside the Wide West mine on Aurora's Lost Chance Hill (a blind lead was a vein not visible from the surface). According to Twain, Higbie sees a specimen of rock purportedly from the Wide West holding and somehow deduces that it had not come from the mine. Lowering himself by rope into the mine shaft, Higbie discovers a blind lead of rich ore cutting diagonally across the Wide West and intersecting their own holdings in the Annipolitan. Convinced that they are rich, or soon will be, the partners spend a pleasant night in their tent imagining what they will do with their newfound wealth. Each intends to build a brownstone mansion on Russian Hill in San Francisco, keep a carriage and coachman to drive him around, and travel to Europe and the Middle East. Meanwhile, they owe the local butcher six dollars, but in typical rich-man fashion, they intend to stiff him. "Hang the butcher!" Highbie says. Due to a mix-up (each thinks the other is working the mine), the partners neglect to put in the necessary ten days required to establish legal ownership. Others jump the claim and walk away with the gold. Clemens and Higbie, "millionaires for ten days," as the dedication to *Roughing It* jokes, go their separate ways, sadder and presumably wiser for their loss.

The true story of the Wide West strike was even more tangled and complicated than Clemens's retelling. The Wide West, the Pride of Utah, and the Annipolitan holdings were inextricably intermingled, with Clemens's two-hundred-foot claim crowded between the others and "most damnably mixed," as he explained to Orion. A cross ledge, presumably Higbie's blind lead, ran across the holdings underground. Pride of Utah's owner, Peter Johnson, legally registered the ledge on July 1, 1862. Clemens conceded to his brother that he did not "own a foot in the 'Johnson' ledge," and the arcane law by which he alleged that he and Higbie were cheated out of their holdings applied only to surface claims—not subterranean finds.

A few days later, Mono County mining officials ruled that the Pride of Utah controlled the ledge for a thousand feet in either direction, a ruling that was legally contested by Wide West owners. In December of that year, Wide West bought out Johnson and consolidated the holdings, which yielded ore assayed at ten thousand dollars per ton. In the end, the strike proved to be a "chamber mine," one that was confined to a single shaft and was not dispersed into other ledges. Within a few months, the strike was played out. The most that could be said for Clemens's and Higbie's blind lead was that it was in the general vicinity.

By then, Sam was tired of being a miner. "Christ! How sick I am of these same old humdrum scenes," he complained to Orion. He had already tongue-lashed his brother for sending down a third party to look into their holdings in Aurora. "God damn it, I don't want any more feet, and I won't touch another foot," he complained. Swearing that he would "never look upon Ma's face again, or Pamela's, or get married, or revisit the 'Banner State' until I am a rich man," Sam was forced to take stock of his present situation. "I had gained a livelihood in various vocations," he said, "but I had not dazzled anybody with my successes." He had been (so he claimed; much of his employment history was undocumented) a grocery clerk, a law student—for "an entire week"—an apprentice blacksmith, a bookstore clerk, a soda jerk in a drugstore, "a tolerable printer," "a good average St. Louis and New Orleans pilot," a private secretary, a miner, and a silver mill operator. "What to do next?" he wondered.

The answer came entirely out of the blue, or so it seemed anyway, when William H. Barstow, the business manager for the Virginia City *Territorial Enterprise*, wrote to Sam in late July to offer him a $25-a-week staff writer's position on the newspaper. The Clemens brothers had gotten to know Barstow when he served as a legislative assistant at the first territorial legislature. For several weeks, simply as a lark, Sam had been sending humorous letters to the newspaper, signing himself "Josh." His favorite target was Nevada chief justice George Turner, whose fondness for constantly referring to himself in his speeches induced Clemens to dub him Professor Personal Pronoun.

When an opening suddenly arose on the paper's staff, Barstow thought of Clemens. With Orion controlling the valuable printing contract for the legislature's official documents, Barstow convinced *Enterprise* editor and publisher Joseph T. Goodman to hire the secretary's brother. What did they have to lose? Clemens came back to his cabin one day, grouchy and dispirited, after shoveling dirt down his neck "on a little rubbishy claim" he was working with Higbie, to find Barstow's unexpected letter waiting for him. "Eureka!" he cried. He had struck gold at last, albeit of a very different grade than the kind he had been digging for all these months.

CHAPTER 4

ENTERPRISE

THE PROFESSIONAL WRITING CAREER OF THE MOST famous writer in American history began modestly, if not quietly, in the autumn of 1862. Sporting a patina of road dust and alkali—to save money he had walked and hitchhiked the entire way from Aurora to Virginia City, 120 miles to the northwest—Sam Clemens burst into the upstairs office of the *Territorial Enterprise* at 27 North C Street one afternoon in late September like the Tasmanian Devil in a Saturday morning cartoon. "Dang my buttons, if I don't believe I'm lousy!" he cried, meaning it literally, not figuratively. "My starboard leg seems to be unshipped. I'd like about one hundred yards of line."

The staffers in the newsroom were not sure at first whether the garrulous newcomer was a miner, a gunslinger, or a landlocked sailor. By his own admission, Clemens was a bit "rusty looking." He wore the typical western costume of blue woolen shirt, denim pants, floppy hat, and high-topped boots, accessorized with a scruffy red beard hanging halfway down his chest and a big navy revolver stuffed into his belt. Given the fact that the newspaper routinely printed stories about its fellow citizens that had only a passing conversance with the truth, no one was entirely certain that the brash young stranger had not come around looking for satisfaction. Not so, it turned out— he was merely there to take his place as the paper's new "local," a combination copy editor/general assignment reporter whose job it was to fill any last-minute holes in the newspaper. Clemens could do that. For years, he had patched similar holes in Orion's various publications, from the Hannibal *Journal* and *Western Union* to the Muscatine *Journal* and the Keokuk city directory. He had also contributed squibs to the New Orleans *Crescent*, most notably his wicked impersonation of Colonel Isaiah Sellers in 1859. As someone had said of Confederate president Jefferson Davis, admittedly in a different context, at the beginning of the Civil War, "The man and the hour had met."

By sheer good luck, of the sort he was routinely blessed with during the first half of his life, Clemens had landed a spot on the best newspaper between St. Louis and San Francisco. The *Territorial Enterprise*—shortened by everyone to the *Enterprise*—was not much older than Virginia City itself, meaning it was quite young. Like its readers, the newspaper was as rootless as a tumbleweed, having begun as a weekly in Genoa in 1858 before moving to Carson City for a year and then relocating to Virginia City in late 1860. Under the energetic leadership of its precocious new owners, twenty-three-year-old editor Joseph Goodman and twenty-one-year-old printing foreman Denis McCarthy, the *Enterprise* began publishing an eight-page daily in September 1861. It had found a home, albeit not much of one. San Francisco writer Frank Soule, visiting at the time, was not impressed. "I have been through one hundred degrees of latitude, north and south," said Soule, "but never have I found so inhospitable, miserable, God-forsaken a spot as this same Virginia City."

Soule's reservations aside, the *Enterprise* was a perfect match for the wide-open town it covered. Fueled by the basket loads of wealth being carted steadily from the Comstock Lode atop which it sat, Virginia City had been scrabbling up the side of Mount Davidson for the past two years, its parallel streets running east to west (but not north to south) along the eastern slope of the mountain. Terraced like its similarly vertical big sister, San Francisco, the West's newest boomtown boasted an ever-shifting population of nearly ten thousand residents, the vast majority of whom were male. There were fifty-one saloons, two opera houses, a dozen quartz mills, and a generous assortment of hotels, restaurants, meat markets, drugstores, and other representatives of the service industry, including a revolving roster of prostitutes, called locally "hurdy-gurdy girls."

Among the most popular saloons lining mile-long C Street were the Sazerac, the Sawdust Corner, and the Bucket of Blood, all serving something called Pisco Punch and the local staple, Forty-rod, a particularly raw and fiery brand of house whiskey so named because that was the approximate distance a tenderfoot could walk before collapsing in a heap. Piper's Opera House, the town's center for performing arts, featured everything from traveling Shakespearean road companies to cage fights between wildcats, bulldogs, bulls, and bears. It also hosted the slightly less bloodthirsty Montgomery Queen's Great Show, which advertised an eye-catchingly capitalized drawing card of "An African Eland, an Abysinnian Ibex, Cassowaries, and the Only Female Somersault Rider in the World."

The business of Virginia City, of course, was mining. There were no mines on Mount Davidson itself, but dozens of subterranean shafts honeycombed the base of the mountain to the east. Peripatetic traveler John Ross Browne luridly described the ongoing and quite literal rape of the land: "Myriads of swarthy, bearded, dust-covered men are piercing into the grim old mountains, ripping them open, thrusting murderous holes through their naked bodies; piling up engines to cut their vital arteries; stamping and crushing up with infernal machines their disemboweled fragments, and holding fiendish revels amid the chaos of destruction." Miners earned upwards of six dollars a day gouging away at the eighty-foot-wide vein of silver stretching like God's own treasury beneath the town. It was called generically the Comstock Lode, after the sharp-eyed thief, Henry T. P. Comstock, who had jumped the claim discovered initially by Peter O'Riley and Patrick McLaughlin three years earlier.

In much the same way, Virginia City owed its somewhat confusing name to an unregenerate desert rat, James "Old Virginia" Fennimore, who immodestly named the town after himself one typically drunken night in camp. None of the four principals had much luck afterward. Old Virginia died first, in July 1861, of a fractured skull after being thrown from a horse while in his usual state of extreme intoxication. Comstock fatally shot himself in the head in Bozeman, Montana, in 1870, after making what was described, a little ungenerously perhaps, as "a feeble struggle against advancing dementia." O'Riley lost his savings and subsequently his mind in disastrous stock speculation, dying in a sanitarium in Woodbridge, California, in 1874. His erstwhile prospecting partner McLaughlin took a job as a forty-dollar-a-week cook at a gold mine in San Bernardino, California, improvidently saved none of his wages, and died a pauper in 1875.

Others got rich. An unlettered rancher named Lemuel Sanford "Sandy" Bowers, described by Clemens as "miraculously ignorant," parlayed an original ten-foot claim in Crown Point Ravine into a $70,000-a-month fortune, making him and his Scottish-born wife, Eilley, the territory's first millionaires. "I've got money to throw to the birds," said Bowers, who pretty much did exactly that. In what was quickly becoming the local custom, the Bowerses' luck soon took a turn for the worse: Sandy died at the early age of thirty-five in 1868, and Eilley lost her inheritance to bad investments and even worse swindlers, ending her life as the self-proclaimed "Washoe Seeress," a mystic whose own lack of financial foresight might have seemed a serious professional handicap.

John W. Mackay, one of the owners of the Kentuck mine, later struck it rich as part of the "Big Bonanza" silver strike in the 1870s. During the Civil War, he supposedly tracked down a missing partner in the Confederate Army of Tennessee, getting him to sign the proper legal papers while dodging Yankee bullets at the Battle of Chattanooga. Mackay's personal lawyer, William M. Stewart, rode his benefactor's connections into a fabulously lucrative legal practice and, later, into five terms as a Radical Republican in the United States Senate from Nevada, during which time he helped author the Fifteenth Amendment, guaranteeing voting rights to former slaves. Missouri-born gold rusher George Hearst bought into the Ophir mine, cashed out early, and sunk his earnings into a San Francisco newspaper, the *Examiner*, which would become the cornerstone of his son William Randolph's global publishing empire. (Papa Hearst spent so much time digging around in the dirt that the local Indians, who observed the white men's back-breaking labors with a stolid mixture of amusement and wonder, dubbed him "Boy That Earth Talks To.")

Even the meek—a few of them, anyway—inherited a part of Virginia City's rich earth. A Mexican prospector named Gabriel Maldonado translated his stake in a trickling creek bed into a million-dollar share of the obviously named Mexican Mining Company. And an eagle-eyed young Canadian telegraph operator named John William Skae used the insider information he gleaned from the various telegrams passing through his hands to invest profitably in choice mining feet. Skae's less than scrupulous success subsequently caused the company he worked for, California State Telegraph, to prohibit its employees from owning personal shares in the mines.

Clemens would come to know many of these silver kings—he called them "nabobs"—during the next few years, but first he had to make the acquaintance of his fellow scribblers on the *Enterprise*. Man for man, they were as varied and colorful as the town itself. First among equals was Joseph Goodman, co-owner and editor of the newspaper. Now twenty-four, Goodman was three years younger than Clemens, but the tall, good-looking newsman had a patina of sophistication that his new reporter did not, compliments of the half decade he had spent as a typesetter in San Francisco before coming to Nevada. A native of Masonville, New York, Goodman had gone west as a teenager, working as a compositor for the *Golden Era*, San Francisco's most prestigious literary journal, before getting the gold bug himself and moving to Nevada in the early 1860s.

Following Goodman eastward were two of his former associates at the *Golden Era*, editor and founder Rollin Mallory Daggett and Australian-born printer Denis McCarthy. After Goodman and McCarthy bought the *Enterprise,* Daggett signed on as associate editor and all-around gadfly. Short, stout, and combative, Daggett drank hard and lived high. At the age of sixteen he had walked all the way from Ohio to California, living for a time with the Sioux Indians, who understandably considered him crazy for doing so and thus left him alone. Using the small fortune he made in the California goldfields, Daggett started up the *Golden Era* in 1852. For the next eight years he tramped the mining camps of the western Sierras, hunting for subscribers among the literature-deprived denizens of the region, before moving to Virginia City and opening a brokerage firm. His work on the *Enterprise* was more a hobby than a full-time job.

Clemens's closest friend on the *Enterprise*, and the man he had been hired to replace temporarily (once he left), was William Wright, better known by his nom de plume, Dan De Quille. Born into a large Quaker family in Knox County, Ohio, in 1829, Wright had moved with his family to West Liberty, Iowa, midway between Iowa City and Clemens's old stomping grounds at Muscatine. There he met and married a local girl, Caroline Coleman, began fathering an eventual five children, and settled on a gently rolling farmstead where, he remembered fondly, he learned "the poetry of corn." Neither the grain's poetic properties nor the familial responsibilities of hearth and home were sufficiently strong to prevent him from joining his brother Hank in a late-season rush to the California goldfields in 1857. Unlike Clemens, Wright was an able and assiduous miner, and his firsthand knowledge of the literally hardscrabble profession induced Goodman to hire him as the *Enterprise*'s resident mining expert, a position he would fill ably and enthusiastically—with brief family vis-its to Iowa—until the newspaper finally folded in 1893. By the time Clemens arrived on the scene, Dan De Quille had begun publishing humorous sketches in the *Golden Era* and *Knickerbocker Magazine*, the same New York publication whose columns of type young Sam Clemens had hand-set a decade earlier during his brief sojourn in the East. De Quille's first bit of advice, which Clemens would carry with him the rest of his career, was wise if succinct: "Get the facts first, then you can distort them as much as you like."

The *Enterprise* staff inhabited, as scholar Henry Nash Smith has observed, "a kind of bachelor's paradise." Most were still in their twenties—De Quille at thirty-three was the graybeard of the group—unmarried, footloose, and more or less fancy free. While hundreds of thousands of men in their age group were fighting and dying on Civil war battlefields in Maryland, Kentucky, Virginia, Tennessee, and even as close by as New Mexico, they existed in a more or less apolitical bubble. Most were northerners or midwesterners by birth, but their long years in the West had largely inoculated them from the internecine war fever back east. Clemens, if he still felt any particular interest or commitment to the Confederate cause, kept it to himself. Instead, the resolutely civilian newsmen drank, smoked, played bil-liards and cards, inflicted and suffered elaborate practical jokes, wrote the occasional breaking news article, and ate endless plates of Chinese food prepared for them by the newspaper's personal cook, "Old Joe."

Like the rest of Virginia City, the *Enterprise* was a man's world, and Clemens, with his boisterous riverboat background, fit right in. He would never be a particularly hard worker—he later boasted that he made a 50 percent profit on his work for the *Enterprise*, being paid six dollars a day and only doing three dollars' worth of work—but he was willing to do his share. He asked Goodman for professional instructions: "He told me to go all over town and ask all sorts of people all sorts of questions," the new reporter recalled, "make notes of the information gained, and write them out for publication." Goodman also gave him a piece of advice that would serve him well when he turned from journalism to fiction writing a decade later: "Never say 'We learn' so-and-so, or 'It is reported,' or 'It is rumored,' or 'We understand' so-and-so, but go to headquarters and get the absolute facts, and then speak out and say 'It *is* so-and-so.' Otherwise, people will not put confidence in your news. Unassailable certainty is the thing that gives a newspaper the firmest and most valuable reputation."

Clemens's assignment was to produce one written column of nonpareil, or six-point type, per day. Being new to the city, he recalled, "I wandered about town questioning everybody, boring everybody, and finding out that nobody knew anything. At the end of five hours my note-book was still barren." Goodman suggested that he check out the comings and goings of hay wagons: "It isn't sensational or exciting, but it fills up and looks business-like." Clemens eventually located "one wretched old hay truck" dragging into town from Truckee, multiplied it by sixteen wagons and sixteen different directions, and generally "got up such another sweat about hay as Virginia City had never seen in the world before."

Even better, Sam stumbled upon one of the town's daily shootings. "A desperado killed a man in a saloon and joy returned once more," he remembered fondly. "I never was so glad over any mere trifle before in my life. I said to the murderer: 'Sir, you are a stranger to me, but you have done me a kindness this day which I can never forget. . . . I was in trouble and you have relieved me nobly and at a time when all seemed dark and drear. Count me your friend this time forth, for I am not a man to forget a favor.'" He was only sorry that the townsfolk did not immediately lynch the desperado on the spot, "so that I could work him up too."

The new reporter caught on quickly. The hard-drudging miners who made up the bulk of the *Enterprise*'s readership wanted to be entertained as well as informed. Raw facts only went so far. It was up to the writer to open a shallow vein of truth, then excavate whatever nuggets of amusement lay buried below. Dan De Quille, with his factual grounding as a miner and his naturally fanciful nature, was a master at one of the newspaper's favorite offerings—the hoax. Shortly before he left on one of his infrequent trips home, De Quille produced a classic. It was headlined "Sad Fate of an Inventor" and concerned one Jonathan Newhouse, "a man of considerable genius" who had invented a suit of "solar armor" to protect him from the broiling desert sun while he was prospecting. According to De Quille, the inventor had devised a loose-fitting jacket and hood made of inch-thick sponge. Before starting into the desert, Newhouse soaked the jacket with water, which he replenished at regular intervals from an India-rubber sack connected to a tube leading to the top of the hood. Thus equipped, Newhouse entered Death Valley for a test run. The next day an Indian discovered his body, frozen solid, his beard covered with frost and a foot-long icicle hanging from his nose. The device had worked too well. De Quille's article was later picked up as far away as London, where the *Daily Telegraph*, in proper English fashion, declared itself "neither prepared to disbelieve it wholly nor to credit it without question."

One week into the job, Clemens produced his own contribution to the genre. "The Petrified Man" reported the discovery, similar to De Quille's frozen inventor, of a naturally preserved hundred-year-old corpse in the mountains south of Gravelly Ford on the Humboldt River. The body, wrote Clemens, "was in a sitting posture and leaning against a huge mass of croppings; the attitude was pensive, the right thumb resting against the side of the nose; the left thumb partially supported the chin, the forefinger pressing the inner corner of the left eye and drawing it partly open; the right eye was closed, and the fingers of the right hand spread apart." In other words, the corpse was simultaneously winking and thumbing his nose at the late, inhospitable world.

Like his evisceration of Colonel Sellers three years earlier, Clemens's article was fueled in part by a grudge the author held against the victim, in this case local judge G. T. Sewall. The cause of the grudge was never stated, but it was probably related to Sewall's cancellation the previous year of a printing contract with Orion Clemens for the official acts and laws of the first territorial legislature. That cancellation had forced Orion to give the contract to a San Francisco firm, which in turn caused U.S. Treasury officials to refuse to pay the costs, since they had been incurred out of state. In "Petrified Man," Clemens had Sewall, in his ex officio role as county coroner, rule ridiculously that the "deceased came to his death from protracted exposure" and refuse to allow sympathetic citizens to dynamite the remains from their limestone resting place and give them a Christian burial. The article was picked up by a number of West Coast publications, including the San Francisco *Bulletin*, giving Clemens his first taste of regional notoriety. It also allowed him the satisfaction of continuing to rub it in to Sewall by having the reprints hand-delivered to his door, heavily underlined by Clemens himself. "I hated Sewall in those days," he confessed a few years later, "and these things pacified me and pleased me. I could not have gotten more real comfort out of him without killing him."

The *Enterprise* staff slept late and stayed up late, putting the paper to bed at 2 A.M. and then repairing to the Sazerac saloon, owned by Virginia City's fire chief and reigning political boss, Tom Peasley, and conveniently located a few doors down from the newspaper on the other side of C Street. The staffers formed what they called the

Companions of the Jug (later renamed the Visigoths), swapping yarns until dawn with the various foot traffic that lurched unsteadily through the bar. The drink of choice was an explosive type of brandy known variously as Washoe, Minie Rifle, or Chain Lightning, whose effect was described by one survivor as "a stomach full of galvanic batteries, yellow hornets, pepper sauce and vitriol." Joe Goodman also provided a daily grog ration for his employees in the form of a ten-gallon barrel of lager beer kept handily in the newspaper's basement. Clemens, said Rollin Daggett, "consumed his portion of the daily allowance with the most astonishing regularity, although he seldom indulged in anything more intoxicating than beer." That would change—in later years, Clemens would famously favor Scotch—but for the time being, he kept to the comparatively softer stuff.

Mostly, he smoked his pipe and watched. There was a lot to take in. Virginia City was a twenty-four-hour town, and Clemens's news beat comprised everything from the silver mines to the police court. Roaming the streets was an adventure in itself. Virginia City, he observed, "had grown to be the 'livest' town, for its age and population, that America had ever produced. The sidewalks swarmed with people. . . . Joy sat on every countenance, and there was a glad, almost fierce, intensity in every eye, that told of the money-getting schemes that were seething in every brain and the high hope that held sway in every heart. Money was as plenty as dust." Years later, he still marveled at the daily spectacle of boomtown life: "There were military companies, fire companies, brass bands, banks, hotels, theatres, 'hurdy-gurdy houses,' wide-open gambling palaces, political pow-wows, civic processions, street fights, murders, inquests, riots, a whisky mill every fifteen steps, a Board of Aldermen, a Mayor, a City surveyor, a City Engineer, a Chief of the Fire Department, with First, Second and Third Assistants, a Chief of Police, City Marshal, and large police force, two Boards of Mining Brokers, a dozen breweries and half a dozen jails and station-houses in full operation, and some talk of building a church."

Like other western towns, Virginia City had more than its share of crime and violence. Clemens, who as a youth in Hannibal had seen one man fatally shot and another fatally stabbed, besides witnessing the usual frontier cavalcade of drownings, accidents, cholera, and yellow fever, was interested but by no means horrified by what he found on the streets of his new home. The first twenty-six graves in the local cemetery were occupied by murder victims, he noted, adding that "more than one man was killed in Nevada under hardly the pretext of provocation," by men who were eager to gain the dubious credit of having "killed his man." The best-known names in the territory belonged to gunslingers—Sugarfoot Mike, Pock-Marked Jake, El Dorado Johnny, Six-fingered Pete, Farmer Pease—"brave, reckless men [who] traveled with their lives in their hands. . . . They killed each other on slight provocation, and hoped and expected to be killed themselves—for they held it almost shame to die otherwise than 'with their boots on,' as they expressed it."

The *Enterprise* duly noted the gunmen's various deeds (some accounts were written by Clemens himself) under such headlines as "Fatal Shooting Affray," "Robbery and Desperate Affray," and "More Cuttings and Shootings." The worst of the lot was Sam Brown, a Texas-born badman who literally cut a broad swathe through Texas, California, and Nevada—his favorite weapon was the bowie knife—leaving a reputed sixteen victims in his wake. When he tried to make Genoa hotel keeper Henry Van Sickle the seventeenth, the alert hotelier beat him to the punch with seven rifle bullets to the body. A jury quickly found Van Sickle innocent, ruling that Brown had died "from a just dispensation of an all-wise Providence," a phrase that Mark Twain himself might have written. Another jury ruled that a suicide victim who had taken arsenic, shot himself in the chest, cut his own throat, and broken his neck by jumping out of a fourth-floor window had met his end "by the visitation of God." What would the world do without such juries? Twain marveled.

Less violent, if not always victimless, crime centered on wide-open C Street, for a time one of the most famous thoroughfares in the United States. In a town where men outnumbered women by a margin of seventeen-to-one, and where many of these same men had pockets bulging with gold and silver nuggets and bags of precious dust, prostitution flourished. An estimated two hundred "fallen angels" and "soiled doves" worked the streets at any one time, from fumbling back-alley assignations and upstairs saloon cribs to well-appointed pleasure houses.

The leading pleasure practitioner was Juliette "Julie" Bulette, a London-born, mixed-blood entrepreneur who had immigrated to New Orleans with her family in the late 1830s and drifted west to San Francisco, where she learned her time-hallowed profession. A one-woman operation, Bulette doled out her favors from a rose- and geranium-entwisted cottage on the corner of D and Union streets. The stereotypical whore with a heart of gold, she raised money for orphans, bought slaves out of bondage, took food and coffee to firemen, nursed sick and injured miners, and pressured city fathers to build cleaner cabins for her less fortunate sisters in their squalid shacks. In the end, all her good works did little to help Bulette herself. In January 1867, she was strangled in her bed by a ne'er-do-well Frenchman named Jean Millian. Some insiders believed Millian had been hired to kill Bulette by the working girl's former San Francisco associates.

Operating alongside the C Street whorehouses were dozens of opium dens, or smoking parlors, where miners could go for a few hours of surcease from their labors. Opium was handled exclusively by Chinese dealers, whose hardworking countrymen had first brought the drug into the West during the 1849 gold rush and still used it avidly while helping build the transcontinental railroad. A pungent cloud of sweet-smelling brown smoke hung continually over the hovels of Chinatown, located at the south end of town. Opium was legal in Virginia City until 1876, when town elders suddenly noticed that many of their own wives and daughters had been seen entering and exiting the dens. Belatedly struck by the drug's insidious menace, the city passed one of the nation's first anti-opium ordinances. A year later, the state legislature codified Nevada's pioneering just-say-no policy.

In November 1862, Clemens talked Goodman into sending him back to Carson City to cover the second territorial legislature. The lawmakers had found a new meeting place, the Great Basin Hotel, owned by the ubiquitous Abraham Curry. Orion Clemens, once again serving as acting governor while James W. Nye was out of state, also had new digs. In anticipation of his wife Mollie's arrival, he had purchased a twelve-thousand-dollar lot on the corner of Spear and Division streets and erected a two-story, three-bedroom house, said to be the finest in town. Exactly where Orion came up with the money is unclear—Sam somewhat dubiously claimed that his brother had made it honestly by selling copies of official charters and certificates to mines and other business interests—but however he found the funds, in October Orion went to San Francisco, picked up his wife and daughter, Jennie, and escorted them by stage to their new home in Carson City. For once in her life with the abjurious Orion, Mollie could live in high style, and she made the most of her position as wife of the acting governor of Nevada. "No one on this planet ever enjoyed a distinction more than she enjoyed that one," her brother-in-law remembered. He moved into their guest room and settled down to cover the legislature.

The solons met for sixty days, and Clemens was there for every one of them. To enliven his reports (and to keep himself from dying of boredom in the process), Clemens contrived a written rivalry with another reporter, Virginia City *Union* correspondent Clement T. Rice, whom he renamed "the Unreliable," in contradistinction to himself, "the Reliable." Yet another native New Yorker who had ventured west for fame and fortune, Rice was a willing and good-natured foil. Together they embarked on a war of words, bringing what brightness they could to the humdrum business of the legislature. Clemens spent most of his time at the opening session observing a particularly ill-bred Washoe delegate, "Colonel" Jonathan Williams, eating an eighteen-pound raw turnip at his desk while simultaneously ushering through committee a sinuous new bill for a toll road that stretched conveniently from one tollhouse to another. The accompanying map, carefully marked with "mule on road" and "dog on road," exhibited, said Clemens, "the wild irregularity of the footprints of birds of prey upon a moist sea shore." The Committee on Internal Improvements, he added, "was struck with the wonderful resemblance of . . . fly-tracks to the map now before your committee."

The parliamentary proceedings, like those of most state legislatures, were regularly relieved by parties, dances, and other get-togethers. The Unreliable was apt to turn up for them in a less than presentable state; Clemens kept his eyes peeled for his rival's next visitation. At one party hosted by former California governor J. Neely Johnson, then living in Carson City, the Unreliable "came and asked Gov. Johnson to let him stand on the porch. That creature has got more impudence than any person I ever saw in my life. Well, he stood and flattened his nose against the parlor window, and looked hungry and vicious—he always looks that way—until Col. [John] Musser arrived with some ladies, when he actually fell in their wake and came swaggering in, looking as if he thought he had been anxiously expected."

Subsequently, the Unreliable descended on the refreshment table. "I never saw a man eat as much as he did in my life," said Clemens. "First, he ate a plate of sandwiches; then he ate a handsomely iced poundcake; then he gobbled a dish of chicken salad, after which he ate a roast pig; after that a quantity of blancmage; then he threw in several glasses of punch to fortify his appetite, and finished his monstrous repast with a roast turkey. Dishes of brandy-grapes, and jellies and such things, and pyramids of fruits, melted away before him as shadows fly at the sun's approach." Had the Unreliable been present at the miracle of the loaves and fishes, said Clemens, "the provisions would just about have held out, I think."

At the gala wedding of Dr. J. A. Wayman and Mrs. M. A. Ormsby (presumably the widow of Carson City founder William Ormsby, slain by Snake Indians in 1860), the Unreliable made another un-invited appearance. "His instincts always prompt him to go where he is not wanted," wrote Clemens, "particularly if anything of an unusual nature is on hand. . . . As soon as the guests found out who he was they kept out of his way as well as they could, but there were so many gentlemen and ladies present that he was never at a loss for somebody to pester with his disgusting familiarity." As usual, the Un-reliable made straight for the food, where "he carried away a codfish under one arm, and Mr. Curry's plug hat full of sauerkraut under the other. . . . I believe he would have eaten a corpse last night, if he had one."

Affronted by the Unreliable's accusation that he had appropri-ated some of his belongings after walking him home to bed, Cle-mens struck back, challenging his opponent to a duel at a hundred paces. "The effect was more agreeable than I could have hoped for," bragged Clemens. "His hair turned black in a single night, from ex-cess of fear; then he went into a fit of melancholy, and while it lasted he did nothing but sigh, and sob, and snuffle, and slobber, and blow his nose on his coat-tail, and say 'he wished he was in the quiet tomb'; finally, he said he would commit suicide—he would say farewell to the cold, cold world, with its cares and troubles, and go and sleep with his fathers, in perdition."

Clemens helpfully wrote a mock obituary for his friend. It began: "He became a newspaper reporter, and crushed Truth to the earth and kept her there." It concluded: "He is dead and buried now. . . . [L]et him rest, let him rot. Let his vices be forgotten, but his virtues be remembered; it will not infringe much upon any man's time."

Even then the Unreliable was true to his name, disrupting his own funeral service—"he could not even be depended upon in death"—by sitting up in his coffin, blowing off the minister, and asking the astonished mourners to borrow a quarter. "He appears to have an insatiable craving for two bits," Clemens noted.

Not everyone was amused by such drolleries. A journalistic competitor on the Virginia City *Bulletin* complained: "We think the funniest part of poor Sammy's character is his claiming the possession of wit. Drawling stupidity, when well acted by an educated, intelligent man, is indeed comical; but when those features are the natural characteristics of an illiterate and by no means bright intellect, the mouthings of such a one it were a misapplication of terms to call wit." The Unreliable, filling in for Clemens while he was sick with bronchitis, offered up a ghostwritten apology: "We have been on the stool of repentance for a long time, but have not before had the moral courage to acknowledge our manifold sins and wickedness. We confess to this weakness." To all the public figures he had offended "from behind the shelter of our reportorial position," including Virginia City mayor Rufe Arick and police chief John V. B. Perry, the bogus Clemens asked for forgiveness. He enclosed particular heartfelt thanks to the Unreliable, who "has saved us several times from receiving a sound thrashing for our impudence." The next day, the real Clemens huffily retracted the apology.

Besides providing a spark of amusement and color to the grindingly dull fulminations of the legislature, the feud with Rice brought Clemens another distinction: it introduced to the world a brand-new pen name—Mark Twain.

Since its first appearance in a "Letter from Carson City" on February 3, 1863, scholars have expended entire careers detailing with Jesuitical exactitude the origins and motives of the famous nom de plume. Some, taking their lead from Clemens himself—never a wise move—have traced it back to the unfortunate Colonel Isaiah Sellers, who, according to Clemens, used it in the 1850s to sign his interminable columns in New Orleans newspapers. There is no evidence that Sellers ever did so, and Clemens had already experimented with a number of different pen names before arriving at Mark Twain. In his apprentice days on Orion's newspapers, he had occasionally signed himself W. Epaminondas Adrastus Perkins, W. Epaminondas Adrastus Blab, Rambler, Grumbler, Peter Pencilcase's Son, John Snooks, and Thomas Jefferson Snodgrass, as well as the vivid but anonymous A Dog-Be-Deviled Citizen. He had published in the New Orleans *Crescent* as Sergeant Fathom, and he had started writing for the Virginia City *Territorial Enterprise* as Josh. (Similarly, Dan De Quille began writing as Ebenezer Queerkut and Picaroon Pax before settling on his pithier alter ego.) Some of Clemens's favorite writers dabbled in pen names: Benjamin Franklin was Poor Richard, Charles Dickens was Boz, and Washington Irving was Geoffrey Crayon, Gent. Certainly, in the West it was an accepted practice for settlers (not just writers) to change their names. Everybody had a past.

However he came by it, "Mark Twain" was a wonderfully terse and evocative name. It harkened back to his days on the Mississippi, when "Mark twain!" was the leadsman's call for two fathoms, demarcating a ship's passage from shallow to safe water. It could also mean the reverse. In *Life on the Mississippi*, Twain recounted a good, if painful, practical joke that had been played on him by Captain Horace Bixby and other crewmen aboard the *Aleck Scott*. Giving the cub pilot the wheel in what he knew to be safe water, Bixby arranged for the leadsman to begin calling out ever more dangerous readings, while Clemens grew increasingly agitated, finally crying out in an agony of doubt and despair: "Quick, Ben! Oh, back the immortal *soul* out of her!"

Bixby's point was that a pilot had to trust his instincts; and for the rest of his career, Samuel Clemens, writing as Mark Twain, would trust his, all the while inhabiting that perilous border between safety and danger, laughter and tears, East and West. By the time he was through, the writer Mark Twain would be subsumed by the performer Mark Twain, and the old man in the white suit with the wild flyaway hair, walrus mustache, and ever-present cigar would be as familiar, if not always as comforting, as one's paternal grandfather or eccentric Uncle Sam. "Mark Twain—Known to Everyone—Liked By All," a well-known tobacco company would advertise beneath his likeness, without fear of contradiction.

All that, of course, was still in the future. For the time being, the newly minted Mark Twain finished his stint at the territorial legislature and took off to San Francisco in May 1863 on a two-month leave of absence. The Unreliable went along for the ride. Joe Goodman, in the *Enterprise*, announced their departure, informing readers on May 3 that "Mark Twain has abdicated the local column of the *Enterprise*, where, by the grace of cheek, he so long reigned Monarch of Mining Items, Detailer of Events, Prince of Platitudes, Chief of Biographers, Expounder of Unwritten Law, Puffer of Wildcat, Profaner of Divinity, Detractor of Merit, Flatterer of Power, Recorder of State Arrivals, Pack Trains, Hay Wagons, and Things in General." Dan De Quille also took note of his friend's impending departure, noting drily that "the atmosphere cannot help but be improved" by his absence.

The two young men took a room at the newly constructed Lick House on Montgomery Street, from whose sumptuous lobby they sallied forth daily to take in the sights. They attended the opera, watched the world-famous sea lions at the Cliff House, waded in the Pacific (Twain remembered doing the same thing in the Atlantic), sailed up the coastline on sleek, fast yachts, and dined like kings at the hotel, whose dining room was modeled on the banquet hall at the palace of Versailles. "I am going to the Dickens mighty fast," Twain informed his mother and sister. "I have lived like a lord—to make up for two years' of deprivation." He subsequently reported on a Lick House fashion show in which society matrons flounced and simpered in "lace embroidered with blue and yellow dogs," "rat-colored bro-caded silk embroidered in violent colors with a battle piece represent-ing the taking of Holland by the Dutch," "a great cataract of white chantilly lace, surmounted by a few artificial worms, and butterflies and things," "a tasteful tarantula done in jet," and "a simple wreath of sardines on a string."

When Twain returned to Virginia City in early July, it seemed a little "like going back to prison." If so, it was a very lively prison. The town was undergoing another of its periodic booms, fueled by a major new silver discovery at the Gould & Curry mine, 430 feet below A Street. The Ophir, too, struck a rich new vein, and thousands of additional fortune hunters rushed into the city to buy and sell stock at inflated prices. "The streets of Virginia City are literally crammed with crazy people who talk incoherently about 'feet' when most of them have no other feet than those they stand on," one San Francisco journalist reported. Housing shortages led to jam-packed hotels and board-ing houses, with rooms going for $250 a month—twice that much if a small woodstove was included. As soon as the foundation went down for one new building, the owner put up a sign: "This building is rented." The undertaking business was booming as well, with one visiting mortician pronouncing the town "the best business place I ever saw. If I had a shop there I could get five coffins a day to make."

As if to underscore that point, Twain added a couple of hasty postscripts to one of his letters home. The first informed his mother and sister: "I have just heard five pistol shots down [the] street—as such things are in my line, I will go and see about it." The second, appended at 5 A.M., reported that "the pistol did its work well—one man—a Jackson County Missourian, shot two of my friends (po-lice officers) through the heart—both died within three minutes. Murderer's name is John Campbell." The dead officers, Dennis

McMahon and Thomas Reed, had confronted Campbell in a beer cellar and accused him of singing "Dixie"—a serious misdemeanor in the increasingly pro-Union town. Campbell shot them down, then fled to a mining tunnel near Gold Hill. A posse followed and trapped the murderer inside, blocking the entrance with a pile of stones. When the rocks were rolled away the next morning, a family of five Indians—three men, one woman, and a child—was found dead inside, smothered by noxious fumes. "The intention of the citizens was good," reported Twain, "but the result was most unfortunate. To shut up a murderer in a tunnel was well enough, but to leave him there all night was calculated to impair his chances for a fair trial." Nothing more was said about the Indians, who were merely collateral damage.

In July 1863, the *Enterprise* moved into a new three-story brick building on South C Street equipped with steam-powered presses and reinforced with twenty new employees. It was a timely move. A few days later a massive fire swept through the city, destroying large swathes of buildings west of A Street. The entire town might have been destroyed if the wind had not been blowing in a southwesterly direction away from the heart. Members of two local volunteer fire departments, Virginia Engine Company No. 1 and Nevada Hook and Ladder No. 1, disputing the honor of arriving first on the scene, fought a free-for-all at the corner of Taylor and C streets. Fifteen firemen were injured and one man was fatally shot. Twain's rooming house on B Street was completely destroyed, costing him a trunk-load of mining stock, whose value he ruefully estimated at between ten cents and two hundred thousand dollars, and a closet full of new suits he had just purchased in San Francisco. He barely escaped with his life, diving through a window as oily black smoke bubbled up the stairs. The next day an acquaintance gave him a sheaf of wildcat stock, and Twain immediately sold it to buy another suit.

When Dan De Quille returned from another foray to Iowa, he and Twain moved in together in a two-room apartment on the second floor of the Daggett and Myers Building, partly owned by their *Enterprise* colleague Rollin Daggett. "We (Mark and I) have the sweetest little parlor and the snuggest little bedroom (and it's only three floors from the ground) all to ourselves," De Quille wrote. "Here we come every night and live—breathe, move and have our being, also our toddies." The new roommates bought on credit several hundred dollars' worth of furniture and furnishings from Moses Goldman's furniture store on West C Street. When Goldman tried to collect his bill, the journalists blew him off. In the end, Goldman had to sue them for his money. Twain told De Quille that "they ought to have known better than to try such a trick with a man whose front name was Moses and whose rear name was Goldman." Their landlady, Mrs. Fitch, developed a sudden aversion to her madcap boarders after reading an account of a "Secret Midnight Hanging" in the Virginia City *Union* and suspecting them of hanging her pet cat in a closet. Given Twain's lifelong love of cats, it was an unlikely crime, and they later discovered that Daggett had planted the story as a practical joke. The cat was found alive in the garden.

Twain came down with a bad cold that August (he had a lifelong susceptibility to respiratory ailments) and went away to Lake Bigler for a few days to recuperate. For company he took with him twenty-two-year-old reporter Adair Wilson of the rival Virginia City *Union*, whom he immediately nicknamed the Unimportant and whose entire baggage consisted of "two excellent silk handkerchiefs and a daguerreotype of his grandmother." A number of wealthy consumptives were summering at the lake, which was undergoing a politically motivated name change to Lake Tahoe, owing to discoverer John Bigler's pro-Confederate sympathies. Twain the former Confederate ranger did not like the change; he considered it a "spoony, slobbering, summer-complaint of a name."

The lake itself was even "more supernaturally beautiful now" than when he had nearly burned it down a year earlier, but it failed to cure his cold. He caught the stage to Steamboat Springs resort, nine miles northwest of Virginia City, where he spent another week taking long steam baths at the hot springs, whose hissing jets of moisture gave the place its name, and hard-boiling eggs wrapped in handkerchiefs that he dipped into the fissures. He tried applying a mustard plaster, but "Young Wilson got hungry in the night and ate it up. I never saw anybody have such an appetite. I am confident that lunatic would have eaten me if I had been healthy." As a last resort, he took a dose of proprietor Joseph Ellis's patented cure-all, Wake-up Jake, "as repulsive a mixture as ever was stirred together in a table-spoon." The nauseating potion left a vile taste in his mouth, "as if I had swallowed a slaughter-house," and he spent the next twelve hours throwing up and bleeding from the nose before deciding that he was "about as waked up now as I care to be."

Restored more or less to health, Twain resumed his duties at the *Enterprise*, where his next written offering proceeded to leave a bad taste in everyone's mouth. On October 28 he published "A Bloody Massacre near Carson," later retitled "The Dutch Nick's Massacre." Purporting to be an eyewitness account by respected citizen Abraham Curry, the article recounted the horrific slaughter of his wife and seven children by one Philip Hopkins, a hitherto respectable mine owner driven mad by bad investments and crooked bankers. "About 10 o'clock on Monday evening Hopkins dashed into Carson [City] on horseback, with his throat cut from ear to ear, and bearing in his hand a reeking scalp from which the warm, smoking blood was still dripping," Twain reported. "The long red hair of the scalp he bore marked it as that of Mrs. Hopkins."

According to the article, the sheriff rushed to the Hopkins home and discovered the scalped body of Mrs. Hopkins "with her head split open and her right hand almost severed from the wrist. . . . In one of the bedrooms six of the children were found, one in bed and the others scattered about the floor. They were all dead. Their brains had evidently been dashed out with a club." The body of the eldest child, nineteen-year-old Mary, was discovered in the attic, "frightfully mutilated, and the knife with which her wounds had been inflicted still sticking in her side."

It was a terrible story, although not a particularly rare one in the West, where men and women routinely lost their minds and went on abrupt killing sprees after cracking under unendurable frontier hardships. The trouble was that, in this particular case, it wasn't true. Twain had made up the whole thing as a way, he explained a little weakly a few days later, to draw attention to dividend-cooking practices by California and Nevada brokerage firms. Careful readers, he said, should have noticed the various hints scattered throughout the story: a "great pine forest" in the middle of the desert; a horseback ride between Empire City and Dutch Nick's, which were one and the same place; the improbability of someone riding all the way to Carson City with his throat cut.

Apparently, Twain was giving his readers too much credit. Most swallowed the whopper in one credulous gulp, although some were unable to finish their breakfasts after doing so. When word got out that the story was another hoax, outraged subscribers put up a howl "from Siskiyou to San Diego." California newspapers, which had picked up the item as a news story, threatened to cancel their reciprocal contracts with the *Enterprise*. After a sleepless night, Twain offered to resign, but Goodman refused to accept his resignation. In years to come, the publisher predicted, the massacre hoax would turn out to be Twain's most-remembered story.

Competing journalists were less forgiving. The Gold Hill *Daily News* reported that the *Enterprise* was working on a new series of articles, "Lives of the Liars, or Joking Justified," and the Virginia City *Evening Bulletin* observed with some justice that "the man who could pen such a story with all its horrors depicted in such infernal detail . . . as a joke, in fun, can have but a very indefinite idea of the elements of a joke." The next day, the *Enterprise* ran a one-sentence correction: "I take it all back," signed "Mark Twain."

Just in time, perhaps, the territorial legislature reconvened in Carson City at the end of October to draw up a constitution and apply formally for statehood. Grateful for the distraction, Twain went down to cover the proceedings. The step was the last one necessary before a territory could be admitted into the Union, as the Lincoln administration clearly wanted Nevada to be. It would also mean the end of Orion's sinecure, since voters in the new state would elect their own governor, senators, and representatives. Sam assured their mother that he would do all he could "to get [Orion] nominated for some fat office under the State Government, so that you can come out and live with him. I am a pretty good hand at such things."

The delegates met for thirty-two days, during which time Twain passed his twenty-eighth birthday. Chastened a little by the massacre hoax, he reported conscientiously on the dry proceedings, filing his daily reports without a byline or as "Sam Clemens." Only his Sunday roundup bore his new pen name. He was so professional in his bearing that his colleagues elected him "governor" of the Third House, a mock legislative body that met at night in various saloons and watering holes to satirize the political events they had been covering that day.

Twain worried, with good cause, that voters would reject the constitution if it contained a clause sponsored by delegate William Stewart calling for the taxation of all mining property within the state. Stewart, said Twain, was "a long legged, bull-headed, whopper-jawed, constructionary monomaniac. Give him a chance to construe the sacred law, and there wouldn't be a damned soul in perdition in a month." And Stewart was a friend. He and other Nevada politicians, wrote Twain, "All owe me something for traducing and vilifying them in the public prints, and thus exciting sympathy for them on the score of persecution, and securing their nomination. I elected those fellows." What he could not do was elect Orion. Nominated to be secretary of state, Orion lost his chance to run for office when voters rejected the proposed constitution—as his brother had predicted—by a five-to-one margin.

By then, Twain had returned to Virginia City, where he glimpsed a promising new path for his own career. His unlikely avatar was a tall, tubercular, homosexual humorist from New England named Charles Farrar Browne, who called himself Artemus Ward in dubious honor of a Revolutionary War general of no particular accomplishments. Although close to the same age as Twain—they were born seventeen months apart—Ward had far outstripped the younger man on the national stage. He had been a columnist for the Cleveland *Plain Dealer* and the editor of *Vanity Fair* magazine in New York before publishing his first book, rather obviously titled *Artemus Ward: His Book*, a year earlier. He was a favorite of Abraham Lincoln, who once interrupted a cabinet meeting at the White House to read aloud one of Ward's humorous stories. The Emancipation Proclamation, the purpose of the day's meeting, had to wait.

Ward's crowd-pleasing shtick, which he took on the road to great profit, involved outlandish puns, head-scratching non sequiturs, purposeful mispronunciation of words, and long, pointless shaggy-dog stories, all delivered with a characteristic deadpan voice and innocent expression. He was a regular drinking partner of New York poet Walt Whitman, joining Whitman and other outré artists at their famous bohemian gatherings in Pfaff's beer cellar in Greenwich Village. Another regular of Pfaff's, hashish-eating poet Fitz Hugh Ludlow, had recently visited San Francisco, where he published a survey of contemporary western humor in Rollin Daggett's old magazine, the *Golden Era*, and singled out for praise "that Irresistible Washoe Giant, Mark Twain." When Ward hit town in Virginia City in mid-December for a two-night speaking engagement at Maguire's Opera

House, one of the first persons he looked up was the Washoe Giant himself.

The two red-haired humorists quickly found that they had much in common. Each had lost his father at a comparatively young age; each had supported himself as a freelance printer and journalist; each had even published an early sketch in the same Boston-based humor magazine, the *Carpet-Bag*. They shared a boy's love for practical jokes, music halls, circuses, and minstrel shows (during his visit to Virginia City, Ward donned blackface and took his place as "end man" in one such show). And owing in large part to their eternal youthfulness, each man in turn became the most popular humorist in America.

The next ten days passed more or less in a brandy-and-water-soaked blur. The slightly built, weak-chinned Ward proved to be a champion drinker, and Twain and the other staffers at the *Enterprise* matched him drink for drink. Twain, Goodman, Denis McCarthy, and Dan De Quille joined forces to give their illustrious visitor a guided tour of Virginia City's fledgling demimonde. One predawn tour of Chinatown almost ended in tragedy when a shotgun-wielding night watchman caught Twain and Ward drunkenly clambering across a rooftop in an impromptu game of follow-the-leader and drew down on them for burglars. Ward defused the situation by giving the guard a couple of complimentary tickets to his performance that night.

Twain was there as well, in the front row at Maguire's, watching transfixed as Ward worked his peculiar magic on the crowd. "I once knew a man in New Zealand who hadn't a tooth in his head," Ward began one story, pausing a beat before adding, "and yet that man could beat a drum better than any man I ever saw." The whole point of the performance, as Twain immediately realized, was not so much what was being said, as how it was being said. Ward wandered the stage like a lost bumpkin, peering into the footlights amiably, his rambling observations and artful pauses always threatening to drift away on a cloud of free associations and mumbled phrases. When the crowd exploded in delayed, defenseless laughter, Ward would gaze vaguely "from face to face, as though astonished and somewhat hurt at being interrupted by the sudden outburst of merriment." He never cracked a smile.

It was a master's-level seminar on the art of the comic delivery, and Twain absorbed it all with the focused intensity of a precocious child. He especially liked Ward's "inimitable way of pausing and hesitating, of gliding in a moment from seriousness to humor without appearing to be conscious of doing so. There was more in his pauses than his words." It was an art that Mark Twain would raise to new heights of perfection a few years later. "The man who is capable of listening to 'Babes in the Wood' from beginning to end without laughing either inwardly or outwardly must have done murder, or at least meditated it at some time during his life," Twain asserted.

Before taking his leave in late December, Ward offered to bring Twain along on his impending tour of Europe and encouraged his newfound protégé to write for more sophisticated eastern publications. He promised to dash off "a powerfully convincing note to my friends" at the New York *Sunday Mercury* in Twain's behalf, but fell dangerously ill with pneumonia in Salt Lake City before he could do so. In the meantime, unaware of Ward's illness, Twain sent off his first submission, "Doings in Nevada," which the *Mercury* published without Ward's help in its February 7, 1864, edition. Two weeks later the newspaper printed a second Twain piece, "Those Blasted Children," describing a brat-disrupted visit to the Lick House in San Francisco and suggesting, in the best Jonathan Swift fashion, that all misbehaving children be soaked in a barrel of vinegar for a week.

Shortly after Ward's epic visit to Virginia City, another veteran of Pfaff's beer cellar arrived for an appearance at Maguire's Opera House. New Orleans–born actress Adah Isaacs Menken (real name:

Dolores McCord) had just completed a wildly successful two-month engagement in San Francisco. Twain, during his stay in the Bay City, had reviewed two of her shows, *Mazeppa* and *The French Spy*, for the *Enterprise*. The first, based on the Lord Byron poem of the same name, showed off Menken's best assets, her lush, well-rounded figure. Called "the most perfectly developed woman in the world" and "the Great Unadorned," the actress upheld her title by wearing flesh-colored tights and a scanty loincloth, which Twain compared to a diaper. He found her "a finely formed woman down to her knees," but judged her acting to be a little busy: "She pitches headforemost at the atmosphere like a battering ram; she works her arms, and her legs, and her whole body, like a dancing-jack. . . . [I]n a word, without any apparent reason for it, she carries on like a lunatic from the beginning of the act to the end of it." As for her performance in *The French Spy*, Twain considered it "as dumb as an oyster," although he conceded that "she plays the Spy, without words, with more feeling than she does Mazeppa with them."

It is doubtful that Menken had read Twain's review when she arrived in Virginia City on February 27, 1864, with her full entourage in tow. This included her manager, her road company of actors, several horses, nineteen dogs, her third husband, humorist Robert Henry Newell, alias "Orpheus C. Kerr," and her beautiful blond friend from bohemian New York, Ada Clare, for whom Menken was planning to write a new play. Clare, in company with Menken, had formed the distaff portion of Walt Whitman's drinking circle at Pfaff's beer cellar. Her real name was Jane McElhenney, and she had relocated to New York from Charleston, South Carolina, to trod the boards. She was rather less successful at that undertaking than Menken—critics found her too thin, in both voice and body—but Whitman considered Clare "gay, easy, sunny, free, loose, but not ungood." As for Menken, the Good Gray Poet had been best man at one of her weddings.

As usual, Menken was a sensation both on stage and off. She

toured the Comstock Lode, boiling an egg in the scalding subterranean waters and accepting a two-thousand-dollar silver bar engraved with the vaguely suggestive name of the Menken Shaft and Tunnel Company. She boxed a couple of rounds at the Sazerac saloon with local bon vivant "Joggles" Wright—her second husband had been heavyweight champion John "the Benicia Boy" Heenan—and became an honorary member of Fire Engine Company No. 2, which gave her a red morocco belt signifying her membership in the clan.

Between visits to the various bars, gambling dens, and hurdy-gurdy parlors along C Street, Menken performed *The French Spy* and *Mazeppa*. The audience predictably favored her less-clothed performance in the latter show; one wag complained that her penchant for performing male roles in drag ensured that she would remain "a thing of beauty and a boy forever." The Virginia City *Union*, reviewing her performance, got in a gratuitous if satisfying dig at its rival, reporting that "Mark Twain is writing a bloody tragedy for her . . . which will excel *Mazeppa* in many respects. It is to be called 'Pete Hopkins, or the Gory Scalp.'"

After her second show, Menken invited Twain and Dan De Quille to dine *en chambres* with her and Ada Clare at the International Hotel. Her husband was pointedly excluded from the dinner, which left him pacing the hallway outside their room, scowling and muttering when the newsmen arrived. The ensuing meal was like something straight out of the stateroom scene in the Marx Brothers' *A Night at the Opera*. Intimidated perhaps by the two lovely actresses—to say nothing of the scorned husband grumbling loudly outside the door— Twain for once was at a loss for words. To enliven matters, De Quille encouraged him to favor them with a song. He managed to cough up several verses of his old standby, "There was an old horse and his name was Jerusalem." Meanwhile, Menken's dogs, which De Quille characterized as "mongrels, puppies, whelps, hounds, and curs of low degrees," snuffled and snarled beneath the table. After one of them peed on Twain's leg, he unleashed a kick in its general direction. De

Quille remembered the ensuing incident with understandable relish: "He missed the dog but hit the Menken's pet corn, causing her to bound from her seat, throw herself on the lounge and roll and roar in agony. This mischance put a sort of damper on the festivities. Mark immediately became sullen as if it had been his own corn that was wounded, and even when Menken came limping back to her chair and begged him not to mind, he refused to be conciliated." Suddenly remembering another engagement, Twain left a few minutes later, thus joining the minuscule ranks of red-blooded men, foreign or domestic, whom Menken and Clare had failed to seduce.

Despite the diverting visits of Ward and Menken, Virginia City by the beginning of 1864 was becoming a little stale. Bullion production was slipping, mining stocks were down, and two hundred different holdings—even those with such optimistic names as "Honest Abe" and "Morning Star"—defaulted on their shares and were auctioned off. A correspondent for the Nevada *Daily Gazette* declared the city "intensely dull" and observed that "all mining towns go up like a rocket and come down like a stick." Residents did what they could to enliven their surroundings: a paddle-footed citizen named John A. Dougherty made news by walking continuously for 108 hours— all within the confines of O'Connor's saloon. Someone else fed his pet lamb chewing tobacco; a cat entertained onlookers by drinking cognac-laced coffee on the sidewalk.

For his part, Twain contributed a sensational account of a "Frightful Accident to Dan De Quille." His roommate, reported Twain, "was coming down the road at the rate of a hundred miles an hour (as stated in his will, which he made shortly after the accident)," when he was thrown from his horse and landed in a heap three hundred yards away. "His head was caved in," wrote Twain with unseemly relish, "one of his legs was jammed up in his body nearly to this throat, and the other so torn and mutilated that it pulled out when they attempted to lift him into the hearse which we had sent to the scene of the disaster under the general impression that he might need it; both arms were indiscriminately broken up until they were joined like a bamboo; the back was considerably fractured and bent into the shape of a rail fence. Aside from these injuries, however, he sustained no other damage."

The humor, like the town, was a little tired. Even a rival at the Gold Hill *Daily News* noticed that "this favorite writer is melancholy; he has got the mulligrubs. . . . We haven't had a good square joke out of poor Mark these four or five days. He sits behind that historic pine table morose and melancholy, and drinking mean whiskey to drown his misery. Cheer up, friend Mark." Partly, it was a carryover from his misbegotten massacre story; it may also have been a function of simple wanderlust. With the exception of his halcyon days on the river, the two years (more or less) that Twain had spent in Nevada was the longest length of time he had spent in one place since leaving home eleven years earlier. He was bored and restless—never the best combination for an inveterate leg puller and peace disturber like Twain. Whether consciously or subconsciously, he was about to do something that would wear out his welcome once and for all in the silver-seeded valleys of the Washoe. As usual, it was his pen that got him into trouble—and his feet that got him out of it.

CHAPTER 5

HEAVEN ON THE HALF SHELL

MARK TWAIN'S SECOND WINTER IN VIRGINIA CITY was also his last. Ironically, the same event that had brought him to Nevada in the first place, the Civil War, was also indirectly responsible for driving him out of the territory. What began as another misconceived newspaper prank rapidly grew into a life-threatening feud and one of the most mortifying events in a life that was not without its share of public and private mortifications—most of them self-inflicted.

As the war entered its third year back east in the spring of 1864, emotions had become increasingly raw, even in far-off Nevada. Pro-Union and pro-Confederate sympathizers jostled one another in the streets, hotel lobbies, and saloons. The southern contingent had its Virginia City headquarters at the aptly named Virginia Hotel, where members gathered daily to drink the success of the Confederacy. Their citadel was breached one day when a Union man named Lance

Nightingill took offense to the treasonous toasts and marched up to the hotel bar with a friend to raise his own defiant glass: "Here's to Abraham Lincoln, God bless him, and God damn everybody who doesn't like him." The secessionists, known collectively as "Southern hell-hounds" or "Copperhead Sneaks," did not respond.

Their lack of response reflected the growing strength of the Unionist movement in Virginia City and the rest of Nevada. Despite the voters' tax-based rejection of the first proposed state constitution in January 1864, the Lincoln administration still nurtured plans for a pro-Union stronghold in the territory. Governor Nye and Secretary Clemens were reliable patriots, and the second territorial legislature had been judged by the political correspondent of the Sacramento *Daily Union* to be "passably loyal, at least so far as test oaths go." Pro-secessionists in Virginia City had run a slate of municipal candidates the previous year, but had lost badly at the ballot box. Their political mouthpiece, the *Democratic Standard*, folded after only two months. Even worse, local Copperhead leader Hal Clayton, a Carson City attorney and personal friend of Twain, was arrested for making disloyal remarks about the government and was sent off to the adobe compound at Fort Churchill for a spell of hard labor and political reeducation. Rumors that a shadowy band of pro-Confederate guerrillas, the Knights of the Golden Circle, was operating at night in the territory brought a mocking response from the *Enterprise*: "We think their numbers are under-rated; it is our firm belief that there are at least 50,000 guerrillas to every acre of ground about the Sink—in the shape of mosquitoes and gallinippers."

Unionism had flourished throughout the war years in Virginia City. As far back as August 1861, when city marshal John Van Buren Perry, a transplanted New Yorker, enlisted fellow Unionists to pummel pro-southern sympathizers celebrating the Confederate victory at Bull Run, local sentiment strongly favored the North. Two months later, the first territorial legislature sent President Lincoln a blaring declaration of support: "Nevada for the Union, ever true and loyal!

The last born of the nation will be the last to desert the flag! Our aid, to the extent of our ability, can be relied upon to crush the rebellion." A false report of the Union capture of Richmond in May 1863 threw residents into patriotic transports. Parades, brass bands, bonfires, and fireworks marked the occasion—only to fall flat when additional information made it clear that "Fighting Joe" Hooker and the Union Army of the Potomac, in fact, had been routed by Robert E. Lee and Stonewall Jackson, and that Hooker himself had been knocked senseless by a piece of falling timber at his headquarters.

There was better news two months later, when Union armies won signal victories at Gettysburg and Vicksburg. A large American flag flew proudly above Mount Davidson, backlit against a rare late-afternoon shower. "How the people were wrought up," Twain wrote. "The superstition grew apace that this was a mystic courier come with great news from the war." When "some creature wearing the shape of a human being" stole the flag, the Virginia City *Union* editorialized that the thief, if caught, should be hanged from the same flagpole. (Luckily for him, he was never found.) That same month Orion Clemens, in his capacity as acting governor, revoked Colonel Jonathan Williams's notary public license for Lander County, calling him "a loud-mouthed Copperhead." Newspaper editorials regularly denounced the "Southern hell-hounds" back east.

Living up to its name, the Virginia City *Union* endorsed Abraham Lincoln for reelection, seconded the Emancipation Proclamation as "a just, righteous, and necessary measure," and thundered editorially: "We are for the Union of the United States—the Union as it was— without equivocation or reserve, and shall break no bread with those who are not, however plausible may be their excuse for treason." And after the Confederate raider CSS *Alabama* sank a transport ship bound for California and bringing a load of gas fixtures to Virginia City, the *Enterprise*'s Dan De Quille noted the civic outrage. "Some of our people have thought pretty well of Jeff Davis," he wrote, "but not a single one of us thought of his wanting our gas-ing machine.

We are all down on him! Every time we break our shins in traveling our dark streets, we curse Jeff Davis . . . and damn the whole Confederacy till everything is black and blue."

A peculiar form of patriotism erupted in the territory that spring, and Mark Twain injected himself into the middle of it. An old Hannibal classmate of his, Reuel C. Gridley, had preceded Twain to Nevada; he owned a grocery store in nearby Austin. Gridley was a Democrat, and after he lost an election bet concerning the outcome of a local race, he had to carry a fifty-pound sack of flour, festooned with American flags and red, white, and blue ribbons, for a mile and a quarter to the winner's house, while a band trailed along playing "John Brown's Body." The victor, Lander County tax collector H. S. Herrick, gave back the flour sack to Gridley, suggesting that he sell it. This gave Gridley the bright idea of auctioning off the sack to the highest bidder, then re-auctioning it again and again, with proceeds going to the United States Sanitary Commission, a humanitarian organization that had been formed in June 1861 by a group of private citizens to assist with the care of sick and wounded Union soldiers. A sort of combination Red Cross and USO, the commission provided volunteer nurses, hospital workers, and ambulance drivers, as well as temporary lodging houses near railroad stations for traveling soldiers and their relatives. Nevada Territory as a whole previously had sent twenty thousand dollars' worth of silver bars to the commission as its contribution to the war effort, but Gridley's imaginative stunt would increase that amount tenfold before he was through.

Twain, long since removed—physically and psychologically—from his Confederate ranger days, had been recruited by his sister, Pamela, to raise funds for the commission in Virginia City. Still living in St. Louis, Pamela was deeply involved in efforts to mount a massive Mississippi Valley Sanitary Fair in the Gateway City. Along with Sam, she also enlisted Orion and his wife, Mollie, to help out in Carson City, where a fancy-dress ball was to be held in conjunction with the St. Louis fair. Such fairs were the chief financial support for the Sanitary Commission, whose members included many of the nation's best-known doctors and civic leaders. Walt Whitman, then serving as a self-appointed hospital visitor in Washington, D.C., was an early member, although he later fell out with the commission over its policy of paying staff members a small salary. Whitman also objected to the quasi-military way in which the commission was run. Such "hirelings," he said, were "always incompetent & disagreeable."

The tenderhearted, unorthodox Whitman was in the minority when it came to the Sanitary Commission. Thousands of Union soldiers and their families greatly appreciated the commission's help—paid or not—which extended from nursing care to assistance in filing pension claims and securing back pay for soldiers. The hard-pressed government gave the commission its full backing—Abraham Lincoln even contributed the original draft of the Emancipation Proclamation to be auctioned off at the Chicago fair.

In Virginia City, Twain did what he could to help the cause, writing editorials in support of the commission, organizing a benefit at Maguire's Opera House, and contributing three hundred dollars in the name of the *Enterprise* while Joe Goodman was off visiting the Sandwich Islands. When his old classmate Gridley showed up en route to St. Louis and the East, Twain and Nevada Sanitary Commission chairman Almarin B. Paul put together a raucous and none-too-sober fund-raising procession from Gold Hill to Virginia City, complete with a brass band and several wagons loaded down with supporters. "The whole population—men, women and children, Chinamen and Indians, were massed in the main street," Twain recalled, "all the flags in town were at the mast head, and the blare of the bands was drowned in cheers." As the cavalcade moved on, it was "refreshed with new lager beer and plenty of it."

The heavy drinking proved to be a problem. A rival reporter for the Gold Hill *Daily News* complained about "Twain and his staff of bibulous reporters, who came down in a free carriage, ostensibly for the purpose of taking notes, but in reality in pursuit of free whiskey." John K. Lovejoy, editor of the Virginia City *Old Piute*, observed somewhat more mildly that Twain had drunk "a sufficient quantity [of beer] to make him good natured."

Lovejoy may have been right about the amount Twain drank, but he was wrong about its effect on his mood. For the past few weeks, Twain had been embroiled in another journalistic feud with the columnists of the Virginia City *Union* and Virginia City *Bulletin* over an April Fool's prank he had played on *Union* editor Thomas Fitch, who lived across the hall from Twain and Dan De Quille on B Street. In an article titled "Another Traitor—Hang Him!" Twain alleged that Fitch had filed a legal complaint against their landlord, W. W. Myers, accusing Myers of slandering the federal government in general, African-Americans and Abraham Lincoln in particular, and giving aid and comfort to the Confederacy.

Fitch let it go (he may even have been in on the joke), but the *Bulletin* for some reason saw fit to take up his defense. "Mark Twain," it wrote, "is notorious for constantly lying. . . . We suppose our neighbor thinks because this is April Fool's Day, he had a greater license than usual. But we don't see it. He who is a fool all the rest of the year, has no special rights on this particular day." Twain was nothing more, the paper concluded, than "an ass of prodigious ear, and a malicious and illiterate cuss generally."

As if to prove the *Bulletin*'s point, Twain went out of his way to pick a fight with the *Union* staff, this time over their allegedly insufficient devotion to the Sanitary Commission. According to Twain, he had been directed by Goodman to contribute exactly $100 more than the *Union* to the fund—whatever the *Union*'s final bid proved to be for Gridley's famous flour sack. For some reason, Twain claimed that the other newspaper had reneged on its $150 offering. This charge, apparently untrue, brought an immediate angry reply from *Union* owner James L. Laird, who took the hide off Twain with a fiery editorial denouncing his "utter and unprecedented meanness" and calling the report "a string of despicable stuff knotted so full of lies that there was not left a space sufficient for the smallest thread of truth." Laird denounced Twain for showing "such a groveling disregard for truth, decency and courtesy, as to seem to court the distinction only of being understood as a vulgar liar." Laird's editorial was accompanied by a letter to the editor from *Union* printer J. W. Wilmington, a former Union infantry captain who had seen action at the Battle of Shiloh, attacking Twain for "slander" and "blackguardism" and concluding that he had "proved himself an unmitigated liar, a poltroon and a puppy."

What had started as a joke, however obscure, was rapidly growing into a dangerous personal standoff. Men in the West did not use—or take—such words lightly. Eight months earlier, Goodman and Fitch had fought a duel of their own with pistols in Stampede Valley, and Goodman had shot Fitch in the knee, leaving him permanently crippled. Twain was undoubtedly aware of the earlier duel, and although he could scarcely hold a pistol in his hand without threatening to shoot himself in the foot, he felt honor-bound to reply in kind to Laird's inflammatory words. Attempting to keep the quarrel on professionally proper levels, he fobbed off Wilmington on one of the *Enterprise*'s printers, his Mississippi-born friend Steve Gillis, who immediately fired off a letter to Wilmington advising him to mind his own business. "A contemptible ass and coward like yourself should only meddle in the affairs of gentlemen when called upon to do so," warned Gillis. Despite weighing only ninety-five pounds and standing less than five feet tall, Gillis was a much-feared saloon brawler, and Wilmington hastily disavowed any quarrel with him, saying that he "had written the communication only in defense of the craft, and did not desire a quarrel with a member of that craft."

In the meantime, Twain issued a string of written challenges to Laird, demanding that he retract his words and, in effect, quit hiding behind Wilmington. "Mr. Wilmington is a person entirely unknown to me in the matter, and has nothing to do with it," wrote Twain, "and any farther attempt to make a catspaw of any other individual and thus shirk a responsibility that you had previously assumed will show that you are a cowardly sneak. I now peremptorily demand of you the satisfaction due to a gentleman—without alternative." More letters flew hotly between them. In later years, Twain portrayed the affair as a mere joke, a matter of "courtesies" and "etiquette" between two people sharing a laugh. "I sent him another challenge, and another and another," he wrote in his autobiography, "and the more he did not want to fight, the bloodthirstier I became." The matter ended, he claimed, when Gillis shot the head off a sparrow during pre-duel target practice and convinced Laird's seconds that Twain had made the fatal shot. "The second took Mr. Laird home, a little tottery on his legs," reported Twain, "and Laird sent back a note in his own hand declining to fight a duel with me on any terms whatever."

It was a good, Tom Sawyeresque story, but there is no evidence that Twain and Laird ever made it as far as the dueling field—bird or no bird. Twain, just then, had other problems to deal with. Indeed, the initial impetus for the feud with Laird may have been a desire to make readers forget about an even more egregious charge Twain had made with regard to the Sanitary Commission, specifically, the disbursal of funds raised by the good ladies of Carson City. He reported in the *Enterprise* that money from the fancy-dress ball "had been diverted from its legitimate course, and was to be sent to aid a Miscegenation Society somewhere in the East." Ever afterward, Twain maintained that he had never intended for the story to run. He had been drunk at the time, he said, and had simply written a spoofing account to amuse Dan De Quille, who to his credit had immediately advised against printing it. According to Twain, he had agreed, leaving the handwritten copy on his desk, where an overeager typesetter found it later and ran it in the next day's edition without Twain's knowledge.

Whatever the true provenance of the article, its publication created an immediate uproar throughout the region. Nevada citizens may have been overwhelmingly pro-Union in their sentiments, but they were no more advanced in their racial attitudes than the rest of the country. The mere whiff of miscegenation and the intermingling of races was enough to bring out the dueling pistol, if not the lynching rope. Twain immediately backtracked, saying that the original article "was a hoax, but not all a hoax, for an effort is being made to divert those funds from their proper course." He apparently had in mind a preliminary discussion among the sponsors of the ball to prevent a portion of their proceeds from going to St. Louis, where it was reported that some of the funds were being earmarked for the Freedmen's Society, an organization assisting freed blacks and escaped slaves.

How he came by the rumor is unclear. Apparently, it did not come from his sister-in-law, Mollie, one of the ball's founders—he told her he had heard it from unnamed parties "in drunken jest," who "meant no harm." Harm did come to Mollie, however, at a time when she could least endure it. Three months earlier, she and Orion had buried their only child, eight-year-old Jennie, a victim of Rocky Mountain spotted fever. Now she was being ostracized by Carson City's society mavens because of her brother-in-law's journalistic faux pas. In an unappealingly self-pitying letter to Mollie two days later, Twain described the drunken sequence of the article, adding that he had suffered, "nothing but trouble & vexation" ever since. "I am sorry the thing occurred, & that is all I can do," he concluded, a little lamely, given the circumstances.

Predictably, the ladies of Carson City fired back, running a paid notice in the Virginia City *Union* under the heading: "The 'Enterprise' Libel of the Ladies of Carson." The ad charged that Twain's miscegenation article had been "a tissue of falsehoods, made for malicious purposes," noting that the funds in question were intended to "go to the aid of the sick and wounded soldiers, who are fighting the battles of our country, and for no other purpose." Having already sworn to Mollie that he would rather die than print a retraction or apology, Twain had backed himself into a very small corner. He attempted, once again, to write himself out of it by sending a note to the president of the Carson City sanitary ball committee, Mrs. W. K. Cutler, explaining that he could not print a retraction while he was still engaged in a public war of words with the owner of a rival newspaper. Nevertheless, he did publish a limited retraction the next day, noting that while he had printed the article alleging that committee funds were going "to aid a 'miscegenation' or some other sort of Society in the East," he had "also stated that the rumor was a hoax." He was "sorry for the misfortune" and "intended no harm."

The labored apology pleased no one. Mrs. Cutler, formerly a holdout, now joined the ranks of ladies publicly cutting Mollie Clemens on the street, and her husband showed up in Virginia City, intending to challenge Twain to yet another duel. Once again, Twain turned to his friend Gillis for help. Gillis showed up at Cutler's hotel room and gave him fifteen minutes to check out of the hotel and another half hour to get out of town altogether. Meanwhile, Twain dashed off a defiant if confusing note to the offended husband, accepting the challenge but saying that he was already planning to leave for California and thus had "no time to fool away on a common bummer like you."

The first part of the note, at least, was true—Twain was indeed planning to leave Virginia City. He informed his brother of his plans on May 26, asking Orion to send him two hundred dollars to help with the move. "Washoe has long since grown irksome to us," he explained. Years later, Twain claimed that he had been motivated to leave because a recent antidueling statute had been passed by the legislature, making it a crime to challenge anyone to a duel in Nevada Territory. The penalty was a prison term of two to ten years. Grand jury foreman Jerry Driscoll, the former business manager of the *Enterprise*, warned Twain that his enemies were planning to lodge just such a complaint. Whether or not Driscoll was right, Twain did not intend to wait around to find out. On May 29, he and Gillis climbed aboard a stage bound for San Francisco, taking the longer route through Henness Pass in order to bypass Carson City. "It was not without regret that I took a last look at the tiny flag . . . fluttering like a lady's handkerchief from the topmost peak of Mount Davidson," he recalled wistfully a decade later. "I was bidding a permanent farewell to a city which had afforded me the most vigorous enjoyment of life I had ever experienced."

The Gold Hill *Evening News*, less inclined to sentiment, enjoyed one last poke in Twain's eye, observing in its May 30 edition that "among the few immortal names of the departed—that is, those who departed yesterday morning per California stage—we notice that of Mark Twain. We don't wonder. Mark Twain's beard is full of dirt, and his face is black before the people of Washoe. Giving way to the idiosyncratic eccentricities of an erratic mind, Mark has indulged in the game infernal—in short, 'played hell.' . . . He has vamosed, cut stick, absquatulated."

However it was characterized, Mark Twain's abrupt departure from Virginia City signaled the end of an era. For the better part of three years, he had been an enthusiastic participant in the gold rush culture of Nevada Territory. At one time or another, either directly or indirectly, he had been a politician, a silver miner, a stock trader, a mill worker, and a newspaper reporter—virtually every role, with the exception of gunfighter or storekeeper, that the wide-open territory offered to a man. (He had spent so much time in bars that he could qualify as an honorary bartender.) Now, with the trusty Gillis at his side, he would try on the role of San Francisco boulevardier, dipping into the rarefied waters of West Coast bohemia, which his brief exposure a few months earlier to Artemus Ward, Adah Isaacs Menken, Ada Clare, and other seasoned culture warriors had encouraged him to sample.

Characteristically, Twain made a joke out of his trip to San Francisco. He and Gillis shared the stage (so he claimed) with a happily inebriated passenger who had been struck on the foot by a hundred-pound silver brick that was being loaded onto the stagecoach. Calling piteously for brandy, the injured party resisted all suggestions that he have a doctor look at his foot at the stage company's expense. "He declined," wrote Twain, "and said that if he only had a little brandy to take along with him, to soothe his paroxysms of pain when they came on, he would be grateful and content." When Twain asked him how he could be so calm in the face of his suffering, the man responded with a smile, "Got a cork leg, you know," and proceeded to get "drunk as a lord all day long, and full of chucklings over his timely ingenuity."

After the chalky deserts of Nevada, windy San Francisco was a literal breath of fresh air. In a celebratory dispatch to the *Enterprise* after checking into his favorite hotel, Twain crowed: "To a Christian who has toiled months and months in Washoe, whose hair bristles from a bed of sand, and whose soul is caked with the cement of alkali dust; whose nostrils know of no perfume but the rank odor of the sagebrush—and whose eyes no landscape but the barren mountains and desolate plains; where the wind blows, and the sun blisters, and the broken spirit of the contrite heart finds joy and peace only in Lindburger cheese and lager beer—unto such a Christian, verily the Occidental Hotel is Heaven on the half shell. He may even secretly consider it to be heaven on the entire shell, but his religion teaches a sound Washoe Christian that it would be sacrilege to say it."

The city itself was equally celestial. It had, observed Twain, the most unvarying climate in the world. "The thermometer stands at about seventy degrees the year round," he wrote. "It is no colder,

A mostly clean-shaven Sam Clemens in 1862, near the outset of his great western adventure. Neither his famous pen name nor his familiar walrus mustache had yet taken hold.

1

Orion Clemens's appointment as secretary to the governor of Nevada Territory in 1861 would be the apogee of his personal and professional career. Sam worried that his brother "hasn't talent enough to carry on a peanut stand."

2

A Concord stage bristling with soldiers prepares to cross hostile Indian territory. On their own "pleasure trip" west, the Clemens brothers did not have the luxury of an armed bodyguard.

3

Mormon leader Brigham Young granted the Clemens brothers a private audience in Salt Lake City. He supposedly advised Sam, "Ten or eleven wives is all you need." Young himself had seventeen.

4

5

D Street in Virginia City, circa 1866. The real action took place one block over, on C Street, where saloons such as the Sazerac, the Sawdust Corner, and the Bucket of Blood catered to a regular clientele of miners, prospectors, gamblers, gunslingers, opium fiends, prostitutes, and journalists.

6

Virginia City, Nevada, was "the livest town that America had ever produced," Mark Twain bragged, adding that the city "afforded me the most vigorous enjoyment of life I had ever experienced." The feeling, for the most part, was mutual.

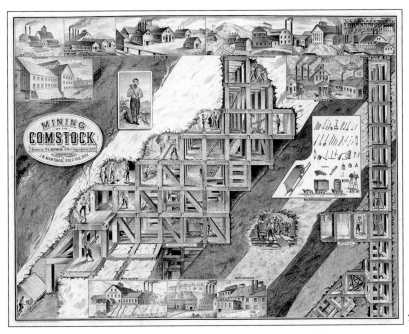

7

Cutaway rendering of a typical Comstock Lode operation. The original silver strike, in 1859, would yield more than $400 million over the next three decades—none of which went to Mark Twain.

The Virginia City *Territorial Enterprise* (seen in later years) was the best newspaper between St. Louis and San Francisco. Its young, rollicking staff quickly welcomed the neophyte Sam Clemens into its ranks.

8

A dapper, if dusty, Dan De Quille sits for a formal portrait. Like his young protégé Mark Twain, Dan was addicted to written hoaxes and practical jokes. "Get the facts first, then you can distort them as much as you like," he advised.

9

LETTER FROM CARSON CITY.

CARSON, Saturday Night.

EDS. ENTERPRISE: I feel very much as if I had just awakened out of a long sleep. I attribute it to the fact that I have slept the greater part of the time for the last two days and nights. On Wednesday, I sat up all night, in Virginia, in order to be up early enough to take the five o'clock stage on Thursday morning. I was on time. It was a great success. I had a cheerful trip down to Carson, in company with that incessant talker, Joseph T. Goodman. I never saw him flooded with such a flow of spirits before. He restrained his conversation, though, un-

what I sang is of no consequence to anybody. It was only a graceful little gem from the horse opera.

At about two o'clock in the morning the pleasant party broke up and the crowd of guests distributed themselves around town to their respective homes; and after thinking the fun all over again, I went to bed at four o'clock. So, having been awake forty-eight hours, I slept forty-eight, in order to get even again, which explains the proposition I began this letter with.

Yours, dreamily,   MARK TWAIN.

The first appearance of the most famous byline in American literature occurred on February 3, 1863, in the pages of the *Enterprise*. Scholars remain divided about its genesis. Was it a Mississippi River sounding, or a Virginia City saloon tally?

A. J. Simmons, Samuel Clemens, and Billy Clagett pose together at a session of the Nevada Territorial Legislature in 1863. Clagett had joined Clemens on a memorable prospecting trip to Unionville the previous year.

12

Earthquake damage at Pine and Montgomery streets in San Francisco. Twain kept a regular "Earthquake Almanac," noting in one characteristic entry: "Nov. 2—Spasmodic but exhilarating earthquakes."

Rival San Francisco newspaper columnist Albert S. Evans, alias "Fitz Smythe," frequently crossed pens with Mark Twain. He called Twain "the Sagebrush Bohemian" and accused him of having a venereal disease.

13

14

In his friend Dick Stoker's cabin on Jackass Hill in the Sierra Nevada foothills of California (pictured in later years), Twain first heard the story of a remarkable jumping frog. "That frog will jump around the world," Twain predicted. He was right.

15

Honolulu was Twain's first stopover in Hawaii, where he spent four blissful months of "luxurious vagrancy" in the spring and summer of 1866. He particularly admired the "long-haired, saddle-colored Sandwich Island maidens."

16

The ill-fated clipper ship *Hornet* smolders in the background as her passengers and crew escape the blaze in hastily loaded lifeboats. Forty-three days later, only one of the boats would reach Hawaii safely, giving Twain his first worldwide scoop.

Olivia Langdon at the age of eighteen. When her future husband first saw her photograph, he described her as "the most perfect gem of womankind that ever I saw in my life." He never wavered in that opinion.

Brash, confident Mark Twain in Constantinople in October 1867, during his six-month voyage to the Holy Land. He would transmute his travels into his first great publishing success, *The Innocents Abroad*.

and no warmer, in the one month than the other." (There is no hard evidence that he ever made the famous quip: "The coldest winter I ever spent was a summer in San Francisco.") One hundred miles away, in Sacramento, the climate was dramatically different. There it was eternal summer. "The people suffer and sweat, and swear, morning, noon and night, and wear out their stanchest energies fanning themselves," Twain noted after passing through town en route to San Francisco. "The thermometer stays at one hundred and twenty in the shade all the time—except when it varies and goes higher." A soldier at nearby Fort Yuma, he said, had died and gone to hell; "the next day he telegraphed back for his blankets."

Happily ensconced in the Occidental, Twain and Gillis made themselves at home in their new surroundings. It was a brief but inspiriting interlude of "butterfly idleness" spent in "the most cordial and sociable city in the Union." With no pressing responsibilities, Twain became for a time a full-fledged dandy. "I lived at the best hotel, exhibited my clothes in the most conspicuous places, infested the opera, and learned to seem enraptured with music," he remembered ruefully a few years later. "I had longed to be a butterfly, and I was one at last. I attended private parties in sumptuous evening dress, simpered and aired my graces like a born beau, and polk[a]ed and schottisched with a step peculiar to myself—and the kangaroo. In a word, I kept the due state of man worth a hundred thousand dollars (prospectively), and likely to reach absolute affluence when that silver-mine sale should be ultimately achieved in the east."

San Francisco was just the place for self-created dandies and prospective millionaires. By the mid-1860s, the city had grown from a sleepy Mexican seaport into a vital, protean city of one hundred thousand commercial-minded Anglos. The 1849 gold rush had temporarily emptied the city, as San Franciscans joined the manic exodus to the nearby goldfields, but the streets quickly filled up again with bankers, shippers, merchants, and saloonkeepers, all dedicated to helping the Forty-niners alternately save, spend, lose, or waste their hard-earned riches. There were 3,117 registered taverns—one for every ninety-six residents—along with an uncountable number of "blind tigers" or "blind pigs," unlicensed, unholy waterfront dives where barnacled old salts waited to drug and shanghai unwary customers onto a literal slow boat to China. "From later afternoon until dawn," one visitor wrote, "all of the dives were thronged with a motley crew of murderers, thieves, burglars, gamblers, pimps and degenerates of every description, practically all of whom were gunning for the sailors, miners, countrymen and others who visited the district through curiosity or in search of women and liquor." The brazenly named Hotel Nymphomania met both needs simultaneously, featuring three floors and 150 cribs for the working girls and their clients. Many of the prostitutes handed out calling cards; Big Matilda, for one, advertised "Three Hundred Pounds of Black Passion, 50 cents."

Not even the six major fires that raged through the city between 1848 and 1851—many of them set by an organized gang of transplanted Australian criminals known as the Sydney Ducks—could slow the explosive urban development, which stretched from the dockside red-light district known as the Barbary Coast to the nouveau riche mansions on 338-foot-high Nob Hill, located above Chinatown and the financial district. English journalist F. W. Rae climbed the hill one day and was surprised to see the city below cloaked by a dense cloud of smoke. "I had supposed San Francisco to be a second Liverpool," he wrote. "I was not prepared to find it was also a second Birmingham." Rae's fellow countryman, novelist Anthony Trollope, was equally unimpressed. "I do not know that in all my travels I ever visited a city less interesting to the normal tourist," Trollope wrote. "Strangers will generally desire to get out of San Francisco as quickly as they can."

✳

Perhaps Rae and Trollope were simply looking in the wrong direction. There was actually a lot to see. Then, as later, San Francisco was home to a decidedly eclectic citizenry. On any given day, residents might encounter on the streets such daffy individualists as the Great Unknown, a mysterious, elegantly dressed old gentleman who paraded down Montgomery Street in funereal silence every afternoon—the victim, some said, of a tragic love affair. Joining the Great Unknown in the citywide cavalcade of cranks were Old Rosie, who wore a trademark flower in the lapel of his threadbare suit; Money King, who lived up to his name by making personal loans in the shadow of the city stock exchange; and Professor Frederick Coombs, a supposed expert of phrenology, which Clemens had dabbled in during his youth. Coombs capitalized on his vague physical resemblance to George Washington by strolling about town in a powdered wig and full Colonial finery, carrying a banner that proclaimed him, perhaps unnecessarily, as "Washington the Second." At any time, these solitaries might find themselves eclipsed by a parade of members from the tongue-in-cheek social club the Ancient and Honorable Order of E Clampus Vitus, which met in the Hall of Comparative Ovations to receive instructions from the Noble Grand Humbug and serve as cochairmen on the Most Important Committee.

The preeminent local character was Joshua Abraham Norton, the self-proclaimed Emperor Norton I, who ruled over his people for more than a quarter of a century with a firm but fond hand after his initial appearance at the desk of the San Francisco *Bulletin* in 1859, where he announced politely, "Good morning, I am the emperor of the United States." The London-born son of a plebeian ship's chandler, Norton had arrived in San Francisco during the height of the gold rush and made a small fortune operating a general store. After losing both his wealth and his mind in an ill-considered scheme to corner the local rice market (he and his partners bought up all the rice in California, only to discover that they had forgotten one small detail—San Francisco Bay was teeming with ships arriving every day loaded to the mast tops with still more rice), the would-be tycoon disappeared from view for several years before making his dramatic reemergence as Emperor Norton I.

Clad in a colonel's uniform, complete with gold epaulettes, cockade hat, and ceremonial sword, which he had somehow wangled from the garrison commander at the local army post, the Emperor held court daily at his imperial residence (actually a low-rent rooming house). From his seat of power he issued well-reasoned edicts abolishing the presidency "because of corruption in high places" and ordering the army to "clear the halls of Congress"—moves that might elicit widespread approval today. He levied taxes of twenty-five cents for small businesses and three dollars for banks and printed his own imperial bonds in denominations of ten, twenty-five, and fifty cents. As a mark of his noble puissance, shops and restaurants throughout the city unhesitatingly honored his money at full face value.

Each day the emperor made his royal progress down Montgomery Street, his subjects duly bowing and scraping as he passed. He was accompanied in his processional by his two royal mastiffs, Bummer and Lazarus. The dogs, like Norton, ate for free and attended the theater in reserved seats—the audience would rise respectfully when the trio made its entrance. The 1870 U.S. Census formally listed Norton's occupation as "emperor," and he was introduced to his fellow potentate, Brazilian Emperor Dom Pedro II, during the South American monarch's state visit to the city. When Bummer passed away in 1865—he was kicked down the stairs by a drunk—Mark Twain composed his epitaph, noting that the decedent had "died full of years and honors and disease and fleas." And when Norton himself quit the scene in 1880, thirty thousand mourners filed past his coffin while flags across the city flew at half-mast and the San Francisco *Chronicle* mourned: "Le Roi Est Mort!" The rival *Bulletin* observed, with some justice, that "the Emperor killed nobody, robbed nobody and deprived nobody of his country, which is more than can be said for most of the fellows in his trade."

During his time at the Occidental, Twain made the acquaintance of another vibrant personality who would become a fixture of San Francisco life for decades to come. Lillie Hitchcock, then twenty-one, was the madcap daughter of Dr. and Mrs. Charles McPhail Hitchcock. Her father was medical director of the Union Army of the Pacific, a position somewhat inconvenienced by the fact that his Virginia-born wife, Martha, and their daughter were ardent Confederates. The female Hitchcocks, in fact, were so pro-southern that the doctor sent them away to Paris for a time. They had just returned to the States when Twain made their acquaintance in the dining room at the Occidental.

Lillie, who supposedly had been engaged fifteen times before she was out of her teens, was well on her way to becoming a true San Francisco eccentric. She smoked cigars, played poker with the men, daringly cross-dressed in denim jeans and plaid miner's shirts, and raced horses and wagons recklessly down city streets. The central focus of her mania, what Twain termed her "wild & repulsive foolery," was firemen in general and Engine Company No. 5 in particular. She had become obsessed with the company after a member saved her life in a hotel fire when she was eight, and in honor of the company's bravery she habitually wore a red blouse, black skirt, and gold-and-diamond badge bearing the number five. She had her own gold fire helmet as well, and she would scramble from debutante balls and drawing room teas into the front seat of a company fire engine whenever the alarm arose, as it frequently did in a city that suffered regularly from major fires and earthquakes. Her fellow rescuers called her "Firebelle."

Like many others, Twain found Lillie fascinating, if a little crazy. She was "stored to the eyelids with energy and enthusiasm," he wrote—so was he, for that matter—and she often waited until noon to eat breakfast with her notoriously late-rising new friend. She was "a brilliant talker," and beneath her wildness was a "tropically warm heart." Twain did not fall entirely under her sway (she was much too unconventional to become a love object for him), but he never forgot Lillie Hitchcock. Much later he featured her as Rachel "Hellfire" Hotchkiss in an unfinished novella about a daredevil young woman who rescues a boy stranded on an ice floe in the middle of the Mississippi River. Adopted by the local fire company, she later performs another rescue of a family trapped in a burning house, clambering over the rooftops in her official belt and helmet. The novella was left unfinished, but Lillie made another appearance as Shirley Tempest, "A San Francisco Belle and Heiress of adventurous spirit," in Twain's ill-starred 1877 play, *Ah Sin*.

One month into his stay in San Francisco, Twain experienced his first earthquake. "As I turned the corner, around a frame house, there was a great rattle and jar," he reported. "Before I could turn and seek the door, there came a really terrific shock; the ground seemed to roll under me in waves, interrupted by a violent joggling up and down, and there was a heavy grinding noise as of brick houses rubbing together. I fell against the frame house and hurt my elbow." Regaining his footing, Twain saw a four-story brick building sprawl across the street in a dusty heap and a passing buggy smashed into bits along a three-hundred-yard track. Passengers poured out of both ends of a damaged streetcar like clowns at the circus, while horses reared and plunged in terror. "One fat man had crashed halfway through a glass window on one side of the car," observed Twain, "got wedged fast and was squirming and screaming like an impaled madman." A woman who had been washing a child ran down the street holding the naked infant by its ankles like a Thanksgiving turkey, while men staggered out of saloons holding pool cues unnoticed in their hands and a frightened dog ran straight up a ladder onto the roof of a swaying building. Thousands of residents, said Twain, were made so seasick by their pitching and rolling floors that they were bedridden for days. He began an "Earthquake Almanac" in his notebook; a characteristic sample read: "Nov. 2—Spasmodic but exhilarating earthquakes, accompanied by occasional showers of rain, and churches and things."

He had scarcely recovered from the shock of the earthquake when he received an even nastier economic blow. Expecting to live on his mining stock, Twain opened a copy of the *Enterprise* to find that his erstwhile partners in Humboldt County had sold their shares out from under him, netting them $3 million in profits in New York and leaving him holding a handful of worthless stock. Worse yet, the bottom had dropped out of the Virginia City market "and everything and everybody went to ruin and destruction! The wreck was complete. The bubble scarcely left a microscopic moisture behind it. I was an early beggar and a thorough one. My hoarded stocks were not worth the paper they were printed on. I threw them all away."

An indication of his financial fall was the plaintive letter Twain sent to Dan De Quille, offering to sell him his half of their furniture for fifty-five dollars. (De Quille, who by that time had found another roommate, did not respond.) Twain and Gillis were forced to move out of the Occidental, beginning a restless round of rent-jumping at various fusty boardinghouses. One landlady, at least, was glad to see them go. When Gillis's father dropped by unannounced to see them, she told him: "They are gone, thank God—& I hope I may never see them again. . . . They were a couple of desperate characters from Washoe—gamblers & murderers of the very worst description." For their amusement, she told the elder Gillis, the two liked to point guns at anyone who annoyed them—there were many—and toss empty beer bottles out of the window at Chinese neighbors passing below. "You'd hear them count 'One—two—three—fire!'" she said. "And then you'd hear the bottles crash on the China roofs and see poor Chinamen scatter like flies."

Very much against his will, Twain was forced to reenter the workforce, taking a job as a general assignment reporter, or "lokulitems," as the position was known within the trade, for the San Francisco *Morning Call*. Gillis went along as a compositor. It was the start of a mutually unsatisfactory relationship. George E. Barnes, the Canadian-born no-nonsense editor of the *Call*, had little use for frontier high jinks. For a salary of forty dollars a week, he expected Twain to give readers the straight news, without hoaxing or embellishing the truth. The *Call* was the city's cheapest newspaper, with a subscription rate of one bit—half a quarter—per week. It unapologetically styled itself "the washerwoman's newspaper," for the large number of Irish domestics who made up the bulk of the paper's readership, and Barnes wanted his reporters to write down to their level.

Unsurprisingly, Twain found the new job "fearful, soulless drudgery," eighteen-hour days spent dashing from courthouse to police station to one of six local theaters, where he would catch just enough action onstage to write a brief review for the morning edition. Forty years later, Twain still shuddered at the soul-killing routine. "By nine in the morning I had to be at the police court for an hour and make a brief history of the squabbles of the night before," he recalled. "They were usually between Irishmen and Irishmen, and Chinamen and Chinamen, with now and then a squabble between the two races for a change. Each day's evidence was substantially a duplicate of the day before, therefore the daily performance was killingly monotonous and wearisome." The only person who found the routine at all interesting, Twain said, was the court-appointed interpreter, a rumpled Englishman who was required to jump between some fifty-six separate Chinese dialects every ten minutes or so, "and this exercise was so energizing that it kept him always awake, which was not the case with the reporters."

The rest of the workday was spent trolling the city for news—"If there were no fires to report we started some." Twain found amusement where he could. One day, he came upon a policeman leaning against a lamppost, asleep on the job. Hurrying to a nearby greengrocer's stand, Twain grabbed the largest cabbage leaf he could find and returned to silently fan the dozing copper while a large crowd gathered, smirking and winking at the spectacle. Another night he happened upon a crowd on Harrison Street that was attempting to make sense of "a pile of miscellaneous articles . . . found heaped up at a late hour." Two policemen arrived on the scene and "solved the difficulty, showing a clean inventory of one horse, one buggy, two men and an indefinite amount of liquor." The two men "were drunk as Bacchus and his brother," Twain reported. "A fight had been on hand somewhere, and one of the men had been close to it, for his face was painted up in various hues, sky-blue and crimson being prominent." The horse, he added happily, "was beyond realizing the sense of his condition."

At the city jail, a series of rat-infested cells in the basement of San Francisco City Hall on Kearny Street, Twain picked through the human refuse for stories. He was under no illusion about his work; he was dealing "in the direct line of misery," surrounded by "dilapidated old hags and ragged bummers." One of the former was a former New York City schoolteacher named Anna Jakes, who had relocated to the West Coast and descended the social ladder immediately and dramatically. "Anna Jakes, drunk and disorderly, but excessively cheerful, make her first appearance in the City Prison last night," Twain reported, "and made the dreary vaults ring with music. It was of the distorted hifalutin kind, and she evidently considered herself an opera sharp of some consequence." Miss Jakes's sister had gotten married a few nights before, and Anna "got drunk to do honor to the occasion—and with a persistency that is a credit to one of such small experience, she has been on a terrific bender." Her choice of music was an invariable and interminable rendition of "Weeping, Sad and

Lonely; or, When This Cruel War Is Over," prompting one member of her captive audience to "curse like a trooper" and another to call out, *"Will* you dry that infernal yowling, you heifer?"

The reporter made a remarkably detailed catalog of another old drunkard's pockets, presumably after they had been emptied by the police. The contents included: "Two slabs of old cheese; a double handful of various kinds of crackers; seven peaches; a box of lip-salve . . . an onion; two dollars and sixty five scents, in two purses . . . a soiled handkerchief; a fine-tooth comb . . . a cucumber pickle, in an imperfect state of preservation; a leather string; an eye-glass, such as prospectors use; one buckskin glove; a printed ballad, 'Call me pet names'; an apple; part of a dried herring; a copy of the Boston Weekly Journal; and copies of several San Francisco newspapers; and in each and every pocket he had two of three chunks of tobacco, and also one in his mouth of such remarkable size as to render his articulation confused and uncertain."

Serious crime was commonplace in San Francisco, and Twain fell back on his Virginia City experience, where readers and reporters were accustomed to having "a man for breakfast," to comb through arrest reports and court dockets for items of interest. There was much to choose from. "Sensation items," as he called them, ranged from violent crimes such as murder, robbery, rape, and suicide to more exotic offenses such as fruit swindling, voyeurism, bigamy, misce-genation, and lost infants. One prominent case involved a deranged soldier named Simon Kennedy, who fatally stabbed a fellow prisoner in the guardhouse at the Black Point artillery post. Kennedy, who was "popularly considered to be insane," had attacked his victim, Private James Fitzgerald, under the delusion that he was about to be hanged. As Twain reported, Kennedy grabbed a guard's bayonet and stabbed Fitzgerald more than a dozen times. "The shrieks of the struggling victim attracted the attention of the sentinel," wrote Twain, and in the ensuing confusion "the murderer rushed out and escaped in the darkness, followed by three or four terrified prisoners." What particularly caught the reporter's eye was the background information that Kennedy was "an extraordinary swimmer, and it is said he once swam the Mississippi at a point where it was more than a mile and half wide, and his bare head being exposed so long to the burning rays of the run, the strength and vigor of his brain were impaired by it, and at intervals since then he has seemed a little flighty."

Another sensational case involved the near-fatal assault and robbery of pawnbroker Harris Myers's eighteen-year-old son, Henry, in broad daylight in August 1864. Myers's shop was located one door down from the *Call*, and Twain arrived on the scene soon after the crime occurred. Young Myers, he reported, had been slugged behind the right ear with a leaded sap, which inflicted "an egg-shaped indentation at the base of the brain." The youth survived, but had no memory of the attack. Twain saved most of his outrage for Chief of Police Martin J. Burke, who ignored an eyewitness account of a fleeing white man with a goatee and instead ordered his men "to detain every suspicious Chinaman they see." "If anybody wants a spry, intelligent thief or two, the same may be obtained at Chief Burke's hotel," wrote Twain, "as all the thieves in the city [along with seventy-two Chinese workers] were arrested on Wednesday night, in the hope of finding among them the robber of the pawnbroker." The crime was never solved, but Twain had created a formidable enemy in Chief Burke, one who like many in his profession would prove to have a long memory.

Twain devoted considerable ink—as well he might—to a case involving the seduction of local schoolgirls for older men by a resourceful fourteen-year-old pimp with the rather prosaic name of Ralph Doyle. The girls, some as young as ten, were supposedly lured away from the playground with salacious drawings and photographs. Twain, who could be surprisingly prudish at times, reported that the various "miscreants" and "scoundrels" involved in the ring "made use of the boys to decoy the girls to their rooms, where their ruin was effected. These rooms were well stocked with obscene books and pictures." At least thirty girls were named in the case, and one willing or unwilling participant, a fifteen-year-old orphan, became pregnant. Her defiler, local businessman George Lambertson, attempted to escape punishment by signing over all his property to the girl. It didn't work; Lambertson was sentenced to three months in the county jail and fined five hundred dollars for "infamous demoralizing practices with young school girls." In an ironic footnote to the case, Rincon School principal John C. Pelton, a friend of Twain, was fired by the school board for devoting too much time and energy to rounding up the dirty books and pictures involved.

In September 1864, a gruesome steamboat accident brought back memories of Henry Clemens's death on the Mississippi six years earlier. The steamer *Washoe* was one of six riverboats operating out of the Broadway wharf and plying the inland rivers and bays between San Francisco and Sacramento. Under Captain George Washington Kidd, the *Washoe* was a notably unlucky vessel. In the five months since she was constructed, the ship had been completely overhauled for faulty boiler flues and collided twice with the same rival ship, *Yosemite*—once on open water in a wide channel above Rio Vista. On the night of September 6, *Washoe* was near Rio Vista again, heading for Sacramento, when her upper deck exploded without warning. Nearly one hundred passengers and crew were killed; another seventy-five were injured.

Twain, perhaps the only San Francisco reporter who could write knowledgeably about such a mishap, attributed the explosion to a faulty boiler. He exonerated the captain from any blame, devoting several hundred lines of type to a detailed description of water pressure, steam gauges, boiler lines, flues, and rivets. Remembering Henry, Twain described the "most horrible" scene of the accident, including the vivid image of "one man, who was scalded from head to foot, got ashore, and in a nude state stood and screamed for help, but would not allow any covering to be put on him." And in a connection that only Twain could have made, he recalled how "the noble little city of Memphis, Tennessee" had raised twenty thousand dollars for the victims of a similar incident "years ago." Memphis, of course, was where Henry had died.

Even in a large city like San Francisco, there was not enough crime and punishment, mayhem, and death to fill up a day's newspaper. Twain had to depend on other tried and true methods. Harking back to the days of "Unreliable" Clement Rice and Dan De Quille, Twain worked mightily to foment a new journalistic feud with rival reporter Albert S. Evans of the *Alta California*. Evans, a "born fool" in the eyes of a rival publication, was a gimlet-eyed theater critic and a sworn enemy of all local artists—stage, canvas, or written page. He fancied himself something of a wit, signing his columns "Fitz Smythe" or "Armand Leonidas Stiggers," the latter identity attached to a limp-wristed, effeminate lover of beauty with "weak blue eyes, delicate pink hair [and] green spectacles" who went about town wearing maroon-colored gloves, accompanied by his flea-infested dog, Rienzi. Evans called Twain, without intending it as praise, "the Sagebrush Bohemian," and described him witheringly as "the aborigine from the land of sagebrush and alkali, whose soubriquet was given him by his friends as indicative of his capacity for doing the drinking for two." On the subject of Twain's drinking, Evans could speak with some authority. Prior to joining the *Alta California*, he had been the Washoe correspondent for the Gold Hill *Daily News*.

As was usually the case with most people who crossed swords, or pens, with Mark Twain, Evans was outmatched from the start. Purposely confusing Evans with his swishy alter ego, Twain referred to him habitually as "Stiggers" and mocked him unmercifully in the *Call*. He accused Evans of drinking up all the liquor at a Chinese temple, of eating a German restaurateur out of business, of toadying up to the police—even of feeding his horse a parsimonious diet of old newspapers. When Evans attempted to wring tears from his readers with a maudlin account of a dying tosspot, writing that "the broad canopy of Heaven . . . had blacked its face with heavy clouds, and was weeping as a mother weeps when she sees her child," Twain suggested—a little late—that the woman in question simply get a job and fix things up with her husband.

Evans's stilted writing style was a frequent Twain target. After Evans unctuously reported the departure of local merchant Moses Ellis, "one of our principal, and, we are pleased to say, prosperous pioneer merchants, who leaves us today on a visit to the home of his nativity," Twain noted that his rival had failed to mention the departure of Ellis's prominent fellow passengers, including Union Major General William S. Rosecrans. "But let Moike Mulrooney, or Tim Murphy, or Judy O'Flaherty, receive a present of real Irish whisky from the ould country, and he will never let you hear the last of it." And when Evans floridly described how two customers had been chiseled by a shoeshine boy—"On examination of their boots they discovered that they had more real estate than blacking on the outer surface, and an examination of their pockets showed conclusively that both parties were teetotally impecunious"—Twain translated the words into simple English: "Their boots were soiled with dust and they had no money."

Not even the feud with Evans could keep Twain sufficiently interested in his job. "It was awful slavery for a lazy man," he wrote in his autobiography, "and I was born lazy. I am no lazier now than I was forty years ago, but that is because I reached the limit forty years ago. You can't go beyond possibility." He managed to talk his editor, George Barnes, into letting him have an assistant, recruiting "a great hulking creature" from the loading docks named William McGrew, whom he called, for no discernible reason, Smiggy McGlural. Twain took a fifteen-dollar-a-week cut in pay and turned over all late-night work to his assistant. "I don't work after 6 in the evening, now," he informed Dan De Quille. "I got disgusted with night work."

Twain's disgust reached critical mass after a run-in with Barnes over a rare bit of morally outraged reporting he had produced concerning the beating of a Chinese laundryman by white toughs. Twain, who was not above tossing the stray beer bottle out his hotel window at random Asian targets below, took offense at the way a local policeman had stood by and let the hoodlums beat this particular victim. He wrote an impassioned account for the *Call*, "with considerable warmth and holy indignation," only to find it spiked on the editor's desk the next morning. Barnes explained that the *Call* could not afford to alienate its Irish readers, who "hated Chinamen" anyway. Accustomed to having everything he wrote printed without question, Twain stewed. A few days later, he and Barnes came to a final meeting of the minds. Whether he resigned or was fired is a matter of semantics—either way, he was out of a job. Forty years later it still hurt, and when news photos of the great San Francisco earthquake of 1906 arrived in the East, showing the *Call*'s building reduced to a skeletal frieze of ruins, Twain exulted, "How wonderful are the ways of Providence!"

Divine retribution notwithstanding, Twain suddenly found himself struggling in the no longer heavenly city. "For two months my sole occupation was avoiding acquaintances," he recalled, "for during that time I did not earn a penny, or buy an article of any kind, or pay my board. I became very adept at 'slinking.' I slunk from back street to back street, I slunk away from approaching faces that looked familiar, I slunk to my meals, ate them humbly and with a mute apology for every mouthful I robbed my generous landlady of, and at midnight, after wanderings that were but slinkings away from cheerfulness and light, I slunk to my bed. I felt meaner, and lowlier and more despicable than the worms."

His replacement at the *Call* lampooned Twain in the newspaper—so much for professional courtesy—as "a melancholy-looking Arab, known as Marque Twein. His hat is an old one, and comes too far down over his eyes, and his clothes don't fit." There was nothing particularly funny about his current plight to Twain, who clung literally to his last dime, afraid, he said, that complete pennilessness "might suggest suicide." He even broached the subject with his religious brother and sister-in-law, noting suddenly in an otherwise serious discussion of marriage that "I am resolved on that or suicide—perhaps." In a later letter, he fretted: "If I do not get out of debt in 3 months—pistols or poison for one—exit *me*." Several years after the fact, he remembered one despairing night when "I put the pistol to my head but wasn't man enough to pull the trigger. Many times I have been sorry I did not succeed, but I was never ashamed of having tried. Suicide is the only really sane thing the young or the old ever do in this life."

Sane or not, he put down the pistol and picked up the pen. As he would do throughout his life, in good times and bad, Mark Twain wrote. Old and new outlets suggested themselves. The *Call* shared a building at 612 Commercial Street with the *Golden Era*, Rollin Daggett's former magazine, to which Twain had contributed earlier pieces about unruly children and matronly fashion shows. Drawing on his experience in police court, he published a new piece, "The Evidence in the Case of Smith vs. Jones," lampooning gaseous lawyers, impenetrable legal jargon, and unreliable witnesses. The *Call* building also housed the local annex of the U.S. Mint, where a bright young writer-editor was emerging on the literary scene while marking time at his government post. Francis Bret Harte, nine months younger than Mark Twain, was yet another easterner (born in Albany, New York) who had come west in the wake of the 1849 gold rush. He had spent time in the raucous mining camps at Jackass Hill and Angel's Camp, collecting experiences that would pay huge dividends a few years later in such stories as "The Outcasts of Poker Flats" and "The Luck of Roaring Camp," before becoming a typesetter and assistant editor on the Uniontown *Northern Californian*.

Relocating to San Francisco, the handsome, cultivated Harte found work on the *Golden Era*, to which he began contributing poetry and stories while tirelessly cultivating influential sponsors such as Jessie Benton Frémont, the wife of pathfinding General John C. Frémont, and the Reverend Thomas Starr King, pastor of the city's largest Unitarian church. Harte's enthusiastic support for the Union cause, to which he contributed specially prepared poems and songs, together with his socially advantageous marriage to the lead contralto in King's choir, helped win him a privileged sinecure at the San Francisco branch of the U.S. Mint. There, his duties as secretary to the superintendent consisted mainly of writing more poems and stories and editing a new literary magazine, the *Californian*, on office time. Somehow Harte managed to do both tasks simultaneously.

Twain and Harte first met in the summer of 1864, while Twain was working upstairs at the *Call*. Despite their radically different Civil War experiences and their inherently opposite personalities, the two men shared a love of writing. Years later, each still remembered vividly his first sight of the other. "His head was striking," wrote Harte of Twain. "He had the curly hair, the aquiline nose, and even the aquiline eye—an eye so eagle-like that a second lid would not have surprised me—of an unusual and dominant nature. His eyebrows were very thick and bushy. His dress was careless, and his general manner one of supreme indifference to surroundings and circumstances." As for Twain, he found his counterpart "distinctly pretty, in spite of the fact that his face was badly pitted with smallpox. He was showy, meretricious, insincere, and he constantly advertised these qualities in his dress. His neckties tended to be either crimson—a flash of flame under his chin, or indigo blue, and as hot and vivid as if one of those splendid and luminous Brazilian butterflies had lighted there."

Personally and professionally, Twain and Harte would always have a complicated relationship. As the first two western writers to achieve national prominence, they would naturally feel a certain amount of competition—Twain perhaps more than Harte. Many years later, in his autobiography, Twain would say memorably: "Bret Harte was one of the pleasantest men I have ever known. He was also one of the unpleasantest men I have ever known." Recalling Harte's much-publicized journey east in 1871 after being hired by the *Atlantic Monthly* to produce a story a month for one year, Twain grumbled that Harte had received "such a prodigious blaze of national interest and excitement that one might have supposed he was the Viceroy of India on a progress, or Halley's comet come again after seventy-five years of lamented absence." Given that Twain felt a proprietary claim on the comet that had heralded his birth in 1835, Harte's celestial linkage would have been considered by Twain to be presumptuous, if not bogus. Even the heavens were not big enough for both of them.

The final break between the two, occasioned mainly by the failure of their collaborative play, *Ah Sin*, a dramatization of Harte's career-making poem, "The Heathen Chinee," was still several years in the future. For the present, Harte generously encouraged Twain's contributions, offering to pay him twelve dollars per article or a flat fifty dollars per month. Twain quickly bragged of his new job to his family. "I have engaged to write for the new literary paper—the 'Californian,'" he informed his mother and sister. "I quit the 'Era,' long ago. It wasn't high-toned enough. I thought that whether I was a literary 'jackleg' or not, I wouldn't class myself with that style of people, anyhow. The 'Californian' circulates among the highest class of the community, & is the best weekly literary paper in the United States—& I suppose I ought to know."

Twain was moving into more rarefied literary territory at the *Californian*, a career change that his inveterate enemy Albert Evans characterized condescendingly as "sundry literature" and "the grave of genius." Twain didn't see it that way. The *Californian* attracted the best and brightest of San Francisco's bohemian culture, including homosexual travel writer Charles Warren Stoddard, a personal friend of Scottish novelist Robert Louis Stevenson. Stoddard, who sometimes styled himself "Pip Pepperpod," had just returned from the Sandwich Islands and Tahiti, where he had tried unsuccessfully to cure himself of his attraction to men by taking long bracing walks on the beach and meditating moistly under the palms. Apparently, it didn't work, since Stoddard was soon writing to his gay New York friend Walt Whitman: "For the first time I act as my nature prompts me. It would not answer in America, as a general principle—not even in California, where men are tolerably bold."

Also tolerably bold was Stoddard's platonic friend and lifelong soul mate, the beautiful bisexual poet Ina Coolbrith. Born Josephine Donna Smith (Coolbrith was her mother's maiden name), Ina was the niece of Mormon founder Joseph Smith. Running full-tilt from her fundamentalist roots, Coolbrith married young, betrothing herself to a wastrel Los Angeles musician named Robert Carsley. Her husband was a mean drunk who threatened his tall, darkly beautiful wife with scissors and knives and once shot off her stepfather's hand when he attempted to intervene. Coolbrith, understandably, sued for divorce and escaped suburban Southern California for the more pacific environs of San Francisco. There under the pen name "Meg Merrilies," she began publishing her breathily apostrophizing poetry—"San Francisco, city of mists and dreams!"—and commenced a half-century-long career as a full-time poet and part-time lesbian. Stoddard, Harte, and Twain were all enamored of her at one time or another, but for various reasons of sexual orientation, marital status, or simple good sense, all declined to press their case. Twain, being neither married nor gay, might have been the most logical suitor, but Ina's Mormon background and her rather prosaic day job as a public librarian across the bay in Oakland may have put him off the chase. He never said—revealingly, perhaps, he never mentioned her at all.

Another of Twain's exotic female acquaintances, poet-actress Ada Clare, reappeared just long enough to provoke from him an angry response. Clare, last seen in the company of Adah Isaacs Menken at their disastrous dinner with Twain and Dan De Quille in Virginia

City in February 1864, had read Twain's Jonathan Swift-like piece, "Those Blasted Children," in the *Californian*, in which he recommended drastic cures for childhood diseases—removing the patient's jaw in the case of stuttering, or parboiling the sufferer in the case of cramps. "I don't quite like Mark Twain's last article on children," Clare ventured to say in the *Golden Era*. "He is funny, of course; but he is guilty of misunderstanding God's little people."

Annoyed and hurt, Twain responded with one of his first recognizably Twainian performances, "The Story of the Bad Little Boy That Bore a Charmed Life." In a spoof of morally uplifting tales, "Grandfather Twain" recounted the tale of Jim, who did not have a sick mother, did not pray for her recovery, did not feel remorse for stealing jam, did not fall out of an apple tree for stealing fruit, did not get expelled for swiping his teacher's penknife, did not drown in the creek for going swimming on Sunday, did not shoot off three or four of his fingers with his father's stolen gun, and did not disappear after running away to sea. Instead, "he grew up, and married, and raised a large family, and brained them all with an axe one night, and got wealthy by all manner of cheating and rascality, and now . . . is universally respected, and belongs to the Legislature."

Twain also got revenge on Clare indirectly by reviewing a concert by her former lover, pianist Louis M. Gottschalk, the father of the out-of-wedlock child with whom she defiantly registered at hotels, "Miss Clare and Son." In a signed review in the *Californian*, Twain unfavorably compared Gottschalk's piano stylings to those of minstrel banjo players Sam Pride and Charley Rhoades, noting that "the piano may do for love-sick girls who lace themselves to skeletons, and lunch on chalk, pickle, and slate pencils"—a direct gibe at the ever-corseted Clare. "Give me the banjo," he said, adding that it produced the same happy physiological effect as hot whiskey punch, strychnine, and the measles. Gottschalk, true to form, was forced to flee from San Francisco a few months later after a couple of schoolgirls from the local female college were caught sneaking back into their dormitory one night following an unauthorized visit to the pianist's hotel room.

Twain's other contributions to the *Californian* were less vengeful, but similarly satirical. In "Aurelia's Unfortunate Young Man," he combined a saccharine love story with the standard advice to the lovelorn newspaper column. A sign for "Love's Bakery" sends the author into a reverie about young lovers "kneaded together, baked to a turn, and ready for matrimony." Aurelia, writing for advice, has a singularly tragic tale: her fiancé has been scarred by smallpox, lost both arms and legs to accidents, lost an eye to erysipelas, and gotten himself scalped by Indians. Twain advises the perplexed young lady to buy her lover wooden arms and legs, a glass eye, and a wig, and marry him "if he does not break his neck in the meantime." If he does, she can always inherit his valuables.

In "The Killing of Julius Caesar 'Localized,'" the author poked fun at sensationalized newspaper accounts by describing how Caesar's death might have been reported in the *Roman Daily Evening Fasces*. "Our usually quiet city of Rome was thrown into a state of wild excitement, yesterday, by the occurrence of one of those bloody affrays which sicken the heart and fill the soul with fear, while they inspire all thinking men with forebodings for the future of a city where human life is held so cheaply, and the gravest laws are so openly set at defiance," the *Fasces* reporter intones. Caesar, "a man whose name is known wherever this paper circulates," has been done in by a gang of bruisers "in the pay of the Opposition" while "talking to some of the back-country members about the approaching fall elections." The reporter's confidential source is Mark Antony, "whose position enables him to learn every item of news connected with the . . . subject."

"Lucretia Smith's Soldier," published in the *Californian* on December 3, 1864, burlesqued "those nice, sickly war stories in *Harper's Weekly*" in which bravely suffering sweethearts pined by the bedsides of their nobly wounded soldiers. Considering the fact that Twain had deserted (more or less) from the war three years earlier, it was a particularly nervy thing to do. Nervy or not, it was undeniably funny. At the start, the author guarantees the veracity of his story, saying it was based on official records of the War Department and inspired by "the excellent beer manufactured by the New York Brewery, in Sutter Street." The story recounts the tragic tale of Miss Smith and her suitor, Reginald de Whittaker, a dry goods clerk from Bluemass, Massachusetts, who has enlisted in the army with the usual dream of coming home "a bronzed and scarred Brigadier-General." Finding her loved one's name on the list of desperately wounded soldiers, Lucretia rushes to his bedside, where she sits vigil beside her heavily bandaged beau. When the bandages come off, she discovers that the soldier is not Reginald de Whittaker of Bluemass, Massachusetts, but Richard Dilworthy Whittaker of rural Wisconsin. "O confound my cats if I haven't gone and fooled away three mortal weeks here, sniffling and slobbering over the wrong soldier!" Lucretia exclaims. "Such is life," the author concludes.

For a war-weary public, "Lucretia Smith's Soldier" struck a much-needed comic chord, and the story was picked up by various East Coast publications. Mark Twain, however, did not stick around long enough to enjoy his first widespread triumph. The day after the story appeared in the *Californian*, he hightailed it out of San Francisco with three hundred dollars in his pocket and a five-hundred-dollar bail bond in his hand for the release of his friend Steve Gillis, who had been arrested by the local police for braining a bartender with a beer mug. (And not just any bartender—Big Jim Casey was a personal friend of Police Chief Martin Burke.) Gillis, it developed, had already left town, heading back to Virginia City, and he strongly advised Twain to do the same.

Having frequently rankled the police with his public criticism of their dedication, honesty, and investigative talents, Twain wisely took his friend's advice. Reasoning, perhaps, that the authorities would be looking for him in Virginia City, the fugitive columnist sought refuge with Gillis's two older brothers, Jim and Billy Gillis, at the ramshackle mining camp of Jackass Hill, a hundred miles east of San Francisco in Calaveras County. It was there, one dark and stormy night, that he first heard a story about a very singular frog. Soon he would make the frog's story his own—and the world's.

CHAPTER 6

LUXURIOUS VAGRANCY

T HE WEATHER WAS LOUSY ON JACKASS HILL. IT rained every day (even California has what passes for winter), and Mark Twain complained that he "couldn't have been colder if I had swallowed an ice-berg." His companions, more inured to the weather, spent the better part of each day "pocket mining" the Sierra Nevada foothills around Angel's Camp, as the decaying settlement across the Stanislaus River was named. At the height of the 1849 gold rush, Angel's Camp had been home to some three thousand treasure seekers. Fewer than half that number still remained, stolidly picking through the mud for stray nuggets of gold. The favored method, as described by Twain, involved shoveling a handful of dirt from the hillside, washing it in a sluice pan, and repeating the process. Miners worked their way downhill in a gridlike pattern, gouging out holes as though dousing for water and occasionally finding a few stray grains of gold. It was a laborious and time-intensive process, and Twain avoided it like the plague, declaring the work "too disagreeable" for one of his delicate constitution. His principal companions, Jim Gillis and Dick Stoker, had been pocket mining together for the past fifteen years. "During the three months I was with them," Twain recalled in his autobiography, "they found nothing, but we had a fascinating and delightful good time trying." Not surprisingly, perhaps, the process "furnish[ed] a very handsome percentage of victims to the lunatic asylum."

When the treasure hunters broke for the day, they repaired to a snugly built cabin atop Jackass Hill. The hill had acquired its less-than-picturesque name from the large number of pack animals picketed there by the teamsters bringing wagonloads of supplies into camp. Stoker had built the cabin in 1850, and Gillis had joined him there five years later. The partners were a good mix: each was quiet, industrious, and surprisingly intellectual. Dan De Quille, who had done some prospecting himself before settling in as a reporter on the *Territorial Enterprise*, called the cabin "the headquarters of all Bohemians visiting the mountains, a sort of Bohemian infirmary. There the sick are made well and the well are made better." Bret Harte, too, had visited the cabin during his mining days, storing up impressions for his breakthrough stories "The Luck of Roaring Camp," "The Outcasts of Poker Flats," and "Tennessee's Partner," among others. While there, Harte had borrowed a twenty-dollar gold piece from Gillis, paying him back years later by making him the speaker of his famous poem, "The Heathen Chinee." The cabin had one great room, twenty feet long and ten feet wide, a packed-dirt floor, and a fireplace equipped with a shoulder-high mantel for ease of leaning. It also housed an extensive library containing works by Gillis's favorite authors, including Byron, Shakespeare, Bacon, and Dickens.

Twain had met Jim Gillis through Jim's brother Steve when Jim came to San Francisco in 1864 as a delegate to the Democratic State Convention. Then and later, Twain considered the elder Gillis one of his best friends. Each night in the cabin, he recalled, Gillis "would stand up before the great log fire, with his back to it and his hands crossed behind him, and deliver himself of an elaborate impromptu lie . . . with Dick Stoker as the hero of it, as a general thing." Among the stories Gillis told was one about a cat named Tom Quartz who had developed an understandable antipathy to quartz mining after being blown sky-high by a dynamite blast in a mine. "We lit the fuse 'n' clumb out 'n' got off 'bout fifty yards," Gillis recounted in dialect. "In 'bout a minute we seen a puff of smoke bust up out of the hole, 'n' then everything let go with an awful crash, 'n' about four million ton of rocks 'n' dirt 'n' smoke 'n' splinters shot up 'bout a mile an' a half into the air, an' by George, right in the dead center of it was old Tom Quartz a goin' end over end, an' a snortin' an' a sneez'n', an' a clawin' an' a reachin' for things like all possessed. . . . An' that was the last seen of *him* for about two minutes 'n' a half, an' then all of a sudden it begin to rain rocks and rubbage, an' directly he come down ker-whop about ten foot off f'm where we stood. Well, I reckon he was p'raps the orneriest lookin' beast you ever see."

Gillis's blown-up cat story would make it verbatim into *Roughing It*. Another Gillis story, about an industrious if rather misguided blue jay that dropped one acorn after another through a knothole in the cabin roof in a vain attempt to fill up the hole below, would reappear as "Baker's Blue-jay Yarn" in Mark Twain's 1880 European travelogue, *A Tramp Abroad*. A third story concerned a stripe-painted man, dubbed the "Royal Nonesuch," who crawled around naked with a lighted candle lodged tightly between his buttocks in front of fascinated, horrified frontier audiences. The "Royal Nonesuch" would reappear in a much expurgated version in *Adventures of Huckleberry Finn*, where it is the Duke who does the crawling. "I have used one of Jim's impromptu tales, which he called 'The Tragedy of the Burning Shame,'" Twain remembered ruefully. "I had to modify it considerably to make it proper for print and this was a great damage. As Jim told it, inventing it as he went along, I think it was one of the most outrageously funny things I have ever listened to.

How mild it is in the book and how pale; how extravagant and how gorgeous in its unprintable form!"

All in all, Twain judged Gillis to be a comic genius, who lacked only "a few years of training with a pen." Describing Gillis's inventive storytelling, he might well have been describing his own—which perhaps he was. "He had a bright and smart imagination," said Twain, "and it was of the kind that turns out impromptu work and does it well, does it with easy facility and without preparation, just builds a story as it goes along, careless of whither it is proceeding, enjoying each fresh fancy as it flashes from the brain and caring not at all whether the story shall ever end brilliantly and satisfactorily or shan't end at all."

It was fortunate that Gillis was such an entertaining storyteller, since there wasn't much else to do at Angel's Camp. The scattering of cabins contained a few prospectors and their families, but they were all dull as dirt to Twain, who had become accustomed to more refined company in San Francisco. The community, he complained, was "always in dire commotion about something or other of small consequence." When a neighboring family welcomed a new addition to its household, Twain groused: "The exciting topic of conversation in this sparse community just at present . . . is Mrs. Carrington's baby. . . . There was nothing remarkable about the baby, but if Mrs. C. had given birth to an ornamental cast-iron dog big enough for an embellishment for the State-House steps I don't believe the event would have created more intense interest in the community."

Somewhat more interesting—to a point, anyway—were the Daniels sisters, Molly and Nelly, who lived close by. Accompanied by Jim Gillis's younger brother Billy, Mark paid attendance to the girls, whom he dubbed "the Chaparral Quails" and who boasted "the slimmest waists, the largest bustles, and the stiffest starched petticoats in the whole locality." Twain walked out with Nelly, once returning her home so late that her mother accused him of attempting to seduce her daughter in a cow pasture. Perhaps he did, but for the most part he found her as tedious as the rest of his neighbors; he griped that the "damned girl [was] always reading novels like 'The Convict, Or The Conspirator's Daughter,' & going into ecstasies about them to her friends."

The quality of food was no better than the company. Twain and his messmates frequently repaired to "the Frenchman's," a local restaurant that served a somewhat limited menu of "beans and dishwater," along with four kinds of soup reserved for special occasions. These soups, apparently some variation on the local staple, chili, were named Hellfire, General Debility, Insanity, and Sudden Death. "It is not possible to describe them," Twain conceded. The Frenchman's beefsteak had the savor and consistency of a tapidero, the leather covering on a Mexican saddle stirrup. "No use, could not bite it," he noted. In desperation, Jim Gillis bought some green fruit from a local Indian woman. Dick Stoker warned him that the fruit was inedible, but Gillis "said that he had eaten it a thousand times; that all one needed to do was to boil it with a little sugar and there was nothing on the American continent that would compare with it for deliciousness." To Twain's vast amusement, Gillis proceeded to do just that, simmering the strange fruit for several hours and periodically tasting it with "fictitious satisfaction." One taste of the "vindictive acid" was all the others could stand, but Gillis "went on sipping and sipping and sipping, and praising and praising and praising and praising, until his teeth and tongue were raw, and Stoker and I nearly dead with gratitude and delight." Gillis couldn't eat or drink for the next two days.

In late January 1865, after a long siege indoors, the weather cleared up long enough for the men to leave the cabin and try some more mining at Angel's Camp. On January 25, at the Angel's Camp Hotel bar, Twain met Ben Coon III, a fellow riverboat pilot from Illinois who now occupied himself with tending bar. Years later, Twain recalled to Gillis "the one gleam of jollity that shot across our dismal sojourn in the rain & mud of Angel's Camp . . . that day we sat around the tavern stove & heard that chap [Ben Coon] tell about the frog & how they filled him with shot. . . . I jotted the story down in my notebook." The jotting, dated February 6, reads: "Coleman with his jumping frog—bet stranger $50—stranger had no frog, & C got him one—in the meantime stranger filled C's frog full of shot & he couldn't jump—the stranger's frog won."

From that brief and tentative seeding came a comic masterpiece that would win Mark Twain his first truly transcontinental fame, and four decades later he could still remember his initial exposure to the jumping frog story and the manner in which it was told. Ben Coon, said Twain, "was a dull person . . . he was entirely serious, for he was dealing with what to him were austere facts . . . he saw no humor in his tale." That was enough for Twain. "If I can write that story the way Ben Coon told it," he assured Billy Gillis, "that frog will jump around the world."

With comedic gold in his pocket, so to speak, Twain decided to return to San Francisco and resume his writing career. He and the others broke camp on February 20 and hiked over the mountains in a driving snowstorm, the first snow Twain had ever seen in California. Then, parting company with the prospectors, he borrowed a horse and rode another twelve miles to the "hell-fired" town of Copperopolis, so named for the giant Union Copper Mine. He toured the three-hundred-foot-deep mine, worth in excess of $1.2 million, but found his accommodations in the inevitably named Copper Hotel "damned poor." The next day he caught a stage for Stockton, pulling into San Francisco the following afternoon.

Checking into his favorite haunt, the Occidental Hotel (on credit—he would have to pay back the proprietor, Lewis Leland, a few months later), Twain found a three-month-old letter waiting for him from Artemus Ward, who was back in New York preparing a book on his recent travels, including a section on Nevada. Ward invited Twain to contribute a story to the book, and he suggested the jumping frog story. Ward responded immediately. "Write it," he urged. "There is still time to get into my volume of sketches. Send it to [George W.] Carleton, my publisher in New York."

For some reason—probably money—Twain delayed writing the frog piece. Instead, he produced three-thousand-word sketches for the *Territorial Enterprise* and the *Californian*, earning a few extra dollars and honing his talent for puncturing the pretentious, the foolish, and the dimwitted with a few judicious pricks of his pen. Answering his mail gave him ample exposure to all three categories of correspondents. In response to a New York minister who wondered whether he should take a pastoral position in San Francisco for a mere seven thousand dollars a year, Twain advised him to accept the offer at once, since "sinners are so thick that you can't throw out your line without hooking several of them" and "you can do such a land-office business." To a correspondent signing himself "Discarded Lover" and lamenting the fact his fiancée had married someone else "during my temporary absence at Benicia last week," the columnist offered the blithe consolation that the man was "to all intents and purposes a widower, because you have been deprived of [a] wife." He was also "a consummate ass for going to Benicia in the first place." Twain advised "Amateur Serenader" and his accompanists to tune their instruments three hundred yards away from their destination, since it would "astonish the dogs and cats out of their presence of mind, too, so that if you hurry you can get through before they have a chance to recover and interrupt you." Then they should "put up your dreadful instruments and go home." Oakland-based reader "Ambitious Learner" received a briefer response: "Yes, you are right—America was not discovered by Alexander Selkirk."

While Twain was busy going through his mail in San Francisco, the Civil War came to an end at Appomattox Courthouse, Virginia, when Robert E. Lee surrendered to Twain's old Marion Rangers bugbear, Ulysses S. Grant. Five days later, Abraham Lincoln was assassinated by John Wilkes Booth at Ford's Theatre in the nation's capital. Whatever his personal reaction was to those events, Twain kept his feelings to himself. In neither his public writing nor his private letters did he refer to the nearly simultaneous conclusion of the war and the death of the president who conducted it. As it had done for all Americans— northern, southern, or bordering—Lincoln's enormous hand had touched Twain's life personally, if indirectly. The war that Lincoln's election had impelled had ended Twain's career as a riverboat pilot, occasioned his brief inglorious career as a Confederate guerrilla, and driven him westward across the continent. The president's casual bestowal of political favor upon Twain's brother Orion had provided Orion with his greatest personal triumph as territorial secretary of Nevada, but Lincoln's insistence on hastening the territory into the Union before the 1864 presidential election effectively eliminated Orion's sinecure. Now, as abruptly as a passing tremor, the war was over, and Mark Twain was stuck again in San Francisco.

In June, making the best of the situation, Twain wrote two pieces for the juvenile publication *Youth's Companion*, "Advice for Good Little Boys" and "Advice for Good Little Girls." He had been nei-ther himself, whether by birth or by inclination, but he thought he could help. For the boys, he advised them "never to take anything that don't belong to you—if you can't carry it off," and "never tell a lie when the truth will answer just as well." They should resist the temptation to "do anything wicked and then lay it on your brother, when it is just as convenient to lay it on some other boy." Finally, they "ought never to knock your little sister down with a club. It is bet-ter to use a cat, which is soft." Good little girls should not take away their little brothers' chewing gum by force—"It is better to rope him in with the promise of the first two dollars and a half you find floating down the river on a grindstone. . . . In all ages of the world this eminently plausible fiction has lured the obtuse infant to financial ruin and disaster." When facing the need to correct their brothers "do not correct him with mud . . . because it will soil his clothes. It is better to scald him a little, for then you attain two desirable results—you secure his immediate attention to the lesson you are inculcating, and at the same time your hot water will have a tendency to remove impurities from his person—and possibly the skin also, in spots." He concluded his advice with what might well have served as his artistic credo: "Never sass old people—unless they sass you first."

Still, with the best of intentions, Twain couldn't seem to get the jumping frog story written. He finished two drafts, began a third—it wouldn't come. Then, as he remembered many years later: "One dismal afternoon as I lay on my hotel bed, completely nonplussed and about determined to inform Artemus [Ward] that I had nothing appropriate for his collection, a small voice began to make itself heard, 'Try me! Try me! Oh, please try me! Please do!' It was the poor little jumping frog . . . that old Ben Coon had described! Because of the insistence of its pleading and for want of a better subject, I immediately got up and wrote out the tale. . . . If it hadn't been for the little fellow's apparition in this strange fashion, I never would have written about him—at least not at that time."

The thought of writing to Ward gave Twain the idea of framing the story as a narrative within a narrative: what Twain is telling Ward, and what Ward's friend, Simon Wheeler, is telling Twain (and by extension the reader). The story itself isn't particularly groundbreaking—at least on the surface. Frontier storytellers had a long repertoire of yarns about city slickers getting outsmarted by canny pioneers. Twain's very first published story, "The Dandy Frightening the Squatter," had involved a would-be smart aleck getting his comeuppance at the hands of a backwoodsman. (He gets knocked into the river for his troubles.) The jumping frog story contains an ironic twist on the old standby. This time it is the local, Jim Smiley, who gets suckered by the city slicker, "a stranger in the camp," who fills Smiley's trick frog with quail shot so that he can't jump, and thus wins the bet.

What made the story hilarious for readers of the time, and what still gives it an important place in the history of American humor, is the way in which it is told. The de facto narrator, Simon Wheeler, is utterly matter-of-fact in both his approach and his affect. He is not trying to tell a joke or even a funny story, but merely to give a straightforward account of Jim Smiley and his frog. The humor comes from his absolute inability to tell the story straight. He works his way through an entire menagerie of Smiley animals, from horses to dogs to chickens to cats, before he even gets to the titular frog. Meanwhile, off camera, the actual narrator, Twain, is doing a comedic slow burn as he waits for Wheeler to get to the point.

Twain's masterstroke, modeled after Ward's style of faux naïf storytelling, is to keep an entirely straight face while recounting (or letting Simon Wheeler recount) a patently ridiculous story. Generations of American comedians—from Ward and Twain to Fred Allen, Robert Benchley, Jack Benny, and Woody Allen—have based their entire careers more on their deliveries than their punch lines. In extreme examples such as the infuriatingly transgressive Andy Kauffman, the "joke" is that there is no joke at all, which is a joke in itself if the listener is disposed to laughing at himself. It can all get to be rather circular.

Carleton sent the completed story to Ward's old friend Henry Clapp, editor of the *Saturday Press*. Clapp was well positioned to be Mark Twain's East Coast champion. For several years, he had functioned as ringleader for the motley circus of New York City bohemians who gathered nightly around a long table in Pfaff's beer cellar, an underground tavern located—appropriately enough—near Phineas

T. Barnum's American Museum on Broadway. With his short stature, high-pitched voice, grizzled beard, and ever-present clay pipe, Clapp looked a little like a down-on-his-luck leprechaun, albeit one of decidedly mixed heritage. Clapp, said a reporter for the New York *Leader*, was "a born Yankee; speaks French like a native; plays poker like a Western man; drinks like a fish, smokes like a Dutchman; is full of dainty conceits as a Spanish or Italian poet, is as rough in his manners as a Russian or a Russian bear."

At Pfaff's, Clapp presided over an ever-changing committee of actors, artists, journalists, short-story writers, and poets, chief among whom, in both talent and charisma, was Walt Whitman, whose poetry Clapp championed long before it was popular to do so. (Adah Isaacs Menken and Ada Clare were also regulars.) Clapp had been to Paris in the 1840s and witnessed the beginning of the bohemian movement, and upon his return to his native shores he became the movement's leading American proselytizer. He was famous for his wit—one of the reasons Carleton had sent him Twain's jumping frog story in the first place—describing fellow editor Horace Greeley as "a self-made man that worships his creator" and recommending that the United States Treasury change its motto from "In God We Trust" to "In Gold We Trust." One of his favorite bits of advice was "Never tell secrets to relatives. Blood will tell." Perhaps you had to be there.

Clapp, to his credit, immediately recognized Twain's piece as comedic gold. On November 16, 1865, he introduced the story, now titled "Jim Smiley and His Jumping Frog," to New York readers. With pardonable exaggeration regarding Twain's future involvement with the magazine, Clapp announced: "We give up the principal portion of our editorial space, today, to an exquisitely humorous sketch . . . by Mark Twain, who will shortly become a regular contributor to our columns." The response was rapturous. Richard Ogden, the New York correspondent for the San Francisco–based *Alta California*, captured the prevailing tone: "Mark Twain's story in the Saturday Press . . . has set all New York in a roar," Ogden wrote. "I have been asked fifty times about it and its author, and the papers are copying it far and near. It is voted the best thing of the day." Newspapers and magazines up and down the eastern seaboard picked up the story, which was published by Bret Harte in the *Californian* a few weeks later.

The only one not amused by the story, it seemed, was the author himself. "To think that after writing many an article a man might be excused for thinking tolerably good, those New York people should single out a villainous backwoods sketch to compliment me on!" Twain complained to his mother and sister. "I wish I was back there piloting up & down the river again." Mindful of Ward's earlier advice to "leave sage-brush obscurity" in the West and seek a broader audience back east, Twain fretted that his out-of-left-field literary triumph would typecast him as precisely that sort of regional humorist. A notice in the *New York Round Table* by Twain's old friend Charles Henry Webb, however well intentioned, must have underscored those fears. "The foremost of the merry men of the California press," wrote Webb, "is one who signs himself 'Mark Twain.' . . . If he will husband his resources and not kill with overwork the mental goose that has given us these golden eggs, he may one day take rank among the brightest of our wits."

Grudgingly and gradually, Twain accepted his fate. In an unusually frank and revealing letter to Orion on October 19, he acknowledged his destiny. After encouraging his brother's new-laid plan to take up preaching, Twain conceded that, with regard to himself, "I never had but two powerful ambitions in my life. One was to be a pilot, & the other a preacher of the gospel. I accomplished the one & failed the other, because I could not supply myself with the necessary stock in trade—i.e., religion." What he did have, Twain thought, was "a 'call' to literature, of a low order, i.e., humorous. It is nothing to be proud of, but it is my strongest suit." From now on, he pledged, he would "turn my attention to seriously scribbling to excite the laughter of God's creatures. Poor, pitiful business!" It calls to mind Mr. Bennet's rueful admission in *Pride and Prejudice*: "For what do we live, but to make sport for our neighbors and laugh at them in our turn?"

By this time, Orion was back to his old ways of failure and frustration, eking out a precarious living as a frontier lawyer in Carson City, a town not notably lacking in lawyers. In true Orion fashion, he had managed to lose both his position as territorial secretary and a very winnable election for Nevada secretary of state through what his exasperated brother termed "one of his spasms of virtue." Not only did he fail to campaign vigorously for election, said Twain, but Orion also sealed his electoral doom when "he suddenly changed from a friendly attitude toward whiskey—which was the popular attitude—to uncompromising teetotalism, and went absolutely dry. . . . He could not be persuaded to cross the threshold of a saloon." In hard-drinking Nevada that was a very unhelpful position to take, and Orion subsequently lost the Republican Party nomination for secretary of state to C. N. Noteware, who tallied forty-four votes to Orion's thirteen. (Twain, in his memoirs, claimed that Orion did not receive a single vote, but that was merely artistic license.)

Twain soon had another reason to be exasperated with his newly abstemious brother. In December 1865, a San Francisco businessman named Herman Camp, an old acquaintance from Virginia City, approached the author out of the blue with an offer to broker a deal for the long-fallow Tennessee land held jointly by the Clemens family. A colony of European winemakers, said Camp, was willing to buy the land for two hundred thousand dollars to establish a grape vineyard. It was not so wild a dream. Two decades earlier Twain's father had tested the land's wild grapes on a prominent Cincinnati winemaker, who thought they would make good Catawba wine. Eager to leave the West Coast and capitalize on his fifteen minutes of fame for "Jim Smiley and His Jumping Frog," Twain implored Orion to sign over his share of the land. Orion refused. He would not be a part of debauching the land for spirituous reasons, Orion said, causing Twain to note despairingly in his journal: "That worthless brother of mine, with his eternal cant about law & religion . . . sends me some prayers, as usual." Once again, Orion had opted for failure, and "the land, from being suddenly worth two hundred thousand dollars, became as suddenly worth what it was before—nothing, and taxes to pay."

Professing himself to be "tired of being a beggar . . . of being chained to this accursed homeless desert," Twain went back to journalistic hackwork with a vengeance. As usual, a favorite target was the local constabulary. In a piece for the *Golden Era*, "What Have the Police Been Doing?" in January 1866, Twain took up the case of an unnamed petty thief whose skull had been crushed by a prominent local merchant, Robert Ziele, in an alleged burglary attempt at his flour mill. The police had left the grievously injured man unattended in a jail cell overnight, where he had lapsed fatally into unconsciousness "with that calm serenity which is peculiar to men whose heads have been caved in with a club." The victim had died, said the columnist, "after four hours of refreshing slumber in that cell, with his skull actually split in twain from front to rear, like an apple." In the same wide-ranging article, Twain also criticized detective Captain Isaiah W. Lees for detailing four of his own men to nursemaid him for a month after he broke his leg, a move that cost the city five hundred dollars in officers' salaries. "Mark Twain is still on the war-path," noted the San Francisco *Examiner* approvingly. "He is after the San Francisco Policemen with a sharp stick."

Twain's criticism of the police was not particularly wise, given the fact that he was drinking heavily himself and hanging out in some of the lowest dives on the Barbary Coast. The same month that his article on police malfeasance appeared, the lawmen managed to exert themselves long enough to arrest one dangerous subject—Mark Twain—for public drunkenness. The arrest predictably attracted the malign attention of Twain's old bête noire, Albert S. Evans, alias

Fitz Smythe, who reported it with unconcealed glee in the Gold Hill *Daily News*. Twain, said Evans, had been arrested in the company of two "Pacific street jayhawkers"—prostitutes—and had thrown himself to the ground and forced the police to drag him off by his legs to the station. While being booked, said Evans, Twain had "cursed and indulged in obscene language," which given the circumstances was not unlikely.

Released without a fine the next morning by Justice of the Peace Alfred Barstow, an old acquaintance, Twain returned to his rented room at the home of Steve Gillis's father, Angus, on Minna Street. From there, he complained to the readers in the next issue of the *Enterprise* that "the air is full of lechery and rumors of lechery." It was indeed. Evans, fanning the flames, charged that Twain had lost forty dollars to the madam of a whorehouse "under peculiar circumstances," and even worse, that he "probably had a venereal disease." "I understand that he is disgusted with San Francisco," said Evans. "Well, my boy, that disgust is mutual." Twain, he continued, "has been a little out of health of late and is now endeavoring to get a chance to go to Honolulu, where he expects to get rid of one disease by catching another."

Evans was right about Twain's immediate ambitions, if not perhaps his underlying reasons. There is no evidence to suggest that Twain ever suffered from a sexually transmitted disease. He seems to have been, so far as can be guessed from a polite distance, unusually virtuous in that regard for a man of his extensive travel experience and unconventional job descriptions. Except for a passing remark to his sister-in-law Mollie about "sleeping with female servants," Twain seldom spoke openly about such matters, and never after he married a prim and proper eastern lady. The vast majority of his fictional women are either maidens or mothers—Becky Thatcher or Aunt Polly—and the longest-lasting infatuation of his life was for a "very little girl with a very large spirit," Laura Wright, who remained an avatar of purity and childish innocence even when, as an elderly mother and widow, she was borrowing money from him nearly fifty years later. It says a lot about his predilections that Twain's favorite character, of all his novels and stories, was Joan of Arc. Unlike many other Victorian-era men, his tastes did not oscillate between the Madonna and the Whore, but rather between the Madonna and the Saint.

But Twain really was trying to get to Hawaii, or the Sandwich Islands, as the chain then was known. In January 1866, the California Steam Navigation Company initiated a new route from San Francisco to Honolulu, 2,500 miles west-southwest across the Pacific. With its screw-propelled, two-thousand-ton flagship, the *Ajax*, leading the way, the company promised to trim the three-month travel time between California and the islands by fully two-thirds. The inaugural voyage had set sail on January 13 and Twain, in his position as San Francisco correspondent for the *Enterprise*, had been one of the fifty-three newsmen, politicians, and society mavens invited to go along. Unable to find a temporary replacement to write his daily column, he had watched sadly as the *Ajax* steamed off into the sunset without him. "Where could a man catch such another crowd together?" he lamented.

Stung by his failure to accept the navigation company's introductory offer, Twain went across the bay to Sacramento, which he described approvingly as "the City of Saloons," to change his luck. After trading quips with the proprietor of his hotel, who described Twain a little puzzlingly as the "young lunar caustic," the reporter made his way to the offices of the Sacramento *Daily Union*. There, with the assistance of mutual friend Charles Henry Webb, Twain convinced the paper's owners, James Anthony, Paul Morrill, and Henry W. Larkin, to underwrite his passage to Hawaii in return for a series of twenty-five or thirty travel letters to be written for the newspaper. "I am to remain there a month & ransack the islands, the great cataracts and volcanoes completely, & write twenty or thirty letters to the Sacramento Union—for which they pay me as much as I would get if I staid [*sic*] at home," Twain informed his family. "Goodbye for the present." He would spend four times that long in "luxurious vagrancy" in the islands, which would ever afterward linger in his memory as "the peacefullest, restfullest, sunniest, balmiest, dreamiest haven of refuge for a worn and weary spirit the surface of the earth can offer."

On the afternoon of March 7, he stood happily at the rail as the *Ajax* steamed out of San Francisco harbor, passed the Golden Gate, and struck the high seas. The *Ajax*, built but never used as a warship, was equipped with auxiliary sails for calm weather and contained accommodations for sixty passengers. It was Twain's first time to leave the American continent and, always a good traveler, he reveled in the experience. "We backed out of San Francisco at 4 P.M.," he reported, "some full of tender regrets for severed associations, others full of buoyant anticipations of a pleasant voyage and a revivifying change of scene, and yet others full of schemes for extending their business relations and making larger profits. The balance were full of whiskey." He had packed carefully for the trip, itemizing "a case of wine, a small assortment of medicinal liquors and brandy, several boxes of cigars, a bunch of matches, a fine-tooth comb and a cake of soap, and . . . a pair of socks." Going up to the hurricane deck, he sat down on a bench and spent the next hour "in that kind of labor which is such a luxury to the enlightened Christian—to wit, the labor of other people."

Matters spiritual and supernatural were much on his mind just then. The *Golden Era* that same month contained his sketch "Reflections on the Sabbath," in which he explained that he had not gone to church for many months because he had been unable to get a pew and had been forced to sit in the gallery among the sinners. This was particularly galling since he considered himself, by virtue of birth and upbringing, to be a sort of brevet Presbyterian himself. "My proper place was down among the elect," he complained, since he had been sprinkled in his infancy and thus conferred "the right to be punished as a Presbyterian," not subjected to the "heterodox hell of remorse of conscience of these blamed wildcat religions." It was his due, and he looked forward—after a fashion—to his reward. "The Presbyterian hell is all misery," he observed, "the heaven all happiness—nothing to do. But when a man dies on a wildcat basis, he will never rightly know hereafter which department he is in—but he will think he is in hell anyhow . . . because in the good place they pro-gress, pro-gress, pro-gress—study, study, study, all the time—and if that isn't hell I don't know what is."

On a less morally elevated level, Twain, before departing, had at-tended numerous séances in the city, many of them at the home of the celebrated medium Ada Hoyt Foye. He served on a self-appointed "investigating committee" for the paranormal, a board whose find-ings were somewhat undercut when one previously sanctioned spiri-tualist was bundled off to the insane asylum at Stockton. The incident did not turn Twain off all séances, however. "Such pleasant corpses," he said, "I find . . . better company than a good many live people." As for the slender, red-haired, good-looking Mrs. Foye, Twain reported attending one of her sessions along with four hundred other spiritual questers. She was "standing on a little stage behind a small deal table with slender legs and no drawers—the table, understand me." When a young German named Ohlendorff attempted to debunk her by trick-ing her into communing with a still-living spirit, Mrs. Foye, thinking quickly, attributed the confusion to a deceitful spirit of the sort which "were ready on the slightest pretext to rush in and assume anybody's name, and rap, and write, and lie, and swindle with a perfect looseness whenever they could rope in a living affinity like poor Ohlendorff to communicate with."

Now, on board the *Ajax*, Twain found himself communing with nature and observing the living, although the rampant seasickness of many of the travelers threw into doubt their continued membership in that company. At one point Twain tallied no less than twenty-two of his fellow passengers throwing up over the side of the ship, not counting a returning United States Army cavalry captain who never got out of bed and, presumably, the dwarf in cabin 2-G, whose attendance at railside was not otherwise noted. Although he had never sailed on anything broader, deeper, or stormier than the Mississippi River during a twister, Twain somehow avoided a bad dose of mal de mer. He did, however, come down with "something like mumps," possibly a urinary tract infection, which caused him to speculate that "I suppose I am to take a new disease to the Islands and depopulate them, as all white men have done before." All joking aside, the islands had indeed been decimated, if not entirely depopulated, by succeeding waves of European-borne diseases, beginning with the sailor's wan companion—syphilis—carried aboard English captain James Cook's arriving fleet in 1797. Cholera and bubonic plague destroyed half the native population in 1804, and thousands more fell victim to influenza, mumps, measles, whooping cough, diarrhea, and smallpox in the next half century.

Despite the weather, the *Ajax* made good time—three hundred miles a day—while Twain committed to memory some of his more colorful companions. Among the most interesting was a trio of "sea-worn old whaleship captains" who were going to Hawaii to rejoin their commands. The captains—James Smith, W. H. Phillips, and A. W. Fish—spent the voyage exuberantly playing euchre in the ship's smoking room (worthless cards, Twain learned, were called "blubbers") and consuming a remarkable nineteen gallons of whiskey among them "without being in the least affected by it," Twain observed, although he reckoned them "the happiest people I think I ever saw."

Less happy, perhaps, but even more colorful was another sea captain, also named James Smith, whom everyone called "the Old Admiral." The Admiral, who had begun his six-decade-long naval career as a cabin boy aboard an American privateer during the War of

1812, had commanded a whaler out of New London, Connecticut, and sailed clipper ships between San Francisco and Honolulu on the original dispatch line between the two ports. Unable to pull himself away from the sea, the Admiral had made a dozen more crossings to Hawaii as a private passenger in the two years since his retirement. "He was a roaring, terrific combination of wind and lightning and thunder, and earnest, whole-souled profanity," wrote Twain. "He was a raving, deafening, devastating typhoon, laying waste the cowering seas but with an unvexed refuge in the centre where all comers were safe and at rest." Invariably accompanied by his female terrier, Fan, the Admiral "was always ready for a political argument, and if nobody started one he would do it himself. . . . It got so, after a while, that whenever the Admiral approached, with politics in his eye, the passengers would drop out with quiet accord . . . and he would camp on a deserted field."

The on-board presence of so many captains underscored Hawaii's importance to the whaling industry. From the moment the first whale was taken off Hawaii in 1819, the islands had been a key refueling and resupplying center. Honolulu on Oahu and Lahaina on Maui became the busiest ports in the Pacific, and many native-born Hawaiians, or Kanakas, joined the whalers on their voyages. A fellow seaman in the 1840s favorably if racially assessed their fitness: "The Kanakas are large and well built men, as active as monkeys and make the best seamen," he said. "It is almost impossible to drown them. In time of a storm they will sport in the surf where a white man could not live for a minute. They will even attack and kill sharks in the water."

From a total of two hundred whalers in 1820, the industry increased 300 percent in ten years' time. Supporting industries of ship chandlery, repair, food supply, and prostitution sprang up on the welcoming green islands. Squadrons of missionaries, Protestant and Catholic, followed close behind, enraging the seamen by pressuring local chiefs to ban consensual contact between sailors and native women. One of the first missionaries was Vermont minister Hiram

Bingham, who took a decidedly dim view of his new flock. The native Hawaiians, he said, were devoted to a life of "unrighteousness, fornication, wickedness, murder, debate, deceit, malignity. They were whisperers, backbiters, haters of God, despiteful, proud, boasters, inventors of evil things, disobedient to parents, without natural affection, implacable, unmerciful." Thanks to such missionaries, a series of port regulations was instituted in Honolulu in 1844, including a two-dollar fine for "desecrating the Sabbath," a five-dollar fine for fornication, six dollars for drunkenness, thirty dollars for adultery, and fifty dollars for rape. Murder, adulterous or not, was a hanging offense.

By the time Mark Twain sailed for Hawaii in March 1866, whaling was a dying industry, done in by the discovery of oil in Pennsylvania in 1859 and the concomitant production of cheap, easily procured kerosene for Americans' reading lamps. Hawaiian agriculture, particularly sugarcane, boomed during the Civil War after the Union naval blockade cut off trade with sugar plantations in the South. In 1866 there were thirty-two prosperous plantations operating in the islands, and Twain, with figures provided by San Francisco Board of Brokers secretary N. Lombard Ingals, estimated the annual customs bill paid by Hawaiian merchants to total nearly $312,000 for sugar, coffee, molasses, salt, pork, and rice. "It is a matter of the utmost importance to the United States that her trade with the islands should be carefully fostered and augmented," observed Twain. "Because—it pays."

On the morning of March 18, Twain got his first look at Hawaii when the distant promontory of Diamond Head on the central island of Oahu wavered into view, bringing with it celestial glimpses of white beaches, coconuts, and palm trees. The *Ajax*, skimming over brilliantly clear blue waters, accompanied by a flock of seabirds and the occasional flying fish, ran up the American Stars and Stripes and the

Hawaiian national flag, a cosmopolitan mixture of English, French, and American influences—eight horizontal stripes of red, white, and blue representing the eight main islands of the group, with a miniature Union Jack in the upper left corner. Straight ahead lay the capital city of Honolulu, population fifteen thousand, which would be Twain's home base for the next four months.

Alighting from the ship with legs a little wobbly from the toss and swell of the voyage, the journalist immediately went exploring. From the very start he liked what he saw of the odd-looking tropical city. Trim white cottages with green shutters and front lawns as smoothly cropped as a billiard table lay scattered amid tall trees and mounds of fragrant flowers—"I had rather smell Honolulu at sunset than the old police courtroom in San Francisco," Twain joked. A confirmed cat lover from youth (notwithstanding his celebrated dosing of the family pet with painkiller, which he would reenact in *The Adventures of Tom Sawyer*), he saw "platoons of cats, companies of cats, regiments of cats, armies of cats, multitudes of cats, millions of cats . . . all of them sleek, fat, lazy, and sound asleep." He also saw, and approved of immensely, the island's contingent of human females, "long-haired, saddle-colored Sandwich Island maidens," sitting in the shade of houses or sweeping by on horseback, "free as the wind . . . with gaudy riding sashes streaming like banners behind them." Invariably clad in red or white sheaths, their long dark hair falling loose behind them, the native women had "comely features, fine black eyes, [and] rounded forms, inclining toward the voluptuous."

Twain was not the first prominent American writer to visit Honolulu and be awed by its beauty. Herman Melville made landfall there in April 1843 as a harpooner aboard the Nantucket whale ship *Charles and Henry*, and, after going AWOL, spent the next three months scraping out a precarious living amid the swarms of prostitutes servicing the sailors when they came ashore. (At one point, the future novelist worked improbably as a pin setter in a local bowling alley.) Melville, who liked missionaries even less than Twain, observed "a robust, red-faced missionary's spouse" being drawn through the streets in a two-man rickshaw. "Not until I visited Honolulu was I aware that natives had been civilized into draught horses," he wrote. "She bawls out Hookee! Hookee! (Pull! Pull!) and rap goes the heavy handle of her huge fan over the naked skull of the old savage, while the young one shies on one side and keeps beyond its range."

In their turn, authors Robert Louis Stevenson and Jack London would also pass time in Hawaii. The frail consumptive Stevenson would content himself with walking the beach in search of seashells, but the physical culture buff London would swim in the bay and spend several sunburned days attempting to master what he called the "royal sport" of surfing, which he described for American readers of *Cosmopolitan* magazine: "Straight on toward shore he flies on his winged heels and the white crest of the breaker. There is a wild burst of foam, a long tumultuous rushing sound as the breaker falls futile and spent on the beach . . . a sunburned, skin-peeling Mercury."

Twain went surfing himself, and the experience inspired him to write the first modern description of the natives' favorite recreation. Coming upon a large group of male and female Hawaiians while canoeing, Twain observed the sport closely: "Each heathen would paddle three or four hundred yards out to sea (taking a short board with him), then face the shore and wait for a particularly prodigious billow to come along; at the right moment he would fling his board upon its foamy crest and himself upon the board, and here he would come whizzing by like a bombshell!" Twain tried to hang ten, "but made a failure of it. I got the board placed right, and at the right moment, too; but missed the connection myself. The board struck the shore in three-quarters of a second, without any cargo, and I struck the bottom about the same time, with a couple of barrels of water in me." He figured wrongly, as future generations of Southern California surfers would prove, that only native-born Hawaiians could master the sport.

It was not all so idyllic. Like other tropical paradises, Honolulu swarmed with a wide variety of pests—insect, animal, and human. Mosquitoes, scorpions, tarantulas, cockroaches, lizards, and centipedes crawled the island, and the squeamish Twain shuddered to think of them. (A particularly horrible illustration in *Roughing It* shows the sleeping Twain with a three-foot-long centipede poised an inch from his face, "with forty-two legs on a side and every foot hot enough to burn a hole through a raw-hide.") Twain's imaginary friend "Mr. Brown" described two such incidents for Sacramento *Union* readers. The first involved a tourist named Mrs. Jones, who was stung on the cheek by a scorpion while washing her face with a sponge. "She felt something grab her cheek," said Brown. "She dropped the sponge and out popped a scorpion an inch and a half long! Well, she just got up and danced the Highland fling for two hours and a half . . . and for three days she soaked her cheek in brandy and salt, and it swelled up as big as your two fists." Another woman, Miss Boone, was out horseback riding when a centipede hiding in a stirrup "clamped himself around her foot and sunk his fangs plum through her shoe; and she just throwed her whole soul into one war whoop and then fainted. And she didn't get out of bed nor set that foot on the floor again for three weeks."

On the third day of his stay in Honolulu, Twain went looking for a horse of his own. Always a terrible horseman, he had not forgotten his misadventures aboard the yellow mule "Paint Brush" during his stint with the Marion Rangers, or his brief but expensive trial by fire on the "Genuine Mexican Plug" in Carson City. This time, the proprietor of the newly opened American Hotel, where Twain and other *Ajax* passengers took their meals, offered him his pick of the stable. "I preferred a safe horse to a fast one," Twain replied. "I would like to have an excessively gentle horse—a horse with no spirit whatever—a lame one, if he had such a thing."

Within five minutes he was mounted on a shambling nag he named "Oahu." Once again, the riding experience left much to be desired. "The first gate he came to he started in," Twain reported. "I had neither whip nor spur, and so I simply argued the case with him. He resisted argument, but ultimately yielded to insult and abuse." Within the next six hundred yards, the horse crossed the street fourteen times and tried to enter thirteen gates, while the journalist sweltered and sweated in the tropical sun, which was "threatening to cave the top of my head in." When the horse grew quiet, Twain was certain it was plotting more deviltry. "The more this thing preyed upon my mind the more uneasy I became, until the suspense became almost unbearable and I dismounted to see if there was anything wild in his eye." The horse was asleep.

Making peace, of a sort, with the animal, Twain toured the island. With his well-developed taste for the ghoulish—even in sunny Hawaii—he stopped in at the government prison on the southeast shore of Diamond Head. There he observed 132 prisoners sleeping in hammocks in roomy, breeze-cooled cells, "the pleasantest quarters in Honolulu." In one cell he came upon a condemned prisoner, "a brown-faced, gray-bearded old scalawag, who, in a frolicsome mood, had massacred three women and a batch of children—his own property, I believe." Another housed "a harmless old lunatic named Captain Tate" who was free to come and go as he pleased, regularly visiting his family in town but returning to prison to read sixty chapters of the Bible each day. A third inmate was "an aged, limping Negro man . . . as crazy as a loon," who called himself General George Washington. A pocket-sized Sampson, the heavily muscled prisoner was kept in shackles since "they have a hard time with him occasionally, and some time or other he will get in a lively way and eat up the garrison." Twain allowed that he did not believe the prisoner to be "the old original General W."

A mile and a half outside Honolulu, Twain visited the site of an ancient temple near the palace of King Kamehameha V, the ruling

Hawaiian monarch, who was fourth in line from the great warrior chief who had unified Hawaii at the turn of the century. Sixty-foot-high coconut trees and grass cottages ringed the temple, which had been constructed with rough blocks of lava. It was "an interesting ruin," Twain reported, "a place where human sacrifices were offered up in those old bygone days when a simple child of nature, yielding momentarily to sin when sorely tempted, acknowledged his error when calm reflection had shown it to him, and came forward with noble frankness and offered up his grandmother as an atoning sacrifice—in those old days when the luckless sinner could keep on cleansing his conscience and achieving periodical happiness as long as his relations held out."

The temple visit inspired Twain to reflect on the blessedly simpler times before the swarms of Christian missionaries had arrived in the islands to "make the natives permanently miserable by telling them how beautiful and how blissful a place heaven is, and how nearly impossible it is to get there." The missionaries had shown the native Hawaiian "how, in his ignorance, he had gone and fooled away all his kinfolks to no purpose; showed him what rapture it is to work all day long for fifty cents to buy food for the next day with, as compared with fishing for pastime and lolling in the shade through eternal summer, and eating of the bounty that nobody labored to provide but nature. How sad it is," Twain concluded, "to think of the multitudes who have gone to their graves in this beautiful island and never knew there was a hell!" Privately, he groused in his notebook that "more row [has been] made about saving these 60,000 people than [it] would take to convert hell itself."

Despite such metaphysical quibbles, he threw himself completely into the Hawaiian experience, touring the marketplace at Honolulu on a Saturday, when the Kanakas gathered to trade, feast, drink a "fearful" brew called awa that was said to cause "premature decrepitude," and watch the maidens dance the restricted hula (an 1859 ordinance required a ten-dollar fee and limited the dance to private

nighttime performances). Twain, as usual, noticed the "gingerbread-
colored" girls' loveliness and gave Sacramento *Union* readers a brief
but vivid description of the hula itself: "It was performed by a circle
of girls with no raiment on them to speak of, who went through with
an infinite variety of motions and figures without prompting, and yet
so true was their 'time,' and such perfect concert did they move that
when they were placed in a straight line, hands, arms, bodies, limbs,
and heads waved, swayed, gesticulated, bowed, stooped, whirled,
squirmed, twisted, and undulated as if they were part and particle of
a single individual; and it was difficult to believe they were not moved
in a body by some exquisite piece of mechanism."

Twain gamely sampled the local fares. The sour, oval-shaped
tamarinds—he called them "aggravated peanuts"—were a dental
nightmare that "sharpened my teeth like a razor, and put a wire edge
of them that I think likely will wear off when the enamel does." He
found Hawaiian bananas to be overrated, did not care much for
mangoes or guavas, and considered the local apples "as good as bad
turnips, but no better." He drew the line at eating poi, the gluey
paste made from taro plants that was the chief food staple of the
islands. It was, said Twain, "a villainous mixture . . . almost tasteless
before it ferments and too sour for a luxury afterward." He also objected to the way in which it was eaten communally. "The forefinger
is thrust into the mess and stirred quickly round several times and
drawn as quickly out, thickly coated, just as it were poulticed," he
noted, "the head is thrown back, the finger inserted in the mouth
and the poultice stripped off and swallowed—the eye closing gently,
meanwhile in a languid sort of ecstasy. Many a different finger goes
into the same bowl and many a different kind of dirt and shade and
quality of flavor is added to the virtues of its contents." An inveterate smoker, Twain was similarly unimpressed with the local cigars,
"trifling, insipid, tasteless, flavorless things they call 'Manilas'—ten
for twenty-five cents; and it would take a thousand to be worth half
the money. After you have smoked about thirty-five dollars worth of

them in a forenoon you feel nothing but a desperate yearning to go
out somewhere and take a smoke."

In late April and early May, Twain spent five blissful weeks touring
the wealthy sugar plantations on Maui. "It has been a perfect jubilee
to me in the way of pleasure," he gushed to his sister-in-law, Mollie.
"I have not written a single line, & have not once thought of business, or care, or human toil or trouble or sorrow or weariness. Few
such months come in a lifetime." One stop on his itinerary was mil-
lionaire James Makee's Rose Ranch, the largest sugar plantation in
the entire islands, which included several guest cottages, hundreds
of acres of lush, peacock-strutting gardens, a billiard room, tennis
court, and bowling alley complete with a small native boy manning
each pin. The sister of Twain's San Francisco friend, Charles Warren
Stoddard, had married into the Makee family, and Twain seems to
have entertained such ambitions himself, getting out of his sickbed
to play cribbage all night with an unnamed heiress for whom he had
conceived a "considerable weakness. . . . If I were worth even $5,000
I would try to marry that plantation—but as it is, I resign myself to a
long & useful bachelordom as cheerfully as I may."

During his stay on Maui, Twain and his party picnicked in the Iao
Valley, "a romantic gorge" shaded by perpendicular, three-thousand-
foot walls and swathed in "passing shreds of cloud." From the
heights of the extinct Haleakala volcano, Twain beheld with a certain
wistfulness his possible dowry—a broad valley shaped like "an ample
checker-board, its velvety green sugar plantations alternating with
dun squares of barrenness and groves of trees diminished to mossy
tufts." The picnickers amused themselves by rolling barrel-sized
boulders down into the "vacant stomach" of the volcano. The sunrise
the next morning, said Twain, was "the sublimest spectacle I ever
witnessed, and I think the memory of it will remain with me always."

While on Maui, Twain also made the unwelcome acquaintance of the latest in a long line of outrageous tall-tale tellers, Francis A. Oudinot. A deputy sheriff by profession, the Kentucky-born Oudinot claimed direct descent from Charles Nicolas Oudinot, one of Napoleon's marshals, and on French national holidays he paraded about the island in a glittering French uniform, flourishing the French tricolor. Renamed "Markiss" in *Roughing It*, Oudinot seemingly turns up everywhere Twain happens to be, boring his listeners to tears with one improbable story after another. In one story, his buggy horse Margaretta outruns a thunderstorm for eighteen miles, and "not one single drop of rain fell on me . . . but my dog was a-swimming behind the wagon all the way." In another, a California acquaintance named Godfrey drills a hole for a mining blast and is literally blown sky-high. "Well, sir, he kept on going up in the air higher and higher, till he didn't look any bigger than a boy," says Markiss, "and he kept going on up higher and higher, till he didn't look any bigger than a doll—and he kept on going up higher and higher, till he didn't look any bigger than a little small bee—and then he went out of sight!" Presently, Godfrey reverses the journey, from bee to doll to boy to full-sized man, and even though he was only gone for sixteen minutes, the mining company docks him for the lost time.

Years later, said Twain, Markiss hanged himself inside his locked bedroom, leaving behind a suicide note in his own handwriting. A local jury, accustomed as it was to the man's colossal lying, refused to believe he was dead simply because he said he was, but after a week they returned a verdict of "suicide induced by mental aberration," reasoning that he would never have told the truth if he had been in his right mind. (The real Oudinot was still alive when Twain wrote his book, allowing one the infrequent satisfaction of turning the tables on the master and declaring that Twain's account of Oudinot's death was "an exaggeration.")

Twain returned to Oahu in time to witness the state funeral of King Kamehameha's sister and heir, Princess Victoria Kamamalu Kaahumanu, who allegedly had died of a botched abortion—her seventh—on May 29, 1866, at the age of twenty-seven. Contradicting her public image as a pious convert to Christianity, the unmarried if somewhat less than virginal princess was said to have kept a harem of "thirty-six splendidly built young native men" for her private recreation, and "it had been her pride and boast that she kept the whole of them busy, and that several times it had happened that more than one of them had been able to charge overtime."

In keeping with Hawaiian custom, the princess lay in state for thirty days before the funeral, clothed in white satin and resting upon the traditional yellow-feathered war cloak worn by previous monarchs. Large crowds of mourners gathered on the palace grounds and "made the place a pandemonium every night with their howlings and wailings, beating of tom-toms and dancing of the (at other times) forbidden *hula-hula* by half-clad maidens to the music of songs of questionable decency chanted in honor of the deceased." Twain, who always liked a good show, went to the funeral and recorded the two-mile-long procession down Nuuanu Street from the royal palace to the royal mausoleum, beginning with the undertaker and concluding with the "Hawaiian population generally." Along with the flower-draped carriages, brightly uniformed riders, and regiments of black-clad women swaying beneath funereal umbrellas came a row of servants carrying four or five of the late princess's poodles. "All the Christianity the Hawaiians could absorb would never be sufficient to wean them from their almost idolatrous affection for dogs," Twain remarked. "And these dogs, as a general thing, are the smallest, meanest, and most spiritless, homely, and contemptible of their species."

From Oahu, Twain sailed to the great island of Hawaii, 150 miles to the south, aboard the packet schooner *Emeline*, which he renamed the *Boomerang*. The ship was so small, said Twain, that he felt like the Colossus of Rhodes when he stood on deck. There the native

Hawaiians sprawled about like the former captives of a southern slave ship, smoking, eating, and picking fleas off each other. Below deck was even more crowded, and Twain's cabin was "rather larger than a hearse, and as dark as a vault. It had two coffins on each side—I mean two bunks." Sleep was out of the question, particularly after he was awakened by a rat running across his face. "Lazarus did not come out of his sepulcher with a more cheerful alacrity than I did out of mine," Twain wrote. Next came a pair of cockroaches as large as peach leaves, "fellows with long, quivering antennae and fiery malignant eyes. They were grating their teeth like tobacco worms, and appeared to be dissatisfied about something." Having heard that the insects were in the habit "of eating off sleeping sailors' toenails down to the quick," Twain stayed awake for the remainder of the voyage, while "a party of fleas were throwing double somersaults about my person . . . and taking a bite every time they struck. I was beginning to feel really annoyed."

Landing at the village of Kailua, on the western shore of the Big Island, "tired of hanging on by teeth and toenails," Twain rode horseback through the Kona coffee district to Kealakekua Bay, the site of English captain James Cook's death on February 14, 1779. The journalist had little sympathy for the explorer, judging Cook's killing by islanders to have been justifiable homicide. "Wherever he went among the islands," said Twain, Cook "was cordially received and welcomed by the inhabitants, and his ships lavishly supplied with all manner of food. He returned these kindnesses with insult and ill-treatment."

Cook had first visited Hawaii a year earlier, when he "discovered" the islands accidentally while searching for the fabled Northwest Passage from Europe to China. Landing on the penultimate western island of Kauai, Cook and his men spent several weeks touring the archipelago, which they dubbed the Sandwich Islands in honor of Cook's chief patron, English naval lord John Montague, the fourth Earl of Sandwich. Twain typically found Cook's choice of names to be wanting, saying the explorer should have called them the Rainbow Islands instead. Believing the light-skinned Cook to be the physical manifestation of the agricultural god Lono, the Hawaiians thronged the flagship *Resolution*. "It was not possible to keep the women out of the ship," Cook recorded, "and no women I ever met with were more ready to bestow their favors. Indeed it appeared to me that they came with no other view."

The festive mood turned ugly when Cook returned a few months later. After natives stole the ship's cutter during the night, the captain led a force of ten marines onto the beach at Kealakekua to recover the vessel. Apparently confusing Cook's seizure of the local chief as part of a ritual mock battle, the islanders pelted the Englishmen with stones. The sailors returned fire, killing one man and infuriating thousands of others. Cook and four of his men were clubbed to death in the shallows of the bay, and the next day a kahuna, or chief priest, returned Cook's severed hands, scalp, skull (minus lower jaw), thigh, and arm bones—nine pounds' worth, according to Twain. It had all been a great misunderstanding, the kahuna said. Twain, touring the fatal area, passed a rock-enclosed barbecue pit that he said marked "the spot where Cook's flesh was stripped from his bones and burned; but this is not properly a monument, since it was erected by the natives themselves, and less to do honor to the circumnavigator than for the sake of convenience in roasting him."

Cook's demise notwithstanding, the undoubted highlight of Twain's visit to the Big Island was his hair-raising tour of Kilauea volcano on the side of fourteen-thousand-foot-high Mauna Loa mountain. Kilauea, the world's most active volcano, has been erupting regularly for at least three hundred thousand years (continuously since 1983). Accompanied by an exasperated Englishman named Howard, whom Twain persisted in calling "Brown" after his imaginary companion, the journalist arrived at Volcano House, a newly opened hotel comprised of twenty thatched cottages. "The surprise of finding a good hotel in such an outlandish spot startled me considerably more than the volcano did," Twain wrote to his family. (The hotel owners, glad for the free publicity, gave him his room free of charge, and Twain returned the favor by noting in the Sacramento *Union* that the hotel was "neat, roomy, well furnished and well kept.")

At the lookout point half a mile above the hotel, Twain got his first look into the boiling crater, which "glowed like a muffled torch and stretched upward to a dizzy height." It put him in mind of the wandering children of Israel, led ever onward by a "pillar of fire" in the sky above them. "I turned to see the effect on the balance of the company," Twain reported, "and found the reddest-faced set of men I almost ever saw. In the strong light every countenance glowed like red-hot iron, every shoulder was suffused with crimson and shaded rearward into dingy, shapeless obscurity! The place below looked like the infernal regions and these men like half-cooled devils just come up on a furlough." The smell of sulfur was strong, he noted, "but not unpleasant to a sinner."

The next night, Twain hiked down the twisting, thousand-foot-long pathway to the crater floor. The floor was hot to the feet, and the native guides refused to venture out onto the lava. A fellow American in the company, Charles W. Marlette of Jacksonville, Illinois, who had visited the volcano at least four times before, offered to lead Twain across the hissing surface. Skipping and jumping from rock to rock, the pair headed toward the north face of the crater. "By and by Marlette shouted 'Stop!' I never stopped quicker in my life," Twain remembered. "I asked what the matter was. He said we were out of the path . . . surrounded with beds of rotten lava through which we could easily break and plunge down a thousand feet. I thought eight hundred would answer for me, and was about to say so when Marlette partly proved his statement by accidentally crushing through and disappearing to his arm-pits."

The resourceful Marlette extricated himself and led them safely across, feeling his way in the glowing dark. Eventually the pair reached the northern shelf, where "stretching away before us was a heavy sea of molten fire of seemingly limitless extent." The glare from the lava flow was so bright that it was like looking into the noonday sun, Twain recalled, and from time to time a bubble would burst, releasing a pale-green trail of vapor—"some released soul soaring homeward from captivity with the damned." Having read of an eruption in 1840 that spewed lava for forty miles across a five-mile-wide swathe that was visible a hundred miles out to the sea, Twain did not tarry long at the bottom. He climbed out of the pit, damned or not, and returned by horseback and *Boomerang* to Honolulu, where the greatest scoop of his journalistic career was about to fall, almost literally, into his lap.

CHAPTER 7

THE TROUBLE BEGINS

ORN OUT FROM ALL HIS VOLCANO CLIMBING, island hopping, and horseback riding, Twain took to his bed at the American Hotel with a bad case of saddle sores. He was nearly expiring from boredom—the only book in the hotel library was a copy of Oliver Wendell Holmes's poetry—when he received an unexpected invitation to call on American diplomat Anson Burlingame, minister to China for the Andrew Johnson administration. Burlingame, a bluff, barrel-shaped, muttonchopped former Republican congressman from Massachusetts, had first won fame ten years earlier, in the summer of 1856, when he accepted a challenge to fight a duel with South Carolina congressman Preston Brooks in the aftermath of Brooks's savage attack on Senator Charles Sumner on the floor of the Senate. A crack shot, Burlingame had offered to meet Brooks at Niagara Falls, New York, for a shootout with rifles at fifty paces. Brooks declined.

An antislavery activist and former Know-Nothing, Burlingame was the very embodiment of what Twain would name indelibly the Gilded Age. A Boston Back Bay lawyer and a strong proponent of the annexation of Hawaii (and anywhere else the United States could extend its coils), Burlingame was en route back to China with his teenage son Edward. Accompanying them to his own Far Eastern posting in Japan was Brigadier General Robert B. Van Valkenburgh, who had commanded the 107th New York Regiment at Antietam, the bloodiest single day in American history, while Samuel Clemens was unconcernedly hitchhiking his way to Virginia City to begin his journalistic career on the *Territorial Enterprise*.

Throwing on a loose-fitting pair of canvas pants, the only trousers he could bear to put on in his present state, Twain took a buggy to the home of the American minister to Hawaii, where Burlingame and his companions were staying during their layover. The trio complimented Twain on his writing—never a bad start with the habitually self-doubting author—and the younger Burlingame recited, apparently from memory, Twain's jumping frog story. He had never been able to successfully deliver the story himself, Twain said smoothly, returning the compliment, and a paternalistic Ambassador Burlingame gave the author a well-meaning piece of advice. "You have great ability; I believe you have genius," Burlingame said. "What you need now is refinement of association. Seek companionship among men of superior intellect and character. Refine yourself and your work. Never affiliate with inferiors; always climb." It was an admonishment Twain would take to heart and follow, virtually to the letter, for the next forty-four years.

Flattered by the diplomat's attention, Twain soon had an even better reason to be glad of Burlingame's largesse. On June 16, while he was still recuperating from his Kilauea exertions, Twain learned along with the rest of the islands of a remarkable occurrence: the landfall on the southern coast of Hawaii the day before of a handful of skeletal shipwreck survivors. Captain Josiah A. Mitchell, twelve crew members, and a pair of passengers from the ill-fated clipper *Hornet* had been at sea for forty-three harrowing days in a fifteen-foot-long lifeboat when they came ashore at the village of Laupahoehoe on the Big Island, two hundred miles south of Honolulu, on the morning of June 15. Their endurance feat was a single-boat record, seven hundred miles and two days longer than the famous voyage completed by English captain William Bligh and eighteen sailors following the mutiny on the *Bounty* in 1789. (Eight surviving members of the whale-smashed vessel *Essex*, the source of Herman Melville's novel *Moby-Dick*, used two lifeboats to sail forty-five hundred miles in ninety-five days in 1820. They also ate several black crewmen and one white cabin boy during their ordeal—something the survivors of the *Hornet* managed to avoid doing by making landfall in the nick of time.)

The *Hornet*'s ordeal began on the morning of May 3, when the ship was one thousand miles due west of the Galapagos Islands in the North Pacific. En route from New York to San Francisco around Cape Horn, the ship had enjoyed such good weather that Captain Mitchell, a forty-three-year-old skipper from Casco Bay, Maine, worried that it was a sign of looming bad luck. He was right. At 7 A.M., a cataclysmic fire erupted belowdecks after a sailor accidentally dropped a lighted lantern on an open barrel of varnish. Within moments the fire spread through the hold, up the stairs, and onto the mainmasts and rigging.

Grabbing what little they could in the face of imminent immolation, the captain, twenty-eight crewmen, and two private passengers scrambled into three lifeboats and set out across the eerily empty ocean. The nearest land was twelve hundred miles north, Clarion Island in the Revillagigedo chain off the western coast of Mexico. With only ten days' rations, the castaways were soon reduced to eating their boots, shoelaces, pieces of wood, strips of canvas, cotton shirts, silk handkerchiefs, and plugs of tobacco. The occasional flying fish that fell into the boat was painstakingly divided into fifteen tiny portions and devoured in seconds. Water was doled out in sips, one in the morning and one at night. Two of the lifeboats drifted away and were lost; mutinous mutterings filled the third. The survivors were less than a day away from drawing straws to kill and eat the loser of the lottery when they sighted the reef-ringed shoreline at Laupahoe-hoe. With the help of heroic villagers who swam out to the boat and guided it through the shallows, they made it ashore.

News of the rescue raced up and down the islands. A few days later, eleven of the surviving crewmen were transferred to the hospital in Honolulu. Twain, still laid up in his own personal hospital room at the American Hotel, sensed a scoop, if only he could get to the men first. Burlingame came to his rescue, arranging for the journalist to be carried by stretcher to the crewmen's ward on June 25. There they located the *Hornet*'s erstwhile third mate, John Sidney Thomas, a "very cool and self-possessed" twenty-four-year-old sailor from Richmond, Maine. While Burlingame asked the questions, Twain carefully took down Thomas's answers in longhand. Thomas talked for three hours. When he was finished, Twain rapidly composed a three-column news story for the Sacramento *Union*, working through the night and just managing (in his retelling, anyway) to toss the heavy package onto a departing mail ship as it was pulling out of Honolulu harbor.

Three weeks and two days later—the time it took the steamer to beat eastward to San Francisco against prevailing headwinds—Twain had his first worldwide scoop. His relatively unvarnished account, written quickly and without any inappropriate humorous flourishes, read like a standard Victorian-era "men against the sea" tale, complete with misty-eyed moral uplift of the sort Twain usually scorned in his writing. Intentionally or not, he omitted any mention of the festering mutiny stoked by French crewman Harry Morris, who ridiculously believed that Captain Mitchell had secreted a million dollars' worth of gold coins in a hole beneath his bench. Instead, Twain's article had nothing but praise for the captain, or "the old man," as he repeatedly identified him.

Always careful with details—he was an inveterate list maker— Twain gave readers a vivid rundown of the men's paltry supplies: "Four hams, seven pieces of salt pork (each piece weighted about four pounds), one box of raisins, one hundred pounds of bread (about one barrel), twelve two-pound cans of oysters, clams, and assorted meats; six buckets of raw potatoes (which rotted so fast they got but little benefit from them), a keg with four pounds of butter in it, twelve gallons of water in a forty-gallon tierce or 'scuttle butt,' four one-gallon demijohns full of water, three bottles of brandy, the property of passengers; some pipes, matches, and a hundred pounds of tobacco."

He was less forthcoming, indeed misleading, about the dramatic parting of the three lifeboats on the eighteenth and twenty-first days of the journey. Mitchell had decided that the boats, until then joined together with towlines, had a better chance of survival if they separated, since they could make better time unconstrained by each other. It was a decision of "magnanimity and utter unselfishness," Twain wrote. "The boats were all cast loose from each other," he said, "and then, as friends part from friends whom they expect to meet no more in life, all hands hailed with a fervent 'God bless you, boys; goodbye!' and the two cherished sails drifted away and disappeared from the longing gaze that followed them so sorrowfully."

It was a touching scene of stiff upper lips and comradely care, but it was almost completely false. The sixteen men in the two smaller quarter boats depended on Mitchell's lifeboat to tow them, as well as the captain's superior navigating skills. Second mate John H. Parr, commanding the smallest boat, flatly refused to cut his line. "Why me?" he demanded. First mate Samuel Hardy offered to go, but only if Parr would exchange boats and give him Parr's compass. "I'll see you in Frisco, Captain," Hardy called. Three days later, Mitchell cut loose from Parr's boat as well, but only after the second mate and his companions had attempted to climb into the larger vessel and had been held off by knives and drawn revolvers. As they pulled away, the men in Mitchell's boat could hear their shipmates screaming furiously after them.

Despite—or because of—its inconsistencies, Twain was convinced that his *Hornet* story would make him famous. "The interest of this story is unquenchable," he wrote. "It is of the sort that time cannot decay, for by some subtle law all tragic human experiences gain in pathos by the perspective of time." Twain personally followed his dispatch back to San Francisco three weeks later, sailing out of Honolulu aboard the Pacific clipper *Smyrniote* on July 19, the same day that his account appeared on the front page of the Sacramento *Union*.

Although still plagued by "a devilish saddle boil," Twain took advantage of the three-week-long crossing to become better acquainted with Captain Mitchell and two of the other *Hornet* survivors, brothers Henry and Samuel Ferguson, whose vivid memories of the ordeal he transcribed into his notebook for use in a longer magazine article he hoped to write after reaching shore. He promised Henry Ferguson that he would leave out any "sensational matter" in his follow-up article, but that agreement would remain very much in doubt. With the ship becalmed in the glassy sea seventeen hundred miles offshore, there was little else for Twain to do—scarcely even a seagull or dolphin to see. The tedium was almost enough to bring Twain back to Jesus, a reconversion that his pious shipmate, the Reverend Franklin S. Riding, attempted manfully to effect. It didn't take; the most Twain would do was to agree to lead the ship's ad hoc choir. The only hymn he knew was "Oh, Refresh Us," which he gamely sang at the beginning and end of the shipboard service. "I hope they will have a better opinion of our music in heaven than I have down here," Twain noted in his journal. "If they don't a thunderbolt will knock this vessel endways." One way or another, the ship survived both the singing and the doldrums.

The *Smyrniote* docked in San Francisco on August 13, and Twain took his leave of Mitchell and the Ferguson brothers. The elder brother, Samuel, had embarked upon the voyage on the *Hornet* as a last-ditch attempt to recover from a fatal case of tuberculosis. In a mordant irony that Twain would have appreciated, had he been aware of Samuel's diagnosis, the twenty-eight-year-old sufferer died in California seven weeks later, having survived one of the worst ordeals in maritime history, only to fall prey to the almost gentlemanly "white death" of tuberculosis before he could make it back home to Stamford, Connecticut.

Twain, for his part, was "home again, no—*not* home again—in prison again," as he groaned in his notebook, "and all the wild sense of freedom gone. The city seems so cramped, & so dreary with toil and care & business anxiety. God help me, I wish I were at sea again!" In his present penurious state that wasn't an option, so Twain went across the bay to Sacramento to present the bill for his Hawaii services to the editors of the *Daily Union*. To his grateful amazement, James Anthony and Paul Morrill agreed to pay him three times the going rate for the *Hornet* scoop, some $100 a column, along with $20 apiece for the twenty-six Hawaiian dispatches. The editors were "the best men that ever owned a newspaper," Twain declared feelingly.

His Hawaiian earnings were not sufficient to live on for very long, so Twain immediately set to work rewriting and expanding his account of the *Hornet* disaster into a lengthy article for *Harper's Weekly* magazine. With the advantage of the Fergusons' journals, which he quoted verbatim for long stretches of the article, Twain added new details about the men's ordeal, including their pitiful efforts to augment their diet by capturing and eating various flying fish, turtles, and seabirds. He also included a frank if brief discussion of the incipient mutiny in the lifeboat, which he termed "a murderous discontent" and ascribed to the men's being "wild with hunger . . . in a manner insane." Twain admitted that the Fergusons had wanted to "improve" their journals before publication, but held to his professional opinion that they did not need improving; Samuel's account, in particular, was "as interesting to me as a novel." Nor did he honor their wishes "that I should leave out all mention of the conspiracy from their published journals." Four decades later, when he came to rework the *Hornet* tragedy in yet another magazine article, Twain did agree—with notable ill humor—to remove the rebellious crewmen's names before reprinting the article in book form, following an angry letter from Henry Ferguson, now an Episcopal minister and college professor. "You should have edited those things out if you didn't want them left in," the author grumbled, but he made the changes Henry requested.

The *Harper's Weekly* article did not have all the impact that Twain expected, partly due to the fact that his name was misprinted in the magazine's table of contents as "Mark Swain." As an old printer himself, he was philosophical about the typo. "I was a Literary Person," he shrugged, "but a buried one; buried alive." Once again, he pondered what to do next. He had a standing offer from Anson Burlingame to tour China as an official visitor, should he choose to travel to the Far East when the inaugural China Mail Steamer left San Francisco in December. Or, like his friendly competitor Bret Harte, he could concentrate his energies in the opposite direction and try to write for the elite literary magazines of Boston and New York. He even briefly considered, but rejected, the notion of returning to the Mississippi, now that the Civil War was over. When his old Hannibal schoolmate and fellow pilot Will Bowen wrote to suggest that alternative, Twain admitted that he had been thinking about it. "You bet your life I do," he told Bowen. "It is about the only thing I'd feel any interest in & yet I can hear least about it. If I were two years younger, I would come back & learn the river over again. But it is too late now. I am too lazy for 14-day trips—too fond of running all night & sleeping all day—too fond of sloshing around, talking with people."

As usual, his brother was no help. Following his defeat for Nevada secretary of state, Orion had drifted out of politics altogether and gone to the Excelsior mining district in northern California to practice law and act as a mining agent—both professions for which he was spectacularly unqualified. Twain had received a letter while en route to Hawaii apprising him of Orion's new career arc, and he had no confidence in either of them working out. "That worthless brother of mine, with his eternal cant about religion and law, [is] getting ready, in his slow, stupid way, to go to Excelsior, instead of the States," Twain confided to his journal. "He sends me some prayers, as usual."

Another letter, this one from Orion's wife, Mollie, had reached Twain in Hawaii, beseeching him to come back home. After urging her to return to Missouri without him, Twain brought up the still-touchy topic of the family's Tennessee land. "It is Orion's duty to attend to that land, and after shutting me out of my attempt to sell it (for which I shall never entirely forgive him) if he lets it be sold for taxes, all his religion will not wipe out the sin," he wrote. "It is no use to quote Scripture to me, Mollie—I am in poverty and exile now because of Orion's religious scruples. Religion and poverty cannot go together."

Having thus discounted the teachings of Christ, at least with regard to his own future plans, Twain apparently tried to convince Orion to follow just such a path. In a stormy meeting with his brother in San Francisco in late August, Twain again urged Orion to become a preacher. Orion, as usual, rejected the advice. Like his father before him, he was still convinced that he could sell the Tennessee land for a huge profit. "Bitter and malignant," Twain refused to join him on the fool's errand. "Orion would make a preacher," Twain told relatives after the meeting, "but he won't touch it. I am utterly and completely disgusted with a member of the family who *could* carry out my old ambition and won't." With money raised from the sale of their twelve thousand dollar home in Carson City, typically at a two-thirds loss, Orion and Mollie sailed for New York City on August 30, 1866. They had sold everything they owned, with the poignant exception of their late daughter Jennie's little chair, which they took with them when they left Nevada. Orion's western adventure was over.

Twain's own adventure still had a few more chapters to go. He fiddled with some short pieces for the Sacramento *Union* and the *Californian* and briefly considered compiling his Hawaiian dispatches into a travel book, going so far as to draft a dedication to his mother praising her "exquisite appreciation of the Good & the Beautiful," while also noting dryly that "she marches over the most elaborately humorous jokes with the tranquil indifference of a blind man treading among flowers." Some time in late September he began seriously discussing with friends a new venture: a public lecture on Hawaii that would capitalize on his current status as "about the best-known honest man on the Pacific coast." Bret Harte and Charles Warren Stoddard, among others, advised against it, saying the talk would damage Twain's "literary reputation"—such as it was. But editors George Barnes at the *Call* and John McComb at the *Alta California* encouraged the idea. Twain, they said, should "take the largest house in town, and charge a dollar a ticket" for the privilege of hearing him speak.

Thus encouraged, Twain went to see the owner of said establishment, Thomas Maguire, the self-proclaimed "Napoleon of the San Francisco stage." Maguire, a transplanted Irishman from the slums of New York City, had worked as a bartender and cabdriver before going into business for himself as an entertainment impresario. During the previous decade he had opened three successively named Jenny Lind Theaters, although the Swedish-born singer herself had no personal or professional connection to any of them. The first two theaters burned down, possibly for the insurance money, and Maguire sold the third to the city of San Francisco for two hundred thousand dollars in a deal that was so overtly shady it became known as the "Jenny

Lind Swindle" or "Jenny Lind Juggle" and brought down the administration of Mayor David C. Broderick.

Landing on his feet, the politically agile Broderick went on to win election to the United States Senate, only to be killed in a duel with political opponent David S. Terry in October 1859. "They have killed me because I was opposed to the extension of slavery and a corrupt administration," Broderick gasped on his death bed. Terry was later shot and killed by a bodyguard of Supreme Court justice Stephen J. Field after attacking that worthy with a knife. For his part in the juggle, Maguire was banished from San Francisco for life, but returned three years later to open Maguire's Opera House. In 1864 he opened the even more resplendent Academy of Music on Pine Street, and it was the latter establishment that Maguire offered to rent to Twain for fifty dollars—half the usual rate—and a share of the profits, if there were any. The night of Tuesday, October 2, was reserved for Twain's public coming-out party.

With three days left before his address, Twain professed himself "the most distressed and frightened party on the Pacific coast." He worked feverishly on what would become an eighty-five-page, ninety-minute-long lecture, shaping his Hawaii travel letters into an artfully artless performance piece complete with carefully practiced stumbles, stutters, blank-outs, and pauses, à la Artemus Ward. He would call the talk "The Sandwich Islands," later refined to "Our Fellow Savages in the Sandwich Islands."

To seed the ground, Twain spent $150 to print and publish handbills advertising his appearance. The ad itself was a classic example of Twainian wit, its blaring, eye-catching headlines immediately undercut by the fine print: "A SPLENDID ORCHESTRA / Is in town, but has not been engaged. A DEN OF FEROCIOUS WILD BEASTS / Will be on exhibit in the next block. MAGNIFICENT FIREWORKS / Were in contemplation for this occasion, but the idea has been abandoned. A GRAND TORCHLIGHT PROCESSION / May be expected; in fact the public are privileged to expect whatever they please." The ad concluded with a snapper that would become a Twain trademark and a staple of performers well into the vaudeville era, which Twain's success before the footlights would do much to create: "Doors open at 7 o'clock. The trouble will begin at 8."

Twain's foray onto the public stage was not as unlikely as it may have seemed to some of his San Francisco friends. Encouraged by his yarn-spinning, innately theatrical mother, he had been fascinated from early childhood by performers of all types—preachers, politicians, actors, singers, Jim Crow dancers, blackface minstrels, low and high comedians. The middle decades of the nineteenth century saw an explosion of traveling lecturers in the United States thanks to the lyceum movement, an autodidactic effort that catered to the hunger for knowledge of a self-educating populace. Spellbinding speakers such as Henry Ward Beecher, William Lloyd Garrison, Susan B. Anthony, Julia Ward Howe, Frederick Douglass, Wendell Phillips, Anna Dickinson, and Thomas Wentworth Higginson, many sprung from the antislavery movement of the 1850s, mixed with an eclectic tribe of wandering divines, faith healers, spirit knockers, temperance lecturers, abstinence promoters, health food advocates, foreign traveloguists, and outright charlatans to entertain and enlighten audiences from New England to California. If anything, the West was even hungrier for such showmen than the East, as hardworking miners, farmers, and cowboys sought to alleviate their lonely, drudging lives with a few hours' diversion at the local theater. As Artemus Ward and Adah Isaacs Menken had demonstrated personally to Twain in Virginia City, a seasoned performer could make good money on the speaking circuit. All he needed was the right act.

Nor was Twain the rank amateur he later claimed to be. One way or another, he had been talking all his life—in fact, it was usually hard to shut him up. He loved to tell stories, and he had learned how to craft and present a crowd-pleasing yarn from such natural-born performers as his mother, Missouri slave Uncle Dan'l, Mississippi River pilot Horace Bixby, Calaveras County raconteur Jim Gillis, and Bay

Area boulevardier Bret Harte. During his time in Carson City, he had served as "governor" of the Third House, an informal gathering of journalists and politicians who regularly met to spoof the territorial legislature's latest idiocies and indiscretions, and he had made scattered speeches from Keokuk to Honolulu. Most recently, on his boisterous tour of the Hawaiian Islands, Twain had seemed so effusive and ebullient, so wildly gesticulating, that many of the local residents thought he was either crazy or drunk. Sometimes, perhaps, he was both.

Whatever his background, training, and inclination, it amused Twain (and still amuses readers) to present himself in the days prior to his stage debut as a panic-stricken tyro. "As those three days of suspense dragged by, I grew more and more unhappy," he wrote. "I had sold two hundred tickets among my personal friends, but I feared they might not come. My lecture, which had seemed 'humorous' to me, at first, grew steadily more and more dreary, till not a vestige of fun seemed left, and I grieved that I could not bring a coffin on the stage and turn the thing into a funeral." As a hedge against such a sepulchral service, he recruited several "stormy-voiced" journalist friends, including John McComb of the *Alta California* and Joe Goodman of the *Enterprise*, to sit in the front row and laugh uproariously at his witticisms. Bret Harte and another claque of confederates planned to station themselves at strategic locations around the hall to further salt the crowd, and Mrs. Mollie Low, wife of current California governor Frederick Low, was placed in an overhanging box to the left of the stage, with instructions to laugh prettily whenever Twain signaled her to do so with a glance.

The local newspapers helped pump up attendance for the speech, printing items (probably ghostwritten by Twain) reporting that he was planning to perform the Hawaiian Hornpipe or "war dance" at his lecture. The *Californian* laughingly pooh-poohed the report, saying that he had trained for the dance, but had collapsed from overexertion while slimming down to a sufficient fighting weight. It was also reported that Twain's imaginary friend, Mr. Brown, would "sing a refrain in the Kanaka tongue." The *Alta California* assured readers that Twain would give a "high-toned" speech, as long as he remembered to speak loudly enough to be heard. On the day of the speech, the San Francisco *Dramatic Chronicle* headlined the "Sensational Rumor" that Twain had been so overcome by stage fright over his impending appearance that he had "secreted himself in the baggage room of the Occidental, with the intention of taking the 4 o'clock boat today, and making his escape to Sacramento." A follow-up report announced that "Mark has been secured and has, after the administration of one dozen bottles of Mrs. Winslow's soothing syrup, become reconciled to the situation. He will positively appear, but holds the public responsible."

On the afternoon of the speech, Twain went down to the theater to get ready for his debut. He was aghast—or claimed to be—when he found the box office closed. "'No sales,' I said to myself. 'I might have known it.'" While standing glumly on the sidewalk contemplating suicide, feigned illness, or flight, Twain ran into a Wells, Fargo driver and volunteer fireman named Bill Slason, whose obituary a few years later would credit him with being "of a jolly, rollicking, boisterous nature, whose love for a joke was only exceeded by a fondness for rye." Openly exhibiting all these tendencies, Slason asked Twain for a complimentary ticket. Renaming him "Sawyer" in *Roughing It* and making him sound very much like Tom Sawyer's ragamuffin partner, Huck Finn, Twain quoted Slason as saying: "You don't know me, but that don't matter. I haven't got a cent, but if you know how bad I wanted to laugh, you'd give me a ticket." After a quick test of Slason's laugh, Twain agreed, adding the fireman to the list of conspirators and giving him "minute instructions about how to detect indistinct jokes."

Arrangements complete, Twain entered the Academy of Music and, if his later account is to be believed, spent the next hour and a half wandering around backstage in the quivering throes of full-on stage fright. "I stumbled my way in the dark among the ranks of canvas scenery, and stood on the stage," he wrote. "The house was gloomy and silent, and its emptiness depressing . . . for an hour and a half [I] gave myself up to the horrors, wholly unconscious of everything else." He hadn't eaten for three days, Twain said—"I only suffered." No doubt he was in some suspense about his reception—even the most seasoned actor is nervous before a performance—but it is also likely that Twain exaggerated his case of the willies. He liked an audience, whether it was one person or one thousand, and he could expect to see many friendly faces in the forest of backlit heads. Whatever the case, he fiddled and fretted in a world of his own until he heard something that made his hair stand on end—the steady stamping of the audience. "Before I well knew what I was about, I was in the middle of the stage, staring at a sea of faces, bewildered by the fierce glare of the lights, and quaking in every limb with a terror that seemed like to take my life away." The trouble, as he had promised, had begun.

No true transcript of the speech survives. Years later, heartily sick of the Hawaiian lecture, Twain burned all his notes. As can best be reconstructed, he simply sauntered onto the stage from the wings, his hands stuffed into his pockets and a sheaf of papers clutched under his arm. He wandered vaguely around the lectern for a bit, looking for the most comfortable place to stand, and then appeared to notice the audience for the first time, the expression on his face registering an equal mixture of surprise, perplexity, and fear. For a long moment he looked silently at the audience while it looked back at him, waiting. "My chief allies, with three auxiliaries, were at hand, in the parquette," he recalled in *Roughing It*, were "all sitting together, all armed with bludgeons, and all ready to make an onslaught upon the feeblest joke that might show its head."

In his lifelong Missouri drawl, slowed down even further for maximum effect, Twain introduced himself: "Ladies and gentlemen, I have the pleasure of introducing to you Mr. Clemens, a gentleman whose numerous accomplishments, I may say, whose historical accuracy and high moral character are only surpassed by his natural modesty and sweetness of disposition." Parenthetically, he added, "I refer in these general terms to myself, for I am the party. I have always been opposed to ceremonious forms of introduction to an audience as being entirely unnecessary after a lecture has been advertised. I had rather introduce myself, because then I can rely on getting in all the facts." Until he reached such prominence that no formal introduction was necessary, he would hold steadfastly to the ploy, telling an audience in Wilmington, Delaware, that he found being introduced by someone else exquisitely embarrassing, since "it put him in mind of that member of his family who was hanged, and of what was said of the affair afterward—that the hanging went off very comfortably but the sheriff's speech was annoying."

Thanks to the uncanny impersonation of Twain by modern actor Hal Holbrook, who has been performing his one-man show, *Mark Twain Tonight*, for more than forty years, we can easily envision the writer onstage in San Francisco that night. Unlike Holbrook's carefully researched costuming, based mainly on Twain's later years, he was not yet wearing his trademark white suit or fiddling with an unlit cigar. His famous deadpan delivery, however, was already in place. Journalist Noah Brooks was in the crowd on opening night, and he recognized immediately that Twain's "method as a lecturer was distinctly unique and novel. His slow, deliberate drawl, the anxious and perturbed expression of his visage, the apparently painful effort with which he framed his sentences, and above all, the surprise that spread over his face when the audience roared with delight or rapturously applauded the finer passages of his word-painting, were unlike anything of the kind they had ever known. All this was original; it was Mark Twain."

Actually, a good bit of it was taken from Artemus Ward, with "some stretchers thrown in," as Twain would later say in another context. It was essentially Ward's country-bumpkin stage act, minus some of its broader cornpone effects, which would not have played well before a sophisticated San Francisco audience. After his self-introduction, Twain apologized for the absence of an orchestra, explaining that despite the setting at the Academy of Music, he wasn't accustomed to putting on an opera. He had engaged a trombone player for the evening, he said, but the man had insisted on having other musicians around to help him, and since Twain had "hired the man to work, and wouldn't stand for any such nonsense, [I] discharged him on the spot." Then, without further ado, he turned to his speech. "When in the course of human events," he began. He was off and running.

For the next ninety minutes, Twain regaled the audience with an alternately humorous and informative account of his visit to Hawaii. The islands, he said, were "composed of lava harder than any statement I have made for three months. There is not a spoonful of legitimate dirt in the whole group." When the islands were discovered by Captain Cook in 1778, Twain said, "The population was about 400,000, but the white man came and brought various complicated diseases, and education, and civilization, and all sorts of calamities, and consequently the population began to drop off with commendable activity." After it had dwindled down to 55,000 souls, it was "proposed to send a few more missionaries and finish them."

Despite their unhealthy exposure to white visitors, he said, the natives were "exceeding hospitable. . . . They will feast you on raw fish, with the scales on, cocoanuts, plantains, baked dogs and fricasseed cats." The Hawaiians were very fond of dogs, "not the great Newfoundland or the stately mastiff, but a species of little mean, contemptible cur, that a white man would condemn to death on general principles." Their bushy tails were the only attractive thing about such dogs, said Twain, adding that "a friend of mine said if he had one of these dogs he would cut off his tail and throw the rest of the dog away." The natives took great care of their dogs—then ate them. "I would rather go hungry for two days than devour an old personal friend in that way," said Twain, but he conceded that many white visitors had eaten "those puppies—and after all it is only our cherished American sausage with the mystery removed." As for the rumor that Hawaiians were cannibals, the speaker adamantly denied it, although he offered to demonstrate the practice on stage "if anyone in the audience would lend me an infant."

The islanders did have some odd customs, Twain conceded. For instance, "They will put a live chicken into hot ashes simply to see it hop about," and they put out an eye or knock out a tooth when a chief died. "If their grief was deep, and they could get relief in no other way, they would go out and scalp a neighbor," said Twain. "In the season of mourning for a great person they permit any crime that will best express sorrow." They used the same word—*aloha*—for "goodbye" and "how do you do." They mounted a horse from the off side, turned left instead of right, and beckoned for a person to approach by waving them away. "They have some customs we might import with advantage," Twain concluded. "I don't call any to mind just now."

Throughout the lecture, Twain studiously maintained a straight face. As he explained in his essay "How to Tell a Story," it was a question of manner over matter: "The humorous story depends for its effect upon the manner of the telling. . . . The humorous story is told gravely; the teller does his best to conceal the fact that he even dimly suspects that there is anything funny about it. . . . Artemus Ward used that trick a good deal; then when the belated audience presently caught the joke he would look up with innocent surprise, as if wondering what they had found to laugh at." At all times, said Twain, "the first virtue of a comedian is to do humorous things with

grave decorum and without seeming to know that they are funny."
That approach was only violated once, when he accidentally made eye
contact with Mrs. Governor Low in her hanging box. "In spite of all
I could do I smiled. She took it for the signal, and promptly delivered
a mellow laugh that touched off the whole audience; and the explosion that followed was the triumph of the evening. I thought that that
honest man Sawyer would choke himself; and as for the bludgeons,
they performed like pile-drivers. . . . All's well that ends well."

He left the stage to a storm of applause. For an encore—he had
none prepared—Twain graciously apologized for any "affliction" he
had forced the audience to endure. It had all been in the service of
a book he intended to write on the Sandwich Islands, he said—and
besides, he needed the money. In the end, he took in some $1,200 in
gate receipts, and after he paid off theater owner Tom Maguire and
the various newspapers, he netted about $400 cash. It was a hand-
some, if far from windfall, profit, and it set him on the path of an
alternate profession. "In October, 1866, I broke out as a lecturer,"
Twain would say later, "and from that day to this I have always been
able to gain my living without doing any work."

The reviews were gratifying. The *Evening Bulletin* raved that "as
a humorous writer Mark Twain stands in the foremost rank," and
the *Dramatic Chronicle* pronounced the lecture "one of the greatest successes of the season." The *Golden Era* caught the prevailing
mood: "We regard this subject with mingled admiration and awe,
and approach him with hesitation. Nature must have been in one of
her funniest moods when she fashioned this mixture of the sublime
and the ridiculous. Never did an aspirant for public favor take more
rapid strides than did the future historian of the Sandwich Islands."
Bret Harte, revealing perhaps the snarky competitiveness that would
underlay his future dealings with his former protégé, worried a little

about Twain's crudeness and coarseness, but judged him "more thoroughly American and national" than Artemus Ward or New England humorist James Russell Lowell. Twain, ever combative, took the broad view. While not addressing Harte specifically, he had some pointed words for the minority who were calling the performance "a bilk" and "a sell." "It's a free country," said Twain. "Everybody has a right to his opinion, if he is an ass. They have the consolation of abusing me, and I have the consolation of slapping my pocket and hearing the money jingle."

After exulting to his mother and sister that he had made "the most sweeping success of any man [I] know of," Twain was ready to take his act on the road. He needed a manager, and he located one in his former *Territorial Enterprise* colleague Denis McCarthy, now working in San Francisco as a stockbroker. Together, the two planned a nine-city swing through northern California and western Nevada— Twain's old stomping ground—commencing with a stop in Sacramento on October 11. They modified slightly the already famous flyer, promising attendees that "THE CELEBRATED BEARDED WOMAN! / Is not with this Circus; THE WONDERFUL COW WITH SIX LEGS! / Is not attached to this Menagerie; THE IRISH GIANT! / Who stands 9 feet 6 inches in height will not be present; and EDWIN FORREST! and EDWIN BOOTH! / Are compelled by circumstance to remain in New York." One man on the street refused to be humbugged by the ad. "I've seen Mark Twain and I know he can't play 'Richard the Third' or 'Richelieu' either," he told the Sacramento *Union*. "You can't get me there tonight." Others went to hear Twain at the Metropolitan Theater, reassured by the promise that although the evening's speaker was "familiar with the Kanaka tongue, he will tell his story in the best California English." The next day, the *Union* praised his "easy colloquial style [which] seasoned a large dish of genuine information with spicy anecdote."

From Sacramento, Twain and McCarthy (nicknamed for some reason "the Orphan") traveled by steamer up the Sacramento River to Marysville, a former boomtown that had fallen on hard times when the gold mines dried up. "It is a pity," said Twain, "to see such a town as this go down." He had barely gotten past "Ladies and gentlemen" when a rush of late-coming miners tramped into the town hall in their heavy boots and "settled down noisily in a clatter of knocked-over benches and a buzz of beery whispers." Twain, used to such a rough crowd from his own gold rush days, carried off the speech without a hitch and retired with his audience to the nearby Como brewery, which would later boast that its lager beer was "the best in the territory, as we can prove by Mark Twain, who has sat in the brewery and drank gallons and gallons of it without arising from his seat." Said an admiring contemporary, "Mark don't drink, except when his spirits are properly amalgamated with sugar, glass, lime, ice and a teaspoon."

The next stop on the itinerary was Grass Valley, thirty-five miles east by stagecoach. Unlike Marysville, Grass Valley was still producing gold, both mineral and animal—it was the home of actress Lola Montez and comedienne Lotta Crabtree, as well as future western historian Josiah Royce. Twain spoke to a standing-room-only crowd inside the town's Hamilton Hall, after first "preparing himself for a clear voice with a copious dose of gin and gum." Given the introduction he received from a notably ill-at-ease citizen, he might have wished for another drink. "Ladies and gentlemen," the introducer stammered, "this is the celebrated Mark Twain from the celebrated town of San Francisco, with his celebrated lecture about the celebrated Sandwich Islands." Following the lecture, Twain and McCarthy made the rounds at Stokes' Oyster Parlor and Ed McSorley's saloon, which advertised "winks understood at the bar" and pushed its hot whiskey punch as "the best spiritual consolation in town."

At Red Dog, appearing at a log cabin schoolhouse on October 24, Twain received another less than rousing introduction from a bulky miner dragooned into service at the last minute. "Ladies and gentlemen," said the miner with admirable honesty, "I shall not waste any unnecessary time in the introduction. I don't know anything about this man; at least I know only two things about him; one is that he has never been in the penitentiary, and the other is that I can't imagine why." Twain liked the introduction well enough to quote it verbatim the next night at nearby You Bet, where he offered to "repeat the unique and interesting feat" of leaving town without paying his hotel bill, an amusing trick he said he had performed "many hundreds of times, in San Francisco and elsewhere, which has always elicited the most enthusiastic comments."

A two-day stagecoach ride brought Twain back to Virginia City for his first return visit in almost three years. The *Daily Union*, still an enemy newspaper, warned readers that Twain was back in town. "Note the articles that are missing," it said, listing "silver spoons, old stoves, worn out amalgamating pans, anything smaller than a 40-stamp quartz mill." Alluding to one of Twain's earliest missteps, his gruesome hoax about the alleged "Dutch Nick's Massacre," the *Union* announced that following Twain's lecture "a grand tableau of the murdered Hopkins family will be given." Then, said the newspaper, Twain would perform the amazing feat of eating three fried eggs, a number of rolls, and a cup of coffee "all without speaking a word." The *Union* said it had heard of "wandering Bohemians" falling so low that they had become governors, congressmen, or senators, "but when one condescends to turn lecturer, well . . ."

Despite his less than valorous "absquatulation" in the spring of 1864, Twain still had many friends in Virginia City. Piper's Opera House was filled with more than eight hundred people, including his old *Enterprise* colleagues Joe Goodman, Dan De Quille, and Steve Gillis, still a fugitive from justice in San Francisco, when the curtain went up on October 31—Halloween night, appropriately enough. There, sitting at a piano, was Twain, lustily singing his familiar drinking song, "I Had an Old Horse Whose Name Was Methusalem." Apparently oblivious to his surroundings, he continued plinking away happily until something got his attention and he rose and wandered down to the foot of the stage, peering querulously through the smoky footlights at the shadows beyond. Something was out there! he realized with a start. It brought down the house.

Three days later Twain returned to the scene of another of his crimes, Carson City, where he had stirred up a hornet's nest of protest over his false miscegenation society report two and half years earlier. He was "mighty dubious" about returning to Carson City, he confessed, until he received a telegram signed by Nevada governor Henry G. Blasdel and several other leading citizens assuring him of "none other than the most kindly remembrances of you." Bygones were bygones. Twain wrote back immediately, promising to "disgorge a few lies and as much truth as I can pump out without damaging my constitution."

His appearance in Carson City on November 3 went off without a hitch, which was more than could be said for his lecture at Gold Hill a few days later. Hiking back to Virginia City in the dark with Denis McCarthy, Twain was suddenly accosted in an isolated gulch by half a dozen masked men flourishing revolvers. Two days earlier, a pair of stagecoaches had been held up nearby, and Twain expected the same treatment when he was ordered to put up his hands. "Throttle him! Gag him! Kill him!" one of the robbers shouted. The leader held his pistol to Twain's head while he ordered his accomplices, "Beauregard," "Stonewall Jackson," and "Phil Sheridan," to search the victim's pockets.

The famous names alone should have been enough to tip off Twain—it was Steve Gillis and some of his other friends playing a rough sort of Washoe joke on the illustrious visitor. The robbers made off with $125 in cash, a $300 gold watch, two jackknives, and three lead pencils, everything Twain had in his pockets. The victim later tried to downplay the incident, claiming that "I never had a thought that they would kill me . . . and so they did not really frighten me bad enough to make their enjoyment worth the trouble they had taken." Perhaps not, but one resident crowed that Twain "was the scaredest man west of the Mississippi," and the always antagonistic

Virginia City *Union* delightedly publicized the incident, conjecturing that the robbers had been "the departed spirits of the Hopkins family, whom Mark murdered (on paper) a short distance from Dutch Nick's." When Twain learned the truth, he abruptly canceled a second lecture in Virginia City, fired McCarthy (who was in on the joke), and returned to San Francisco on the next stage. "Since then I play no practical jokes on people and generally lose my temper when one is played upon me," he said, not altogether accurately—at least the first part.

Nursing a bad cold, which he attributed to being forced to stand with his hands over his head for fifteen minutes in the frosty night air at Gold Hill, Twain pondered what to do next. The lecture tour had gone well, fake holdup notwithstanding, but it was a lot of work and a lot of traveling for the money earned, a fact brought home forcibly to Twain when the local sheriff attached some of his earnings to cover various outstanding debts in Nevada and California, possibly including his two-year-old five-hundred-dollar bail bond for Steve Gillis. "Between the highwaymen and the police, Mark seems to be getting the worst of it these days," the Washoe *Evening Slope* noted sympathetically.

A second San Francisco lecture, at Platt's Hall on November 16, did not go over nearly as well as the first. The theater critic from the *Chronicle* complained that Twain apparently had been "alkalied in the savage wilds of Washoe, and had become a little demoralized." Worse than that, he had become "too familiar with his audience." The *Call* echoed the criticism, noting that "whether owing to native bashfulness"—not likely—"or the effect exercised upon his nerves by the late robbery in Nevada . . . the lecture became confused, facts and factiae intermixed." Harshest of all was the verdict of the *Daily Times* that "Mark Twain fulfilled his promise of perpetrating a robbery."

After a final swing around the bay for appearances at San Jose, Petaluma, and Oakland, where he endured small crowds, bad weather, scheduling conflicts, and an inexhaustible high school band that tooted away at maddening length while the speaker fumed and fretted in the wings, Twain announced plans for a farewell "benefit"—with himself as sole beneficiary—in San Francisco on December 10. He promised to revisit his first Hawaiian lecture, with newly added descriptions of the Kilauea and Haleakala volcanoes and many "uncommonly bad jokes." It would positively be his last local appearance, he swore, and he had already written an "impromptu farewell address" especially for the occasion.

The valediction, given at Congress Hall to "my friends and fellow-citizens," was heartfelt, even sentimental. "I have been treated with extreme kindness and cordiality by San Francisco," Twain told the audience, "and I wish to return my sincerest thanks and acknowledgements. . . . While I linger here upon the threshold of this, my new home, [I] say to you, my kindest and my truest friends, a warm good-bye and an honest peace and prosperity attend you." He predicted a brilliant future for his adopted city, stating that when "the clouds shall pass away from your firmament . . . a splendid prosperity shall descend like a glory upon the whole land."

Once again the reviewers were kind. Twain, said the *Evening Bulletin*, "departs with a brilliant reputation. Men of this sort never overstock the market, and Mark will find room for an honorable career in the field to which he is going." Added the *Daily Times*: "This popular lecturer has struck a new lead in literary research, and his multitudinous friends all hope that his prospects will pan out rich." The new lead, as reported in the *Alta California* five days later, involved Twain's assignment as the paper's roving travel correspondent, "not stinted as to time, place or direction—writing his weekly letters on such subjects and from such place as will best suit him."

The proposed itinerary was ambitious, to say the least: France, Italy, the Mediterranean, India, China, and Japan, and the *Alta* was confident that Twain's appointment would "give him a world-wide reputation." Twain took advantage of his new position to say good-bye publicly to his "highway-robber friends" from Gold Hill. "Good-bye, felons—good-bye," he jeered. "I bear you no malice. And I sincerely pray that when your cheerful career is closing, and you appear finally before a delighted and appreciative audience to be hanged, that you will be prepared to go, and that it will be a ray of sunshine amid the gathering blackness of your damning recollections, to call to mind that you never got a cent out of me. So long, brigands."

Privately, he wrote to his mother and family in St. Louis, inform-ing them of his travel plans and permitting himself some last-minute bragging. "I sail tomorrow," he announced, "leaving more friends behind me than any newspaper man that ever sailed out of the Golden Gate." Allowing for a little forgivable exaggeration, he was speaking the truth. He had come west as Sam Clemens, out-of-work riverboat pilot and (technically, at least) Confederate Army deserter. He was returning east as Mark Twain—increasingly renowned journalist, lecturer, and short story writer.

The next day he boarded the steamship *America*, bound for New York City by way of the isthmus of Nicaragua. There were 399 other passengers on board, including a fifteen-year-old runaway bride named Emma Bayer whose father attempted to remove her forcibly from both the ship and the insufferable clutches of her husband, only to be beaten back by her fellow shipmates, Twain included. Then the ship cast off, steaming southward down the California coast toward Mexico. Like other departing travelers at such moments, Twain grew reflective. With the late-afternoon sun slanting off the Pacific waves, he took stock of his now-concluded time in the West. "Thus, after seven years of vicissitudes, ended a 'pleasure trip' to the silver mines of Nevada which had originally been intended to occupy only three months," he recalled, before adding the carefully timed snapper: "However, I usually miss my calculations further than that."

SIVILIZED

MARK TWAIN'S RETURN TRIP EAST BY OCEAN steamer was considerably less pleasant than his stagecoach journey west five and a half years earlier. In fact, it was a stomach-churning ordeal, beginning with the first leg of the journey. *America* was beset by storms almost from the moment she lost sight of the California coast. By nightfall, she was fighting for her life through the worst tempest her captain, Edgar "Ned" Wakeman, had seen in the Pacific in many years. Water flooded the decks and holds; a case of wine and a man's boots floated away in six inches of backwash. Twain, confined to his cabin with an undefined illness (probably persistent diarrhea), avoided the worst of the deckside weather, which sent many of his fellow passengers dropping to their knees in abject prayer. Lifeboats were readied for emergency offloading, but the sea was too heavy to launch them. All anyone could do was ride out the storm. It was, said Twain with eloquent brevity, "a long, long night."

Worse was yet to come when they reached Nicaragua. Changing ships at Greytown after a twelve-mile horse and wagon journey across the isthmus aboard "the hellfiredest sorebacks in the world," Twain and the others boarded the *San Francisco*, a bad-luck steamer that already had broken down several times on her way to Central America and that would, in short order, turn into a literal plague ship. Hundreds of passengers coming the opposite way from New York had been stranded in port for weeks, awaiting transportation to California. While stuck in tropical, rain-soaked Nicaragua, many had come down with cholera, which spread inevitably to the new arrivals.

San Francisco had only been at sea for a day when Twain reported two cases of cholera among his shipmates. The outbreak spread rapidly, particularly in steerage, and dozens fell ill. In all, seven passengers died, including twenty-one-year-old barber Andrew Nolan whom Twain had nicknamed "Shape"; an infant girl named Harlan (no first name), who was buried at sea on Christmas Day; and Episcopal minister S. Michael Fackler of Boise City, Idaho, who had nursed the others tirelessly during their suffering before succumbing himself. The ship's doctor, a fellow Mason, confided to Twain that the disease was "cholera of the most virulent type" and that he had already run out of medicine. The report caused Twain to reflect—as well it might—that he himself could be dead tomorrow. The ship, he said, was "fast becoming a floating hospital."

After a fortuitous one-day stopover in Key West—Twain took advantage of the brief respite to stock up on the island's renowned Cuban-made cigars while the hard-pressed doctor replenished his medical supplies—the *San Francisco* turned north into the Gulf Stream and headed up the Atlantic coast to New York. With the advent of cooler temperatures, the number of sick fell from eighteen to thirteen to eight, and the weather beyond Cape Hatteras turned so cold that Twain stayed in bed much of the time. Spirits rose with the decrease in illness, and Twain, joining in the fun, soaked a banana in brandy and gave it to the company's pet monkey, which the women in the shipboard sewing society had dressed in black pants and vest and a cutaway coat trimmed with red and yellow cuffs. The monkey, which Twain promoted to correspondent for the *Nicaragua Transcript*, got satisfyingly "tight" on the concoction while the crowd in the smoking room capered and sang (no mention of whether the monkey joined in). Finally, on January 12, 1867, after twelve frequently hellish days at sea, the *San Francisco* made port in New York harbor.

The next morning, relieved and revived, Twain walked down the ice-encrusted gangplank and made his way to the Metropolitan Hotel on south Broadway. It was his first visit to the blizzard-stricken metropolis in thirteen years and much had changed, for both the city and himself, since he left the East "a pure and sinless sprout" in the spring of 1854. To begin with, it was more crowded and spread out, and the returning author found that he had to "walk the legs off [him]self" to get anywhere. It was also damnably cold, and a former newspaper colleague from San Francisco who bumped into Twain on the streets of Manhattan found him "shivering and chattering his teeth."

Undeterred, Twain trudged through the slushy streets of Soho for a meeting with Charles Henry Webb, his old editor at the *Californian*. Webb, who had returned to his bohemian haunts in New York after a contentious career on the West Coast, looked over Twain's clippings and suggested that they collaborate on a collection of Twain's western sketches, built around the celebrated jumping frog story. With Twain's permission—Webb promised to do most of the actual work—a meeting was set up with publisher George Carleton to finalize plans for the book. Much to the author's surprise, the choleric Carleton took one look at Twain's disreputable appearance and turned him down flatly, "swelling and swelling until he had reached the proportions of a god of about the second or third degree." His shelves were loaded down with books awaiting publication, Carleton said, and he did not want any more—not completely true, since he had recently agreed to publish a similar collection of Bret Harte's California sketches. Whatever the case, Carleton's brusque rejection was a professional misstep of such gargantuan proportions that the publisher would reintroduce himself to Twain, many years later, as "the prize ass of the nineteenth century."

Stepping into the breach, Webb offered to publish and market the book himself, in return for 90 percent of the profits. Twain agreed. He had already fixed his eyes on a new endeavor, another sea voyage and packet of letters similar to those he had produced in Hawaii. This time around, he was looking even further afield. The Plymouth Congregational Church, home to flamboyant minister Henry Ward Beecher, was sponsoring a five-month cruise to Europe, the Mediterranean, and the Middle East, ostensibly to enable Beecher to complete his research for a biography of Jesus Christ. Several other prominent Americans, including Civil War general William Tecumseh Sherman, Massachusetts congressman Nathaniel Banks, and Broadway actress Maggie Mitchell, were on the prospective passenger list.

Twain went on a fact-finding mission to Beecher's church in Brooklyn, where he paid close attention to the minister's charismatic stage presence. "He forsook his notes and went marching up and down his stage," Twain informed readers of the *Alta California*, "swaying his arms in the air, hurling sarcasms this way and that, discharging rockets of poetry, and exploding mines of eloquence, halting now and then to stamp his foot three times succession to emphasize a point." Fighting back an urge to applaud in sheer admiration, the newly fledged lecturer watched the veteran evangelist at work. Beecher, said Twain, had "a rich, resonant voice, and a distinct enunciation, and made himself heard all over the church without very apparent effort. . . . [P]oetry, pathos, humor, satire and eloquent declamation were happily blended."

Perhaps seeing a little of himself in the minister, Twain added: "Mr. Beecher is a remarkably handsome man when he is in the full tide of sermonizing, and his face is lit up with animation, but he is as homely as a singed cat when he isn't doing anything." That wasn't often. When Beecher wasn't busy exhorting, he was cutting a secret but extensive swathe through the female half of his congregation. A few years later, his sexual transgressions would come to light in the most celebrated adultery trial in American history, but for the time being Beecher's indiscretions were entirely sub rosa. Twain, for his part, had seen enough. "Send me $1,200 at once," he wired his editors at the *Alta California*. "I want to go abroad."

Introducing himself to the leader of the expedition, Captain Charles Duncan, as "the Reverend Mark Twain, Baptist minister and Sandwich Islands missionary," Twain booked passage on the aptly named *Quaker City*, a 1,428-ton former Union Navy supply ship. "You don't look like a Baptist minister," Duncan observed shrewdly, "and really, Mr. Clemens, you don't smell like one either." For such a tireless advocate of alcoholic abstinence, Twain thought, Duncan seemed to be a pretty good judge of secondhand whiskey, but the writer sheepishly confessed his real identity and made a $125 down payment for a private stateroom. On June 10, after weeks of delays and the bowing out of virtually the entire star-studded roster of fellow travelers—Beecher, Sherman, Banks, and Mitchell all found better things to do with their time—the *Quaker City* finally steamed out of New York harbor. Mark Twain and five or six dozen other comparative innocents (estimates vary—on numbers, not innocence) went abroad.

Once again, Twain's restless nature served him well. The subsequent twenty-three weeks he spent touring and scoffing at the various cultural, religious, artistic, and architectural wonders of the Old World gave him both the inspiration and the raw material for *The Innocents Abroad*, his first great publishing success and the biggest-selling book in the United States since Harriet Beecher Stowe's *Uncle Tom's Cabin* seventeen years earlier. (Stowe, coincidentally, was Henry Ward Beecher's sister.) Besides finding, as it were, *The Innocents Abroad*, Twain also found a girl—or rather, he found the girl's brother, and then he found the girl. Her name was Olivia Louise Langdon—Livy to her wealthy Elmira, New York, family—and she was to be the love of his life. Had he not gone on the voyage to the Holy Land, Twain would never have met fellow pilgrim Charley Langdon on the trip and so discovered, in a cameo photograph of Langdon's exceedingly proper and well-brought-up sister, his future wife. His career most likely would have mirrored that of his recently deceased drinking companion Artemus Ward—a one-man Chautauqua show (minus the religious overtones) lived out in smoky lecture halls, clattering railroad stations, seedy hotel rooms, and raucous late-night bars.

Instead, much to the wonderment of his western friends, Mark Twain set about rehabilitating himself (or at least the frontier version of himself) in the single-minded interests of winning the girl. He dutifully requested letters of recommendation from various respectable West Coast acquaintances, particularly the ministers he had met in San Francisco. The character references he got back were so universally bad—"I would rather bury a daughter of mine than have her marry such a fellow," one respondent wrote—that Livy's good-natured father, Jervis Langdon, actually took pity on her dejected suitor and gave the couple his blessing. He also gave them a fully furnished mansion in Buffalo as a surprise wedding gift and, when he died unexpectedly of stomach cancer six months later, a quarter-million-dollar legacy. Livy Langdon, Twain assured his old Hannibal friend Will Bowen, was "the most perfect gem of womankind that ever I saw in my life—& I will stand by that remark till I die." Against all odds, he would prove as good as his word.

The couple was married in the flower-filled parlor of the Langdon home on the evening of February 2, 1870. The officiating minister was Thomas K. Beecher, the family's pastor and the half-brother—

small world—of Henry Ward Beecher. Afterward, the wedding party ate boned turkey and drank appropriately nonalcoholic cider. At the housewarming in Buffalo the next day, they sang the old Congregationalist hymn "Heaven Is My Home," which was only fitting since that would be the couple's approximate address for the next two decades, before the encroaching shadows of debt and death began to shroud "the great dark" of Twain's latter years.

The unlikely marriage of the hard-knock humorist from backwoods Missouri and the fragile, stay-at-home heiress from upstate New York worked surprisingly well. Twain showed the previously sheltered Livy the world; she in turn "sivilized" him, toning down the worst of his inveterate clowning. For the next thirty-four years, in good times and bad, the couple presented a unified front, a model mid-Victorian marriage blessed with three spirited daughters and innumerable cats, Twain's favorite billiards companions, even if he occasionally crammed them—the cats, not the girls—into a corner pocket for fun. Meanwhile, the contentedly housebroken author produced the remarkable stream of novels, short stories, essays, and travel pieces that today stands as one of the great bodies of work in English literature. The first book he completed after his marriage was *Roughing It*, a sunny and expansive account of his cross-country stagecoach trip with his brother Orion a decade earlier and his subsequent adventures in the raw and rollicking West. In it, as Huckleberry Finn would say of his creator in another context a few years later, he told the truth mainly, with some stretchers thrown in. "That ain't no matter," says the ever-forgiving Huck. "I never seen anybody but lied, one time or another." It went with the territory.

NOTE ON SOURCES

Befitting his extraordinarily eventful life, Mark Twain has never lacked for biographers, beginning with himself. *Roughing It*, published in 1872, is the touchstone for his western adventures; and the annotated 1993 edition published by the University of California Press is, as it states on its cover, "the authoritative text." Anyone studying this seminal period of Twain's life owes a sincere debt of gratitude to the editors of the project—Harriet Elinor Smith and Edgar Marquess Branch. The same goes for the various editors of *Mark Twain's Letters*, also published by the University of California Press, who have allowed us to see the author plain and unvarnished, without the whitewash added to the fence.

Twain's various autobiographical reminiscences, both fiction and nonfiction, continue to amuse and inform—if not always with complete factual accuracy. *The Autobiography of Mark Twain*, edited by Charles Neider in 1959, brought some much-needed chronological order to Twain's intentionally disordered remembrances, which contain patches of the author's best and most heartfelt writing. And no one can go wrong by reading Twain's lovingly rendered *Life on the Mississippi* for an example of a marvelous writer writing at the top of his powers.

The first official biography of Twain, a massive, three-volume work by his friend and amanuensis Albert Bigelow Paine, appeared in 1912. Paine's biography is crucial for its unrivaled access to the subject himself, although scholars have been continually frustrated by Paine's tendency to gloss over and at times conceal unflattering aspects of his subject's life. Justin Kaplan's Pulitzer Prize–winning 1966 biography, *Mr. Clemens and Mark Twain*, which begins at the exact moment that Twain leaves San Francisco and returns to the East, is a wonderfully written and entertaining account of the second half of Twain's life. More recent and equally entertaining biographies include Fred Kaplan's *The Singular Mark Twain* (2003) and Ron Powers's *Mark Twain: A Life* (2006). *Mark Twain A to Z*, by R. Kent Rasmussen, is a comprehensive and enlightening encyclopedia of Twainian lore.

Specialized studies of Twain's early life and career include *Sam Clemens of Hannibal*, by Dixon Wecter; *Mark Twain, Business Man*, by Charles Webster; *Dangerous Water: A Biography of the Boy Who Became Mark Twain*, by Ron Powers; and *Mark Twain and Orion Clemens: Brothers, Partners, Strangers*, by Philip Ashley Fanning. Previously published studies of Twain's western experience—none completely comprehensive—include *Mark Twain's Western Years*, by Ivan Benson; *Mark Twain in Nevada*, by Effie Mona Mack; *Mark Twain in Virginia City*, by Paul Fatout; *The Sagebrush Bohemian: Mark Twain in California*, by Nigey Lennon; and George Williams III's idiosyncratic trilogy, *Mark Twain: His Adventures at Aurora and Mono Lake; Mark Twain: His Life in Virginia City, Nevada*; and *Mark Twain and the Jumping Frog of Calaveras County*.

General studies of the West useful in writing this book include *Desert Between the Mountains: Mormons, Miners, Padres, Mountain Men, and the Opening of the Great Basin, 1772–1869*, by Michael

S. Durham; *The Plains Across: The Overland Emigrants and the Trans-Mississippi West, 1840–60*, by John D. Unruh, Jr.; and *Star-Spangled Eden: 19th Century America Through the Eyes of Dickens, Wilde, Frances Trollope, Frank Harris, and Other British Travelers*, by James C. Simmons.

Invaluable collections of Twain's early journalism include *Mark Twain of the Enterprise*, edited by Henry Nash Smith; *Clemens of the Call*, edited by Edgar M. Branch; and *Mark Twain's Letters from Hawaii*, edited by A. Grove Day. *Mark Twain: Unsanctified Newspaper Reporter*, by James E. Caron, is a good recent study of Mark Twain the budding journalist, and Joseph E. Coulombe's *Mark Twain and the American West* insightfully considers how Twain manipulated his public image to create a marketable persona as a westerner. Indispensable studies of Twain's speaking career include *Mark Twain on the Lecture Circuit*, by Paul Fatout, and *The Trouble Begins at Eight*, by Fred Lorch. Joe Jackson's book-length account of the *Hornet* disaster, *A Furnace Afloat*, is the rare work of nonfiction that reads like a novel.

NOTES

INTRODUCTION

Page

1 "to light out": This and subsequent Huck quotes are from Samuel Langhorne Clemens, *Adventures of Huckleberry Finn* (New York: Norton, 1977), p. 7.

CHAPTER 1: A CAMPAIGN THAT FAILED

Page

5 "the only unfettered": Mark Twain, *Life on the Mississippi* (New York: Penguin Putnam, 2001), p. 166.

6 "to follow the river": Ibid., p. 246.

6 "Great rejoicing": John Lauber, *The Making of Mark Twain* (New York: American Heritage Press, 1985), p. 89.

7 "so much for eggs": Edgar Marquess Branch, Michael B. Frank, and Kenneth M. Sanderson, eds., *Mark Twain's Letters*, vol. 1, 1853–66 (Berkeley: University of California Press, 1988), p. 103. Hereafter cited as *Letters*.

7 "flamboyantly secessionist": Ibid., p. 121.

7 "perched all solitary": Twain, *Life on the Mississippi*, p. 144.

8 "Good Lord Almighty": Albert Bigelow Paine, *Mark Twain: A Biography*, 3 vols. (New York: Harper & Brothers, 1912), vol. 1, p. 162.

8 "with the fear that he might be arrested": Samuel Charles Webster, ed., *Mark Twain, Business Man* (Boston: Little, Brown, 1946), p. 60.

8 "should have guarded": Ibid., pp. 61–62.

9 "the Worshipful Master": *Letters*, pp. 106–7.

10 "There was nothing": Charles Neider, ed., *The Autobiography of Mark Twain* (New York: Harper & Row, 1959), p. 32. Hereafter cited as *Autobiography*.

11 "a silent, austere man": Ibid., p. 25.

11 "My own knowledge": Justin Kaplan, *Mr. Clemens and Mark Twain* (New York: Simon & Schuster, 1966), p. 16.

12 "You don't expect": Dixon Wecter, *Sam Clemens of Hannibal* (Boston: Houghton Mifflin, 1952), p. 44.

12 "She had a slender": *Autobiography*, pp. 27–28.

12 "She was the most": Ibid., pp. 28–29.

13 "uncashable promises": Ibid., p. 103.

13 "You will doubtless": *Letters*, pp. 3–4.

14 "If books are not": Ibid., p. 10.

14 "the greatest wonder yet": Ibid., p. 13.

14 "borne, and rubbed": Ibid., p. 10.

14 "She is a pretty": Ibid., p. 31.

15 "abominable foreigners": Ibid., p. 29.

15 "free-and-easy": Ibid.

15 "Being of a *snaillish*": Edgar Marquess Branch and Robert H. Hirst, eds., *Mark Twain's Early Tales and Sketches*, vol. 1, 1851–64 (Berkeley: University of California Press, 1979), p. 62. Hereafter cited as *ET&S*.

15 "a fierce hater": Ibid., p. 72.

16 "real *dog*-gertype": Ibid., p. 75.

16 "failing in the patriotic": Ibid.

16 "obscene and despicable": Ibid., p. 73.

16 "rather rough": Ibid., p. 74.

16 "TERRIBLE ACCIDENT!": Ron Powers, *Dangerous Water: A Biography of the Boy Who Became Mark Twain* (New York: Basic Books, 1999), p. 204.

17 "sadly out of place": *Letters*, p. 40.

17 "a fine looking old man": Ibid., p. 41.

17 "a lion imprisoned": Ibid.

18 "in self-defense": Paine, *Mark Twain*, vol. 1, p. 102.

18 "threatened to carve": Kaplan, *Mr. Clemens and Mark Twain*, pp. 51–52.

19 "then I branched off": Twain, *Life on the Mississippi*, p. 272.

19 "a hotbed of rest": Ron Powers, *Mark Twain: A Life* (New York: Free Press, 2006), p. 69.

20 "I believe it was": Fred Kaplan, *The Singular Mark Twain: A Biography* (New York: Anchor, 2003), p. 56.

20 "voluptuous, inhibitive, combative": David S. Reynolds, *Walt Whitman's America: A Cultural Biography* (New York: Knopf, 1995), p. 248.

20 "activity, quickness, suppleness": Frederick Anderson, Michael B. Frank, and Kenneth M. Sanderson, eds., *Mark Twain's Notebooks & Journals*, vol. 1, 1855–73 (Berkeley: University of California Press, 1975), p. 22. Hereafter cited as *N&J*.

20 "nervous temperament": Ibid., pp. 28–29.

21 "good average St. Louis": Mark Twain, *Roughing It* (Berkeley: University of California Press, 1993), p. 272.

21 "Taking you by and large": Twain, *Life on the Mississippi*, p. 48.

22 "The face of the water": Ibid., p. 54.

22 "Your true pilot": Ibid., p. 40.

24 "me and De Soto": "River Intelligence," in Walter Blair, ed., *Selected Shorter Writings of Mark Twain* (Boston: Houghton Mifflin, 1962), p. 10.

24 "I cannot correspond": *Letters*, p. 77.

25 "in fine, fancy, splendid": Ibid., p. 88.

25 "You write well": Ibid., p. 108.

25 "not remarkably pretty": Ibid.

25 "never break through the ice": Ibid., p. 110.

25 "too visionary": Ibid., p. 111.

26 "You could follow": Absalom Grimes, *Absalom Grimes: Confederate Mail Runner* (New Haven: Yale University Press, 1926), pp. 4–5.

29 "to a shady": "The Private History of a Campaign That Failed," *Selected Shorter Writings*, p. 210.

29 "We did learn": Ibid., p. 211.

29 "that if I": Ibid., p. 212.

29 "because no government": Ibid., p. 215.

30 "took a soldier": Ibid., p. 214.

30 "They couldn't undo": Ibid.

30 "a first-rate fellow": Ibid., pp. 217–18.

31 "Presently, a muffled sound": Ibid., p. 219.

31 "The thought shot": Ibid., p. 220.

32 "We told him": Ibid., p. 222.

32 "I could have become": Ibid., p. 223.

33 "incapacitated by fatigue": *Autobiography*, p. 111.

33 "I thought he needed": Webster, *Mark Twain, Business Man*, p. 39.

34 "used his chin": Doris Kearns Goodwin, *Team of Rivals: The Political Genius of Abraham Lincoln* (New York: Simon & Schuster, 2005), pp. 22–23.

34 "an honest man": Twain, *Roughing It.*, p. 574.

35 "such majesty": Ibid., p. 1.

35 "It was a sad parting": Ibid., p. 4.

36 "weighed about a thousand": Twain, *Autobiography*, p. 112.

36 "was armed to the teeth": Twain, *Roughing It*, p. 5.

36 "to guard against": Ibid.

CHAPTER 2: A FINE PLEASURE TRIP

Page

38 "unpoetic and repulsive": George Constable, ed., *Time-Life Books: The Old West* (New York: Prentice Hall, 1990), p. 175.

38 "I have seen nothing": Ibid., p. 182.

38 "so dull and sleepy": Twain, *Roughing It*, p. 2.

38 "a confused jumble": Ibid., pp. 2–3.

39 "she was walking": Ibid., p. 3.

39 "a bully boat": Ibid.

39 "had the deep sagacity": Ibid.

39 "Navigating the Missouri": Ibid., p. 576.

41 "I was personally acquainted": Ibid., pp. 53–54.

41 "a great swinging": Ibid., p. 7.

42 "for the Injuns": Ibid.

43 "I starved him": Twain, *Autobiography*, p. 9.

43 *Huck Finn and Tom Sawyer*: R. Kent Rasmussen, *Mark Twain A to Z: The Essential Reference to His Life and Writings* (New York: Facts on File, 1995), pp. 214–15.

44 "To enjoy such a trip": John D. Unruh, Jr., *The Plains Across: The Overland Emigrants and the Trans-Mississippi West, 1840–60* (Urbana: University of Illinois Press, 1979), p. 414.

44 "The air of the plains": James C. Simmons, ed., *Star-Spangled Eden: 19th Century America Through the Eyes of Dickens, Wilde, Frances Trollope, Frank Harris, and Other British Travelers* (New York: Carroll & Graf, 2000), p. 192.

44 "beautifully dressed": Twain, *Roughing It*, p. 770.

45   "an exhilarating sense": Ibid., p. 6.

45   "Our perfect enjoyment": Ibid., pp. 11–12.

46   "He was the only": Twain, *Autobiography*, p. 93.

46   "To aim along": Twain, *Roughing It*, p. 5.

47   "Bemis did not": Ibid.

47   "tilted Bemis's nose": Ibid., p. 19.

47   "Bemis said he was": Ibid., p. 77.

47   "the vilest whisky": Ibid., pp. 88–89.

48   "the uneasy Dictionary": Ibid., p. 18.

48   "and consequently no swearing": Ibid., p. 15.

48   "His diabolical notions": *Letters*, pp. 180–81.

48   "a fine pleasure trip": Twain, *Roughing It*, p. 137.

49   "It is not putting": Ibid., p. 13.

49   "is a long, slim": Ibid., pp. 30–31.

49   "his first cousins": Ibid., pp. 33–34.

50   "unspeakably picturesque": Ibid., p. 22.

50   "a great and shining": Ibid., p. 20.

50   "old as the hills": Ibid.

50   "Pass the bread": Ibid., pp. 24–25.

50   "At last, when he came to": Ibid., p. 25.

51   "till every noxious principle": Richard F. Burton, *The City of the Saints and Across the Rocky Mountains to California* (New York: Knopf, 1963), p. 92.

51   "It'll be a most": Edward Rice, *Captain Sir Richard Francis Burton* (New York: Charles Scribner's Sons, 1990), p. 330.

51   "Both have the same wild": Simmons, *Star-Spangled Eden*, p. 200.

52   "refused indignantly": Burton, *City of the Saints*, pp. 126–27.

52   "a bustling, growing village": Horace Greeley, *An Overland Journey: From New York to San Francisco in the Summer of 1859* (New York: Knopf, 1964), p. 9.

52   "The Indians are children": Ibid., p. 119.

52   "squalid and conceited": Ibid., p. 121.

52   "I could not help": Ibid., p. 120.

52   "There are too many": Ibid., p. 52.

53   "assumed that [they]": Ibid., p. 187.

53   "generally idle and depraved": Ibid., p. 298.

53   "virtuous, educated, energetic women": Ibid.

53   "making their pile": Ibid., p. 303.

53   "nearly destitute": Ibid., p. 108.

53   "The broad landscape": Ibid., p. 112.

53 "the meanest river": Ibid., pp. 229–30.

53 "one of the pleasantest": Twain, *Roughing It*, p. 184.

54 "in whose presence": Ibid., p. 35.

55 "Wanted: Young, skinny": Albert Hemingway, "Riders in Hostile Land," *Wild West*, August 1990, p. 20.

56 "We had had a consuming desire": Twain, *Roughing It*, pp. 51–52.

56 "Help! Help! Help": Ibid., p. 57.

57 "but before I could": Ibid., p. 771.

58 "Slade was about": Ibid., pp. 67–68.

58 "those who met him": Ibid., p. 69.

59 "cold and disagreeable": Burton, *City of the Saints*, p. 102.

59 "He had gray eyes": Twain, *Roughing It*, p. 779.

59 "clean up on": Richard O'Connor, *Wild Bill Hickok* (New York: Curtis, 1959), p. 19.

61 "This wild, unflinching": Burton, *City of the Saints*, p. 248.

61 "was murderous enough": Twain, *Roughing It*, p. 86.

61 "no common man": Burton, *City of the Saints*, p. 271.

61 "quiet, kindly, easy-mannered": Twain, *Roughing It*, pp. 92–93.

61 "merely looked around": Ibid.

61 "a grubbing": Ibid., p. 595.

62 "You are going": Ibid.

62 "Now the yoke": Michael S. Durham, *Desert Between the Mountains: Mormons, Miners, Padres, Mountain Men, and the Opening of the Great Basin, 1772–1869* (New York: Henry Holt, 1997), p. 251.

62 "a vast improvement": Burton, *City of the Saints*, p. 221.

62 "looked like a soup-kettle": Simmons, *Star-Spangled Eden*, p. 319.

62 "Some portly old frog": Twain, *Roughing It*, p. 99.

62 "Take my word": Ibid., p. 106.

62 "poor, ungainly": Ibid., pp. 97–98.

63 "chloroform in print": Ibid., p. 107.

63 "a prosy detail": Ibid., p. 97.

63 "a community of traitors": Durham, *Desert Between the Mountains*, p. 298.

63 "concentrated hideousness": Twain, *Roughing It*, p. 122.

64 "the wretchedest type": Ibid., p. 126.

64 "a silent, sneaking": Ibid., p. 127.

64 "threw the animal": Unruh, *The Plains Across*, p. 418.

64 "one would as soon": Twain, *Roughing It*, p. 127.

65 "The difference between": Ibid., p. 233.

65 "The poetic Indian": Greeley, *An Overland Journey*, p. 119.

65 "They are called deserts": Twain, *Roughing It*, p. 772.

65 "one prodigious boneyard": Ibid., p. 130.

65 "a region whose uses": Unruh, *The Plains Across*, p. 411.

65 "assemblage of mere": Twain, *Roughing It*, pp. 137–38.

CHAPTER 3: THE DAMNEDEST COUNTRY UNDER THE SUN

Page

67 "consisted of four": Twain, *Roughing It*, p. 138.

68 "His death was generally": Effie Mona Mack, *Mark Twain in Nevada* (New York: Charles Scribner's Sons, 1947), p. 85.

69 "did all the talking": Durham, *Desert Between the Mountains*, p. 277.

70 "I'll have to get": Twain, *Roughing It*, p. 138.

70 "general esteem": Ibid., p. 612.

70 "and began to rebuke": Ibid., p. 138.

71 "I never saw": Ibid.

71 "a pretty regular wind": Ibid., p. 140.

71 "a soaring dust-drift": Ibid., p. 138.

71 "the vast dust-cloud": Ibid., p. 139.

71 "It was something": Ibid.

72 "came from the four": Mack, *Mark Twain in Nevada*, pp. 178–79.

73 "a white frame": Twain, *Roughing It*, p. 140.

74 "He was a fine": Twain, *Autobiography*, p. 112.

74 "By the time": Ibid., p. 115.

74 "The Governor's official": Ibid., pp. 113–14.

75 "were paid assassins": Twain, *Roughing It*, p. 143.

75 "If you stood": Ibid., p. 141.

75 "with recreation amid": Ibid., p. 143.

75 "Turn out, boys": Ibid., pp. 145–46.

76 "I know I am not": Ibid.

76 "a festering border": Philip Ashley Fanning, *Mark Twain and Orion Clemens: Brothers, Partners, Strangers* (Tuscaloosa: University of Alabama Press, 2003), p. 61.

77 "the prettiest seal": Ibid., p. 63.

77 Orion termed the idea: Ibid.

77 "rowdyish and bully": Twain, *Roughing It*, p. 147.

77 "a first-rate fellow": *Letters*, p. 124.

78 "three or four thousand": Twain, *Roughing It*, p. 147.

78 Sam "superintended" Kinney: Ibid., p. 150.

78 "expanded[ed] your soul": *Letters,* p. 133.

78 "Three months of camp": Twain, *Roughing It,* p. 149.

78 "made a failure": Ibid.

78 "Within half an hour": Ibid., p. 156.

79 "hunger asserted itself": Ibid.

79 "This is the damnedest": *Letters,* pp. 132–33.

79 "thieves, murderers, desperadoes": Ibid., p. 137.

80 "would come tomorrow": Fanning, *Mark Twain and Orion Clemens,* p. 64.

80 "had other business": Ibid.

80 "The Secretary of the Territory": Ibid., p. 65.

80 "There is something": Twain, *Roughing It,* p. 168.

80 "a fine collection": Ibid., p. 171.

80 "sat under prayers": Mack, *Mark Twain in Nevada,* p. 89.

81 The assault was so severe: Ibid., p. 104.

81 "The United States": Twain, *Roughing It,* p. 171.

81 "it looked like": Ibid.

81 "It went through": Ibid.

81 "Nothing in this world": Ibid., p. 170.

82 "nothing in his instructions": Ibid., p. 173.

82 "hasn't business talent": *Letters,* p. 159.

82 "a prissy chucklehead": Powers, *Mark Twain,* p. 107.

82 "had as many humps": Twain, *Roughing It,* p. 158.

82 "Oh, *don't* he": Ibid., p. 161.

82 "Imagination cannot conceive": Ibid.

82 "Any child, any Injun": Ibid., p. 162.

82 "a notoriously substanceless": Ibid., p. 164.

82 "my idea being": Ibid.

83 "everybody I loaned": Ibid., p. 163.

83 "whom fortune delivered": Ibid., p. 165.

83 "the richest mineral": Ibid., p. 176.

83 "composed of equal parts": *The Californian,* June 17, 1865.

84 "much addicted to fleas": *Letters,* p. 148.

84 "a little mean": Ibid.

84 "bituminous from long": Twain, *Roughing It,* p. 180.

84 "If a word was long": Ibid., p. 181.

84 "meretricious in his movements": Ibid., p. 182.

85 "too technical for him": Ibid., p. 183.

85 "well stocked in liquor": *Mining and Scientific Press,* June 14, 1862.

85 "expected to find": Twain, *Roughing It*, pp. 184–85.

85 "a lot of granite": Ibid., p. 188.

85 "nothing that glitters": Ibid.

86 *Contained* it!": Ibid., p. 189.

86 "about deep enough": Ibid., p. 193.

86 "We wanted a ledge": Ibid.

86 "bloated millionaires": Ibid., p. 195.

86 "drunk with happiness": Ibid., p. 193.

87 "By'm-by, heap water": Ibid., p. 197.

87 "a great turmoil": Ibid., p. 198.

87 "Boys," said Tillou: Ibid., p. 208.

88 "I have scarcely exaggerated": Ibid., p. 217.

88 "necessary adjustments": Fanning, *Mark Twain and Orion Clemens*, p. 68.

88 "a man can't hold": Mack, *Mark Twain in Nevada*, p. 143.

89 Orion was forced to repay: Twain, *Roughing It*, p. 212.

89 "in deference to popular": Ibid., p. 274.

89 "The Ophir": *Letters*, p. 154.

90 "It always snows": Ibid., p. 196.

90 some 250 "helpers": Mack, *Mark Twain in Nevada*, p. 156.

90 If all else failed: *Letters*, p. 156.

91 "a dead sure thing": Ibid., pp. 220–21.

91 "uncongealable sanguine personality": Ibid., p. 157.

92 "It is a pity": Twain, *Roughing It*, p. 233.

92 "I was ordered off": Ibid., p. 237.

92 "I came near getting": *Letters*, p. 225.

93 "He is a damned": Ibid., p. 228.

93 "a large, strong man": Ibid., p. 225.

93 "lumps of virgin gold": Twain, *Roughing It*, p. 240.

93 "The vein was about": Ibid., p. 239.

94 "during the still hours": *Sacramento Bee*, July 3, 1862.

94 "the fly people": Twain, *Roughing It*, p. 638.

94 "lies in a lifeless": Ibid., p. 245.

94 "It was bad judgment": Ibid.

95 "Once capsized": Ibid., pp. 250, 253.

95 "Dam stove heap gone": Ibid., p. 255.

96 "Hang the butcher": Ibid., p. 262.

96 "most damnably mixed": *Letters*, p. 220.

96 "own a foot": Ibid., p. 228.

96 "Christ! How sick": Ibid., p. 221.

97 "God damn it": Ibid., p. 195.

97 "I had gained": Twain, *Roughing It*, pp. 271–72.

97 "on a little rubbishy claim": Ibid., p. 272.

CHAPTER 4: ENTERPRISE

Page

99 "My starboard leg": Paine, *Mark Twain*, vol. 1, p. 205.

99 "rusty looking": Twain, *Roughing It*, p. 274.

100 "The man and the hour": James McPherson, *Battle Cry of Freedom: The Civil War Era* (New York: Oxford University Press, 1988), p. 259.

100 "I have been through": Durham, *Desert Between the Mountains*, p. 279.

101 "An African Eland": Ivan Benson, *Mark Twain's Western Years* (Stanford, Calif.: Stanford University Press, 1938), p. 65.

101 "Myriads of swarthy": Mack, *Mark Twain in Nevada*, pp. 185–86.

102 "a feeble struggle": Benson, *Mark Twain's Western Years*, p. 61.

102 "miraculously ignorant": Twain, *Roughing It*, p. 300.

102 "I've got money": Durham, *Desert Between the Mountains*, p. 282.

103 "Boy That Earth Talks To": H. W. Brands, *The Age of Gold: The California Gold Rush and the New American Dream* (New York: Doubleday, 2002), p. 415.

104 "the poetry of corn": Richard A. Dwyer and Richard E. Lingenfelter, *Dan De Quille, the Washoe Giant* (Reno: University of Nevada Press, 1990), p. 8.

105 "Get the facts first": Ibid.

105 "a kind of bachelor's paradise": Henry Nash Smith, ed., *Mark Twain of the Enterprise: Newspaper Articles and Other Documents 1862–1864* (Berkeley: University of California Press, 1957), p. 5.

106 "He told me to go": Twain, *Roughing It*, p. 274.

106 "I wandered about town": Ibid., p. 275.

106 "A desperado killed": Ibid., p. 276.

107 "a man of considerable genius": Dwyer and Lingenfelter, *Dan De Quille*, p. 185.

107 "neither prepared to disbelieve": Ibid., p. 189.

107 "was in a sitting posture": "A Washoe Joke," *Selected Shorter Writings of Mark Twain*, p. 11.

108 "deceased came to his death": Ibid.

108 "I hated Sewall": *ET&S*, p. 156.

109 "a stomach full": Fatout, *Mark Twain in Virginia City* (Bloomington: Indiana University Press, 1964), p. 73.

109 "consumed his portion": George Williams III, *Mark Twain: His Life in Virginia City, Nevada* (Dayton, Nev.: Tree By The River, 1986), p. 103.

109 "had grown to be": Twain, *Roughing It*, pp. 281–82.

109 "There were military": Ibid., p. 282.

110 "more than one man": Ibid., pp. 318–19.

110 "brave, reckless men": Ibid., p. 323.

110 "from a just dispensation": Ibid., p. 672.

110 "by the visitation": Ibid., p. 308.

112 "No one on this planet": Twain, *Autobiography*, p. 115.

113 "mule on road": Smith, ed., *Mark Twain of the Enterprise*, pp. 37–38.

113 "came and asked": Ibid., p. 50.

113 "I never saw a man": Ibid., p. 51.

114 "the provisions would": Ibid.

114 "His instincts always prompt": Ibid., p. 58.

114 "The effect was more": Ibid., pp. 53–54.

114 "He became a newspaper reporter": Fatout, *Mark Twain in Virginia City*, pp. 40–41.

115 "he could not even": Smith, ed., *Mark Twain of the Enterprise*, p. 50.

115 "We have been on the stool": Mack, *Mark Twain in Nevada*, pp. 233–34.

116 "Quick, Ben!": Twain, *Life on the Mississippi*, p. 79.

117 "Mark Twain has abdicated": Virginia City *Territorial Enterprise*, May 3, 1863.

117 "the atmosphere cannot": Ibid.

117 "I am going": *Letters*, p. 255.

118 "lace embroidered with blue": *ET&S*, pp. 310–11.

118 "like going back": *Letters*, p. 256.

118 "The streets of Virginia City": San Francisco *Evening Bulletin*, June 14, 1863.

118 "This building is rented": Fatout, *Mark Twain in Virginia City*, p. 60.

118 "the best business": Ibid.

118 "I have just heard": *Letters*, p. 246.

119 "The intention of the citizens": Fatout, *Mark Twain in Virginia City*, p. 43.

120 "We (Mark and I)": Dwyer and Lingenfelter, *Dan De Quille*, p. 228.

120 "they ought to have": *Letters*, p. 310.

120 "two excellent silk": "How to Cure a Cold," in *Collected Tales, Sketches, Speeches, & Essays 1852–1890* (New York: Library of America, 1992), p. 40.

120 "spoony, slobbering": San Francisco *Golden Era*, September 13, 1863.

121 "Young Wilson got": "How to Cure a Cold," *Collected Tales*, pp. 41–42.

121 "as repulsive a mixture": Ibid., p. 35.

121 "About 10 o'clock": Virginia City *Territorial Enterprise*, October 8, 1862.

122 "from Siskiyou to San Diego": Dwyer and Lingenfelter, *Dan De Quille*, p. 208.

122 "Lives of the Liars": Gold Hill *Daily News*, November 21, 1863.

122 "the man who could pen": Virginia City *Evening Bulletin*, November 2, 1863.

123 "I take it all back": Virginia City *Territorial Enterprise*, October 9, 1863.

123 "to get [Orion]" nominated: *Letters*, p. 264.

123 "a long legged": Virginia City *Territorial Enterprise*, December 12, 1863.

123 "All owe me something": Virginia City *Territorial Enterprise*, June 4, 1864.

124 "That Irresistible Washoe Giant": San Francisco *Golden Era*, November 22, 1863.

125 "I once knew a man": Powers, *Mark Twain*, p. 132.

126 "from face to face": Paul Fatout, *Mark Twain Speaking* (Iowa City: University of Iowa Press, 1976), p. 45.

126 "inimitable way": Ibid.

126 "The man who is capable": Virginia City *Evening Bulletin*, December 28, 1863.

126 "a powerfully convincing": Fatout, *Mark Twain in Virginia City*, p. 131.

127 "the most perfectly": Albert Parry, *Garrets and Pretenders: A History of Bohemia in America* (New York: Covici, Friede, 1933), p. 34.

127 "a finely formed": Virginia City *Territorial Enterprise*, September 13, 1863.

127 "gay, easy, sunny": Parry, *Garrets and Pretenders*, p. 35.

128 "a thing of beauty": Fatout, *Mark Twain in Virginia City*, p. 162.

128 "Mark Twain is writing": Virginia City *Union*, November 16, 1863.

128 "There was an old horse": Mack, *Mark Twain in Nevada*, p. 304.

128 "mongrels, puppies, whelps": Ibid., p. 305.

129 "He missed the dog": Ibid., p. 306.

129 "intensely dull": Nevada *Daily Gazette*, May 24, 1864.

129 "was coming down the road": Mack, *Mark Twain in Nevada*, pp. 254–55.

130 "this favorite writer": Gold Hill *Daily News*, November 2, 1863.

CHAPTER 5: HEAVEN ON THE HALF SHELL

Page

132 "Southern hell-hounds": Smith, ed., *Mark Twain of the Enterprise*, p. 18.

132 "passably loyal": Sacramento *Union*, December 18, 1862.

132 "We think their numbers": Virginia City *Territorial Enterprise*, September 20, 1862.

132 "Nevada for the Union": Mack, *Mark Twain in Nevada*, p. 123.

133 "How the people": Twain, *Roughing It*, p. 383.

133 "some creature wearing": Marysville *Daily Appeal*, July 18, 1863.

133 "a loud-mouthed Copperhead": Fanning, *Mark Twain and Orion Clemens*, p. 84.

133 "a just, righteous": Virginia City *Union*, May 15, 1863.

133 "We are for the Union": Ibid., May 9, 1863.

133 "Some of our people": Fatout, *Mark Twain in Virginia City*, p. 72.

135 Such "hirelings": Edward Haviland Miller, ed., *Walt Whitman: The Correspondence*, 6 vols. (New York: New York University Press, 1961), vol. 1, pp. 110–11.

135 "the whole population": Twain, *Roughing It*, p. 297.

136 "Twain and his staff": Gold Hill *Daily News*, May 17, 1864.

136 "a sufficient quantity": Virginia City *Old Piute*, May 17, 1864.

136 "Mark Twain is notorious": Quoted in Fatout, *Mark Twain in Virginia City*, p. 181.

136 "an ass of prodigious ear": Ibid.

137 "utter and unprecedented": Virginia City *Union*, May 24, 1864.

137 "A contemptible ass": *Letters*, p. 295.

137 "had written the communication": Ibid.

138 "Mr. Wilmington is": Virginia City *Territorial Enterprise*, May 24, 1864.

138 "courtesies" and "etiquette": Twain, *Autobiography*, 126.

138 "The second took": Ibid., p. 128.

138 "had been diverted": Virginia City *Territorial Enterprise*, May 17, 1864.

139 "was a hoax": Ibid.

139 "in drunken jest": *Letters*, p. 287.

139 "nothing but trouble": Ibid., pp. 287–88.

140 "a tissue of falsehoods": Virginia City *Union*, May 21, 1864.

140 "to aid a 'miscegenation'": Virginia City *Territorial Enterprise*, May 24, 1864.

140 "no time to fool": *Letters*, p. 301.

140 "Washoe has long since grown": Ibid., p. 299.

141 "It was not without": Twain, *Roughing It*, p. 382.

141 "among the few": Gold Hill *Evening News*, May 30, 1864.

142 "He declined": Twain, *Roughing It*, p. 380.

142 "To a Christian": San Francisco *Golden Era*, June 26, 1864.

142 "The thermometer stands": Twain, *Roughing It*, p. 387.

143 "The people suffer": Ibid., p. 389.

143 "butterfly idleness": Ibid., p. 396.

144 "From later afternoon": Mick Sinclair, *San Francisco* (Northampton, Mass.: Interlink, 2004), p. 74.

144 "Three Hundred Pounds": Ibid., p. 80.

144 "I had supposed": Oscar Lewis, *This Was San Francisco* (New York: David McKay, 1962), p. 169.

144 "I do not know": Ibid., pp. 179–80.

145 "Good morning": Jon Guttman, "Emperor Norton I," *Wild West*, February 1989, p. 8.

146 "because of corruption": Ibid., pp. 55–58.

146 "died full of years": Virginia City *Territorial Enterprise*, November 8, 1865.

146 "Le Roi Est Mort!": Doris Muscatine, *Old San Francisco: The Biography of a City* (New York: G. P. Putnam's Sons, 1975), p. 170.

146 "the emperor killed": Ibid.

147 "wild & repulsive foolery": Margaret Sanborn, *Mark Twain: The Bachelor Years* (New York: Doubleday, 1990), p. 245.

147 "stored to the eyelids": Ibid.

148 "As I turned": Twain, *Roughing It*, p. 398.

148 "One fat man": Ibid., p. 399.

149 "Nov. 2—Spasmodic": Edgar Marquess Branch and Robert H. Hirst, *Mark Twain's Early Tales & Sketches*, vol. 2, 1864–65 (Berkeley: University of California Press, 1981), p. 319.

149 "and everything and everybody": Twain, *Roughing It*, p. 397.

149 "They are gone": Quoted in Nigey Lennon, *The Sagebrush Bohemian: Mark Twain in California* (New York: Paragon House, 1993), p. 47.

150 "the washerwoman's newspaper": Twain, *Autobiography*, p. 131.

150 "fearful, soulless drudgery": Ibid.

150 "By nine in the morning": Ibid., p. 130.

150 "and this exercise": Ibid.

151 "If there were no fires": Ibid.

151 "a pile of miscellaneous": San Francisco *Morning Call*, August 13, 1864.

151 "was beyond realizing": Ibid.

151 "in the direct line": "In the Station House," *Selected Shorter Writings of Mark Twain*, p. 31.

151 "dilapidated old hags": San Francisco *Morning Call*, July 31, 1864.

151 "Anna Jakes, drunk": Ibid., July 14, 1864.

152 "Two slabs of old": Ibid., July 16, 1864.

152 "a man for breakfast": Edgar M. Branch, ed., *Clemens of the Call: Mark Twain in California* (Berkeley: University of California Press, 1969), p. 139.

152 "popularly considered to be": San Francisco *Morning Call*, August 5, 1864.

153 "an egg-shaped indentation": Ibid., August 18, 1864.

153 "as all the thieves": Ibid., August 20, 1864.

153 "miscreants" and "scoundrels": Ibid., July 23, 1864.

154 "infamous demoralizing practices": Ibid., July 24, 1864.

154 "most horrible" scene: Ibid., September 7, 1864.

154 "the noble little city": Ibid., September 9, 1864.

155 "born fool": *Californian*, April 6, 1867.

155 "weak blue eyes": *Alta California*, June 3, 1864.

155 "the Sagebrush Bohemian": Ibid., August 24, 1864.

156 "the broad canopy": San Francisco *Morning Call*, August 23, 1864.

156 "one of our principal": *ET&S*, vol. 2, p. 331.

156 "On examination of their": Ibid.

156 "Their boots were soiled": Ibid., p. 343.

156 "It was awful slavery": Twain, *Autobiography*, p. 131.

156 "a great hulking creature": Ibid., p. 133.

156 "I don't work": *Letters*, p. 310.

157 "with considerable warmth": Twain, *Autobiography*, p. 131.

157 "How wonderful are": Ibid., p. 134.

157 "For two months": Twain, *Roughing It*, p. 405.

157 "a melancholy-looking Arab": San Francisco *Morning Call*, October 29, 1865.

158 "might suggest suicide": Twain, *Roughing It*, p. 406.

158 "I am resolved": *Letters*, p. 315.

158 "If I do not get out": Ibid., p. 324.

158 "I put the pistol": Ibid., p. 325.

159 "His head was striking": Powers, *Mark Twain*, p. 147.

159 "distinctly pretty": Twain, *Autobiography*, p. 136.

160 "Bret Harte was": Ibid.

160 "such a prodigious": Ibid., p. 137.

160 "I have engaged": *Letters*, p. 312.

160 "the grave of genius": Gold Hill *Evening News*, October 15, 1864.

161 "For the first time": Andrew Hoffman, *Inventing Mark Twain: The Lives of Samuel Langhorne Clemens* (New York: William Morrow, 1997), p. 102.

161 "Meg Merrilies": Lennon, *The Sagebrush Bohemian*, pp. 77–82.

162 "I don't quite like": San Francisco *Golden Era*, April 3, 1864.

162 "he grew up": "Story of the Bad Little Boy," *Selected Shorter Writings of Mark Twain*, p. 21.

162 "the piano may do": *ET&S*, vol. 2, p. 235.

163 "kneaded together": "Whereas," *Collected Tales*, p. 92.

163 "if he does not": "Aurelia's Unfortunate Young Man," in Charles Neider, ed., *The Comic Mark Twain Reader* (New York: Doubleday, 1977), p. 346.

163 "Our usually quiet": "The Killing of Julius Caesar 'Localized,'" *Collected Tales*, p. 103.

163 "a man whose name": Ibid.

163 "whose position enables": Ibid., p. 106.

164 "the excellent beer": "Lucretia Smith's Soldier," *Collected Tales*, p. 108.

164 "a bronze and scarred": Ibid., p. 109.

164 "O confound my cats": Ibid., p. 112.

CHAPTER 6: LUXURIOUS VAGRANCY

Page

167 "couldn't have been colder": *N&J*, p. 84.

168 "During the three months": Twain, *Autobiography*, p. 328.

168 "furnish[ed] a very handsome": Twain, *Roughing It*, p. 413.

168 "the headquarters of all": Dwyer and Lingenfelter, *Dan De Quille*, p. 214.

168 "would stand up": Twain, *Autobiography*, p. 152.

169 "We lit the fuze": Twain, *Roughing It*, p. 418.

169 "I have used one": Twain, *Autobiography*, p. 152.

170 "a few years": Ibid., p. 151.

170 "He had a bright": Ibid.

170 "always in dire commotion": *N&J*, p. 81.

170 "The exciting topic": Ibid.

170 "the Chaparral Quails": Ibid., p. 68.

171 "damned girl [was]": Ibid., p. 69.

171 "beans and dishwater": Ibid., p. 76.

171 "It is not possible": Ibid., p. 78.

171 "No use, could not bite": Ibid.

171 "said that he had eaten it": Twain, *Autobiography*, p. 153.

171 "fictitious satisfaction": Ibid.

171 "vindictive acid": Ibid., p. 154.

171 "went on sipping": Ibid.

171 "the one gleam": Victor Fischer and Michael B. Frank, eds., *Mark Twain's*

Letters, vol. 4, 1870–71 (Berkeley: University of California Press, 1991), p. 36.

172 "Coleman with his": *N&J*, p. 80.

172 "was a dull person": *ET&S*, vol. 2, p. 264.

172 "If I can write": *Letters*, vol. 1, p. 321.

172 "hell-fired" town: *N&J*, 82.

172 "damned poor": Ibid.

173 "Write it," he urged: Paine, *Mark Twain*, vol. 1, p. 277.

173 "sinners are so thick": "Important Correspondence," *Collected Tales*, p. 114.

173 "during my temporary": Ibid., p. 121.

173 "a consummate ass": Ibid., p. 122.

173 "astonish the dogs": Ibid., p. 124.

173 "Yes, you are right": Ibid., p. 126.

174 "Never to take": "Advice for Good Little Boys," *Collected Tales*, p. 163.

174 "ought never to knock": Ibid.

174 "It is better to rope": "Advice for Good Little Girls," *Collected Tales*, p. 164.

175 "do not correct him": Ibid.

175 "Never sass old people": Ibid., p. 165.

175 "One dismal afternoon": *ET&S*, vol. 2, p. 266.

176 "a stranger in the camp": "The Notorious Jumping Frog of Calaveras County," *Selected Shorter Writings of Mark Twain*, p. 17.

177 "a born Yankee": Parry, *Garrets and Pretenders*, p. 42.

177 "a self-made man": Ibid., p. 43.

177 "Never tell secrets": Ibid., p. 44.

177 "We give up": New York *Saturday Press*, November 16, 1865.

177 "Mark Twain's story": *ET&S*, p. 271.

178 "To think that": *Letters*, vol. 1, p. 327.

178 "The foremost of the merry": Ibid., p. 325.

178 "I never had but two": Ibid., pp. 322–23.

179 "one of his spasms": Twain, *Autobiography*, p. 116.

179 "he suddenly changed": Ibid.

180 "That worthless brother": *N&J*, p. 112.

180 "tired of being a beggar": *Letters*, vol. 1, p. 326.

180 "with that calm serenity": "What Have the Police Been Doing?" *Collected Tales*, pp. 197–98.

180 "Mark Twain is still": San Francisco *Examiner*, February 10, 1866.

181 "Pacific street jayhawkers": Gold Hill *Daily News*, January 22, 1866.

181 "cursed and indulged": Ibid., January 29, 1866.

181 "the air is full of lechery": Virginia City *Territorial Enterprise*, January 23, 1866.

181 "under peculiar circumstances": Gold Hill *Daily News*, February 12 and 19, 1866.

181 "sleeping with female": *Letters*, vol. 1, p. 145.

181 "very little girl": Ibid., p. 114.

182 "Where could a man": Fatout, *Mark Twain on the Lecture Circuit*, p. 40.

182 "young lunar caustic": Lennon, *The Sagebrush Bohemian*, p. 118.

182 "I am to remain": *Letters*, vol. 1, p. 333.

183 "the peacefullest, restfullest, sunniest": A. Grove Day, ed., *Mark Twain in Hawaii* (Honolulu: Mutual, 2000), p. xxvi.

183 "We backed out": A. Grove Day, ed., *Mark Twain's Letters from Hawaii* (New York: Appleton-Century, 1966), p. 1.

183 "a case of wine": Ibid., p. 2.

183 "in that kind of labor": Ibid., p. 4.

183 "My proper place": "Reflections on the Sabbath," *Collected Tales*, p. 208.

184 "The Presbyterian hell": Ibid., p. 209.

184 "Such pleasant corpses": San Francisco *Golden Era*, February 4, 1866.

184 "standing on a little stage": Ibid.

184 "were ready on the slightest": "The Spiritual Séance," *Collected Tales*, p. 201.

185 "something like mumps": *N&J*, p. 189.

185 "I suppose I am": Ibid.

185 "sea-worn old whaleship captains": Twain, *Roughing It*, p. 421.

185 "without being in the least": Ibid.

186 "He was a roaring": Ibid., pp. 421–26.

186 "The Kanakas are large": John H. Chambers, *Hawaii* (Northampton, Mass.: Interlink, 2004), p. 112.

187 "unrighteousness, fornication, wickedness": Ibid., pp. 102–3.

187 "desecrating the Sabbath": Ibid., pp. 115–16.

187 "It is a matter": Day, *Mark Twain's Letters from Hawaii*, p. 20.

188 "I had rather smell": Ibid., p. 28.

188 "platoons of cats": Ibid., pp. 30–31.

188 "long-haired, saddle-colored": Twain, *Roughing It*, p. 433.

188 "comely features": Ibid., p. 432.

189 "a robust, red-faced": Chambers, *Hawaii*, p. 127.

189 "Straight on toward shore": Alex Kershaw, *Jack London: A Life* (New York: St. Martin's, 1998), p. 186.

189 "Each heathen would": Twain, *Roughing It*, p. 501.

190 "with forty-two legs": Ibid., pp. 434–35.

190 "She felt something": Day, *Mark Twain's Letters from Hawaii*, p. 32.

190 "clamped himself around": Ibid., pp. 32–33.

190 "I preferred a safe horse": Twain, *Roughing It*, p. 437.

191 "The first gate": Ibid.

191 "The more this thing preyed": Ibid.

191 "the pleasantest quarters": Day, *Mark Twain's Letters from Hawaii*, p. 72.

191 "a brown-faced, gray-beaded": Ibid.

191 "a harmless old lunatic": Ibid., p. 73.

191 "an aged, limping Negro": Ibid., pp. 75–76.

191 "they have a hard time": Ibid., p. 75.

192 "an interesting ruin": Ibid., pp. 52–53.

192 "make the natives permanently": Ibid., p. 53.

192 "more row [has been] made": *N&J*, p. 233.

192 "premature decrepitude": Day, *Mark Twain's Letters from Hawaii*, p. 69.

193 "It was performed": Ibid., pp. 70–71.

193 "sharpened my teeth": Twain, *Roughing It*, p. 435.

193 "as good as bad turnips": Day, *Mark Twain's Letters from Hawaii*, p. 39.

193 "a villainous mixture": Ibid., pp. 68–69.

193 "trifling, insipid, tasteless": Ibid., p. 38.

194 "It has been a perfect": *Letters*, vol. 1, p. 341.

194 "considerable weakness": Ibid., p. 337.

194 "a romantic gorge": Twain, *Roughing It*, p. 520.

194 "an ample checker-board": Ibid., p. 522.

194 "the sublimest spectacle": Ibid., p. 525.

195 on French national holidays: *N&J*, p. 120.

195 "not one single drop": Twain, *Roughing It*, p. 528.

195 "Well, sir, he kept": Ibid., p. 530.

195 "suicide induced by": Ibid., p. 531.

196 "thirty-six splendidly built": *N&J*, p. 129.

196 "made the place a pandemonium": Twain, *Roughing It*, p. 466.

196 "Hawaiian population generally": Ibid., p. 468.

196 "all the Christianity": Day, *Mark Twain's Letters from Hawaii*, pp. 182–83.

197 "rather larger than a hearse": Ibid., p. 196.

197 "Lazarus did not come": Ibid., p. 197.

197 "fellows with long": Ibid.

197 "of eating off sleeping sailors'": Ibid.

197 "tired of hanging on": Ibid., p. 203.

197 "Wherever he went": Ibid., p. 215.

198 "It was not possible": Chambers, *Hawaii*, p. 54.

198 "the spot where Cook's flesh": Twain, *Roughing It*, p. 492.

199 "The surprise of finding": *Letters*, vol. 1, p. 343.

199 "neat, roomy, well furnished": Day, *Mark Twain's Letters from Hawaii*, p. 298.

199 "glowed like a muffled torch": Ibid.

199 "I turned to see": Ibid., p. 294.

199 "By and by Marlette": Twain, *Roughing It*, p. 514.

200 "stretching away before us": Ibid., pp. 514–15.

200 "some released soul": Ibid., p. 515.

CHAPTER 7: THE TROUBLE BEGINS

Page

202 "You have great ability": Lennon, *The Sagebrush Bohemian*, p. 132.

203 "The *Hornet*'s ordeal": For the *Hornet* disaster, see Joe Jackson, *A Furnace Afloat: The Wreck of the* Hornet *and the Harrowing 4,300-mile Voyage of Its Survivors* (New York: Free Press, 2003).

204 "very cool and self-possessed": Day, *Mark Twain's Letters from Hawaii*, p. 138.

205 "Four hams, seven pieces": Ibid., p. 142.

205 "magnanimity and utter unselfishness": Ibid., p. 145.

205 "Why me?" Jackson, *A Furnace Afloat*, p. 94.

205 "I'll see you in Frisco": Ibid., p. 104.

206 "The interest of this": "Forty-Three Days in An Open Boat," *Harper's New Monthly Magazine*, December 1866.

206 "a devilish saddle boil": *N&J*, p. 58.

206 "I hope they will have": Ibid., p. 137.

207 "home again, no": Ibid., p. 163.

207 "the best men that ever owned": *Letters*, vol. 1, p. 355.

207 "a murderous discontent": "Forty-Three Days in An Open Boat."

208 "as interesting to me": Ibid.

208 "You should have edited": Jackson, *A Furnace Afloat*, p. 219.

208 "I was a Literary Person": "My Debut as a Literary Person," *Century Magazine*, December 1899.

208 "You bet your life": *Letters*, vol. 1, p. 358.

209 "That worthless brother": *N&J*, p. 112.

209 "It is Orion's duty": *Letters*, vol. 1, p. 341.

209 "Orion would make": Ibid., p. 367.

210 "exquisite appreciation": *N&J*, p. 176.

210 "about the best-known": Fatout, *Mark Twain on the Lecture Circuit*, p. 35.

210 "take the largest house": Twain, *Roughing It*, p. 533.

210 "Jenny Lind Swindle": Sinclair, *San Francisco*, pp. 64–65.

211 "the most distressed": Twain, *Roughing It*, p. 533.

211 "A SPLENDID ORCHESTRA": Ad reproduced in Fred Lorch, *The Trouble Begins at Eight: Mark Twain's Lecture Tours* (Ames: Iowa State University Press, 1968), p. 27.

213 "As those three days": Twain, *Roughing It*, p. 533.

214 The *Californian* laughingly: *Californian*, September 29, 1866.

214 a "high-toned" speech: *Alta California*, October 2, 1866.

214 "Sensational Rumor": San Francisco *Dramatic Chronicle*, October 2, 1866.

214 " 'No sales,' I said": Twain, *Roughing It*, p. 534.

214 "of a jolly, rollicking": San Francisco *Chronicle*, April 11, 1876.

214 "You don't know me": Twain, *Roughing It*, p. 534.

215 "I stumbled my way": Ibid., pp. 534–35.

215 "I only suffered": Ibid.

215 "Before I well knew": Ibid.

215 "My chief allies": Ibid., pp. 535–36.

216 "Ladies and gentlemen": Reproduced in Lorch, *The Trouble Begins at Eight*, p. 216.

216 "method as a lecturer": Ibid., p. 32.

217 "hired the man": San Francisco *Evening Bulletin*, October 3, 1866.

217 "When in the course": Fatout, *Mark Twain on the Lecture Circuit*, p. 43.

217 "composed of lava": Ibid., pp. 276–77.

217 "The population was about": Ibid.

217 "exceeding hospitable": Ibid., p. 278.

217 "not the great Newfoundland": Ibid., p. 279.

218 "I would rather go hungry": Ibid.

218 "if anyone in the audience": Ibid., p. 280.

218 "They will put a live chicken": Ibid., p. 282.

218 "If their grief was deep": Ibid.

218 "They have some customs": Ibid.

218 "The humorous story": "How to Tell a Story," *Selected Shorter Writings of Mark Twain*, pp. 239–40.

218 "the first virtue": Ibid.

219 "In spite of all": Twain, *Roughing It*, p. 536.

219 "as a humorous writer": San Francisco *Evening Bulletin*, October 3, 1866.

219 "one of the greatest": San Francisco *Dramatic Chronicle*, October 3, 1866.

219 "We regard this subject": San Francisco *Golden Era*, October 7, 1866.

220 "more thoroughly American": Springfield *Republican*, November 10, 1866.

220 "It's a free country": Oakland *Daily News*, October 10, 1866.

220 "the most sweeping success": *Letters*, vol. 1, p. 121.

220 "THE CELEBRATED BEARDED": Sacramento *Union*, October 10, 1866.

220 "I've seen Mark Twain": Ibid., October 13, 1866.

220 "familiar with the Kanaka": Ibid., October 12, 1866.

220 "easy colloquial style": Ibid., October 13, 1866.

221 "It is a pity": Fatout, *Mark Twain on the Lecture Circuit*, p. 48.

221 "settled down noisily": Ibid.

221 "the best in the territory": Como *Sentinel*, June 4, 1867.

221 "Mark don't drink": Virginia City *Daily Trespass*, April 27, 1868.

221 "preparing himself for a clear": Sacramento *Union*, October 21, 1866.

221 "Ladies and gentlemen": Paine, *Mark Twain*, vol. 1, p. 295.

221 "winks understood at the bar": Fatout, *Mark Twain on the Lecture Circuit*, p. 50.

221 "I shall not waste": Twain, *Autobiography*, p. 180.

222 "repeat the unique": Nevada City *Gazette*, October 19, 1866.

222 "Note the articles": Virginia City *Daily Union*, October 19, 1866.

222 "a grand tableau": Ibid., October 17, 1866.

222 "but when one condescends": Ibid., October 19, 1866.

222 "I Had an Old Horse": Fatout, *Mark Twain on the Lecture Circuit*, pp. 54–55.

223 "mighty dubious": *Letters*, vol. 1, p. 365.

223 "disgorge a few lies": Ibid., p. 364.

223 "Throttle him!": Twain, *Roughing It*, p. 539.

223 "I never had a thought": Ibid., p. 541.

223 "was the scaredest man": Lorch, *The Trouble Begins at Eight*, p. 337.

224 "the departed spirits": Virginia City *Daily Union*, November 12, 1866.

224 "Since then I play": Twain, *Roughing It*, p. 542.

224 "Between the highwaymen": Washoe *Evening Slope*, November 21, 1866.

224 "alkalied in the savage": San Francisco *Chronicle*, November 17, 1866.

224 "whether owing to native": San Francisco *Morning Call*, November 17, 1866.

224 "Mark Twain fulfilled": San Francisco *Daily Times*, November 17, 1866.

225 "uncommonly bad jokes": Fatout, *Mark Twain on the Lecture Circuit*, p. 64.

225 "I have been treated": *Alta California*, December 15, 1866.

225 "departs with a brilliant": San Francisco *Evening Bulletin*, December 11, 1866.

225 "This popular lecturer": San Francisco *Daily Times*, December 11, 1866.

225 "not stinted as to time": *Alta California*, December 15, 1866.

226 "Good-bye, felons": Ibid., December 14, 1866.

226 "I sail tomorrow": *Letters*, vol. 1, p. 373.

226 "Thus, after seven years": Twain, *Roughing It*, p. 542.

EPILOGUE: SIVILIZED

Page

227 "a long, long night": *N&J*, p. 246.

228 "cholera of the most": Ibid., p. 258.

228 "fast becoming": Ibid., pp. 277–78.

229 got satisfyingly "tight": Ibid., p. 292.

229 "a pure and sinless sprout": *Alta California*, March 27, 1867.

229 "walk the legs off": Ibid., March 28, 1867.

229 "shivering and chattering": Kaplan, *The Singular Mark Twain*, p. 173.

229 "swelling and swelling": Twain, *Autobiography*, p. 167.

230 "the prize ass": Ibid.

230 "He forsook his notes": *Alta California*, March 30, 1867.

230 "a rich, resonant voice": Ibid.

230 "Mr. Beecher is a remarkably": Ibid.

231 "Send me $1,200": Harriet Elinor Smith and Richard Bucci, eds., *Mark Twain's Letters*, vol. 2, 1867–68 (Berkeley: University of California Press, 1989), p. 17.

231 "the Reverend Mark Twain": Kaplan, *Mr. Clemens and Mark Twain*, p. 28.

231 "You don't look": *Letters*, vol. 2, p. 16.

232 "I would rather bury": Victor Fischer and Michael B. Frank, eds., *Mark Twain's Letters*, vol. 3, 1869 (Berkeley: University of California Press, 1990), p. 57.

232 "the most perfect gem": *Letters*, vol. 4, p. 52.

233 "That ain't no matter": Clemens, *Adventures of Huckleberry Finn*, p. 7.

BIBLIOGRAPHY

Aaron, Daniel. *The Unwritten War: American Writers and the Civil War.* New Haven, Conn.: Yale University Press, 1973.

Anderson, Frederick, Michael B. Frank, and Kenneth M. Sanderson, eds. *Mark Twain's Notebooks & Journals.* Vol. 1. 1855–73. Berkeley: University of California Press, 1975.

Benson, Ivan. *Mark Twain's Western Years.* Stanford, Calif.: Stanford University Press, 1938.

Blair, Walter, ed. *Selected Shorter Writings of Mark Twain.* Boston: Houghton Mifflin, 1962.

Branch, Edgar M., ed. *Clemens of the Call: Mark Twain in California.* Berkeley: University of California Press, 1969.

Branch, Edgar Marquess, Michael B. Frank, and Kenneth M. Sanderson, eds. *Mark Twain's Letters.* Vol. 1. 1853–66. Berkeley: University of California Press, 1988.

Branch, Edgar Marquess, and Robert H. Hirst, eds. *Mark Twain's Early Tales and Sketches.* 2 vols. Berkeley: University of California Press, 1979–81.

Brands, H. W. *The Age of Gold: The California Gold Rush and the New American Dream.* New York: Doubleday, 2002.

Burton, Richard F. *The City of the Saints and Across the Rocky Mountains to California.* New York: Knopf, 1963.

Caron, James E. *Mark Twain: Unsanctified Newspaper Reporter.* Columbia: University of Missouri Press, 2008.

Carpenter, Allan. *The Encyclopedia of the Far West.* New York: Facts on File, 1991.

Chambers, John H. *Hawaii.* Northampton, Mass.: Interlink, 2004.

Clemens, Samuel Langhorne. *Adventures of Huckleberry Finn.* Edited by Sculley Bradley, Richmond Croom Beatty, E. Hudson Long, and Thomas Cooley. New York: Norton, 1977.

Constable, George, ed., *Time-Life Books: The Old West.* New York: Prentice Hall, 1990.

Coulombe, Joseph L. *Mark Twain and the American West.* Columbia: University of Missouri Press, 2003.

Cunningham, Robert D., Jr. "Under the Lash of the Jehu." *American History Illustrated*, May 1985, pp. 16–21.

Day, A. Grove, ed. *Mark Twain in Hawaii.* Honolulu: Mutual, 2000.

———. *Mark Twain's Letters from Hawaii.* New York: Appleton-Century, 1966.

Delbanco, Andrew. *Melville: His World and Work.* New York: Knopf, 2005.

Durham, Michael S. *Desert Between the Mountains: Mormons, Miners, Padres, Mountain Men, and the Opening of the Great Basin, 1772–1869.* New York: Henry Holt, 1997.

Dwyer, Richard A., and Richard E. Lingenfelter. *Dan De Quille, the Washoe Giant.* Reno: University of Nevada Press, 1990.

Emerson, Everett. *Mark Twain: A Literary Life.* Philadelphia: University of Pennsylvania Press, 1999.

Fanning, Philip Ashley. *Mark Twain and Orion Clemens: Brothers, Partners, Strangers.* Tuscaloosa: University of Alabama Press, 2003.

Fatout, Paul. *Mark Twain in Virginia City.* Bloomington: Indiana University Press, 1964.

———. *Mark Twain on the Lecture Circuit.* Bloomington: Indiana University Press, 1960.

———. *Mark Twain Speaking.* Iowa City: University of Iowa Press, 1976.

Faust, Patricia L., ed. *Historical Times Illustrated Encyclopedia of the Civil War.* New York: Harper & Row, 1986.

Fischer, Victor, and Michael B. Frank, eds. *Mark Twain's Letters.* Vol. 3. 1869. Berkeley: University of California Press, 1990.

———. *Mark Twain's Letter.* Vol. 4. 1870–71. Berkeley: University of California Press, 1991.

Gerber, John. "Mark Twain's 'Private Campaign.'" *Civil War History* 1 (March 1955), pp. 37–60.

Bibliography

Goodwin, Doris Kearns. *Team of Rivals: The Political Genius of Abraham Lincoln.* New York: Simon & Schuster, 2005.

Graham, Adele. "Irrepressible Ab Grimes." *America's Civil War*, May 1991, pp. 10, 72–74.

Grant, Bruce. *Concise Encyclopedia of the American Indian.* New York: Bonanza, 1989.

Greeley, Horace. *An Overland Journey: From New York to San Francisco in the Summer of 1859.* New York: Knopf, 1964.

Grimes, Absalom. *Absalom Grimes: Confederate Mail Runner.* New Haven, Conn.: Yale University Press, 1926.

Guttman, Jon. "Emperor Norton I." *Wild West*, February 1989, pp. 8, 55–58.

Hemingway, Albert. "Riders in Hostile Land." *Wild West*, August 1990, pp. 18–25.

Hoffman, Andrew. *Inventing Mark Twain: The Lives of Samuel Langhorne Clemens.* New York: William Morrow, 1997.

Howells, William Dean. *My Mark Twain: Reminiscences and Criticism.* Baton Rouge: Louisiana State University Press, 1967.

Jackson, Joe. *A Furnace Afloat: The Wreck of the* Hornet *and the Harrowing 4,300-mile Voyage of Its Survivors.* New York: Free Press, 2003.

Kaplan, Fred. *The Singular Mark Twain: A Biography.* New York: Anchor, 2003.

Kaplan, Justin. *Mr. Clemens and Mark Twain.* New York: Simon & Schuster, 1966.

Kershaw, Alex. *Jack London: A Life.* New York: St. Martin's, 1998.

Lauber, John. *The Making of Mark Twain.* New York: American Heritage, 1985.

Lennon, Nigey. *The Sagebrush Bohemian: Mark Twain in California.* New York: Paragon House, 1993.

Lewis, Oscar. *This Was San Francisco.* New York: David McKay, 1962.

Lorch, Fred W. "Mark Twain and the 'Campaign That Failed.'" *American Literature* 12 (January 1941), pp. 454–70.

———. *The Trouble Begins at Eight: Mark Twain's Lecture Tours.* Ames: Iowa State University Press, 1968.

Mack, Effie Mona. *Mark Twain in Nevada.* New York: Charles Scribner's Sons, 1947.

Mattson, J. Stanley. "Mark Twain on War and Peace: The Missouri Rebel and 'The Campaign That Failed.'" *American Quarterly* 20 (1968), pp. 783–94.

McPherson, James M. *Battle Cry of Freedom: The Civil War Era.* New York: Oxford University Press, 1988.

Miller, Edward Haviland, ed. *Walt Whitman: The Correspondence.* 6 vols. New York: New York University Press, 1961–77.

Monachello, Anthony. "Missouri in the Balance: Struggle for St. Louis." *America's Civil War*, March 1988, pp. 44–49, 74.

Morris, Roy, Jr. *Ambrose Bierce: Alone in Bad Company*. New York: Crown, 1996.

———. *The Better Angel: Walt Whitman in the Civil War*. New York: Oxford University Press, 2000.

———. *The Long Pursuit: Abraham Lincoln's Thirty-Year Struggle with Stephen Douglas for the Heart and Soul of America*. New York: Smithsonian, 2008.

———. "The Sullen and Dangerous 'Big Muddy,'" *Wild West*, August 1992, p. 6.

Muscatine, Doris. *Old San Francisco: The Biography of a City*. New York: G.P. Putnam's Sons, 1975.

Charles Neider, ed. *The Comic Mark Twain Reader*. New York: Doubleday, 1977.

O'Connor, Richard. *Wild Bill Hickok*. New York: Curtis, 1959.

Paine, Albert Bigelow. *Mark Twain: A Biography*. 3 vols. New York: Harper & Brothers, 1912.

Parry, Albert. *Garrets and Pretenders: A History of Bohemia in America*. New York: Covici, Friede, 1933.

Powers, Ron. *Dangerous Water: A Biography of the Boy Who Became Mark Twain*. New York: Basic Books, 1999.

———. *Mark Twain: A Life*. New York: Free Press, 2006.

Rasmussen, R. Kent. *Mark Twain A to Z: The Essential Reference to His Life and Writings*. New York: Facts on File, 1995.

Reynolds, David S. *Walt Whitman's America: A Cultural Biography*. New York: Knopf, 1995.

Rice, Edward. *Captain Sir Richard Francis Burton*. New York: Charles Scribner's Sons, 1990.

Sanborn, Margaret. *Mark Twain: The Bachelor Years*. New York: Doubleday, 1990.

Simmons, James C., ed. *Star-Spangled Eden: 19th Century America Through the Eyes of Dickens, Wilde, Frances Trollope, Frank Harris, and Other British Travelers*. New York: Carroll & Graf, 2000.

Sinclair, Mick. *San Francisco*. Northampton, Mass.: Interlink, 2004.

Smith, Harriet Elinor, and Richard Bucci, eds. *Mark Twain's Letters*. Vol. 2. 1867–68. Berkeley: University of California Press, 1989.

Smith, Henry Nash, ed. *Mark Twain of the Enterprise: Newspaper Articles and Other Documents 1862–1864*. Berkeley: University of California Press, 1957.

Thomas, Diane Stine, ed. *Time-Life Books: The Old West*. New York: Prentice Hall, 1990.

Twain, Mark. *The Autobiography of Mark Twain*. New York: Harper & Row, 1959.

———. *Collected Tales, Sketches, Speeches, & Essays 1852–1890*. New York: Library of America, 1992.

———. *Collected Tales, Sketches, Speeches, & Essays 1891–1910*. New York: Library of America, 1992.

———. *The Celebrated Jumping Frog of Calaveras County, and Other Sketches*. New York: Oxford University Press, 1996.

———. "Forty-Three Days in an Open Boat." *Harper's New Monthly Magazine* 34 (December 1866), pp. 104–13.

———. *Life on the Mississippi*. New York: Penguin Putnam, 1961.

———. "My Debut as a Literary Person." *Century Magazine* 69 (November 1899), pp. 76–88.

———. *Roughing It*. Edited by Harriet Elinor Smith and Edgar Marquess Branch. Berkeley: University of California Press, 1993.

Unruh, John D., Jr. *The Plains Across: The Overland Emigrants and the Trans-Mississippi West, 1840–60*. Urbana: University of Illinois Press, 1979.

Waldman, Carl. *Atlas of the North American Indian*. New York: Facts on File, 1985.

Webster, Samuel Charles, ed. *Mark Twain, Business Man*. Boston: Little, Brown, 1946.

Wecter, Dixon. *Sam Clemens of Hannibal*. Boston: Houghton Mifflin, 1952.

Williams, George III. *Mark Twain and the Jumping Frog of Calaveras County*. Carson City, Nev.: Tree By The River, 1999.

———. *Mark Twain: His Adventures at Aurora and Mona Lake*. Riverside, Calif.: Tree By The River, 1986.

———. *Mark Twain: His Life in Virginia City, Nevada*. Dayton, Nev.: Tree By The River, 1986.

Williams, Robert C. *Horace Greeley: Champion of American Freedom*. New York: New York University Press, 2006.

Willis, Resa. *Mark and Livy: The Love Story of Mark Twain and the Woman Who Almost Tamed Him*. New York: Atheneum, 1992.

ACKNOWLEDGMENTS

One of the best things about writing this book has been the opportunity to reunite with my old editor at Simon & Schuster, Roger Labrie. As I first discovered eight years ago when working with Roger on *Fraud of the Century: Rutherford B. Hayes, Samuel Tilden, and the Stolen Election of 1876*, his understated but acute editorial skill is combined with an enthusiastic commitment to the project at hand, and his willingness to seek and suggest imaginative promotional possibilities is not—trust me on this—an industry-wide standard. Thanks also to my long-ago thesis advisor and professor at the University of Tennessee, Dr. Allison Ensor, an eminent Mark Twain scholar for many years, for reading and improving the book in manuscript.

Friends and family (often both) who have generously and consistently encouraged my endeavors throughout the years include Tony Morris, Ellyn and Ken Bivin, Lindy and Don Oakes, Burton and Lois Pierce, David Pierce, Paula and David Shuford, Susan and Dan Gilmore, Jim Bob and Debra Wilson, Barry Parker, Mike Haskew, Nat Hughes, Mike McKee, Jim Balentine, Steve Ellis, Lamont Ingalls, and Amy Dyer. Special thanks to Carl Gnam, my publisher at *Military Heritage*, for enabling me to continue my self-education at his expense.

As always, my deepest thanks go to my long-suffering but unfailingly supportive nuclear family—my wife, Leslie, and our children, Phil and Lucy, whose own talents and accomplishments continue to grow at such a rate that fatherly pride cannot always keep up with them, though it tries.

INDEX

Index

ABOUT THE AUTHOR

Roy Morris, Jr., is the editor of *Military Heritage* magazine and the author of five previous books on the Civil War era. A former newspaper reporter himself, Morris has served as a consultant for A&E Network and the History Channel. He lives in Chattanooga, Tennessee.